fat talk

fat talk

**WHAT
GIRLS
AND
THEIR
PARENTS
SAY
ABOUT
DIETING**

Mimi Nichter

HARVARD UNIVERSITY PRESS
Cambridge, Massachusetts
London, England
2000

Library of Congress Cataloging-in-Publication Data

Nichter, Mimi.
Fat talk : what girls and their parents say about dieting / Mimi Nichter.
p. cm.
Includes bibliographical references and index.
ISBN 0-674-00229-6 (alk. paper)
1. Teenage girls—Nutrition. 2. Reducing diets. 3. Obesity in
adolescence. 4. Body image in adolescence. I. Title.

RJ399.C6 N53 2000
613.2′5′08352—dc21

99-059521

For Mark, Simeon, and Brandon

Contents

Preface

THIS BOOK has been personally as well as professionally motivated. This became evident to me soon after the project began. I was having dinner with my mother, who was celebrating her seventieth birthday. To my surprise, she refused to indulge in a piece of chocolate cake for dessert. After some persuasion from my sister and me she relented, agreeing to eat a sliver. Her rationale was clear—she was dieting to lose the weight she had gained over the holiday season. When I jokingly told her that she could be a participant in my research project, she smiled broadly and said, "Yes, me and the rest of the women in my community! We're still concerned with our weight . . . you know, it doesn't stop when you get older. We're always watching what we eat!" After a moment she added, "You can never be too rich or too thin!"

As I reflected on her comments later that evening, I considered how age-centric my thinking was about the issue of weight. Had I naïvely assumed that as women got older they became less concerned with their weight? Had my own awareness of body weight diminished as I matured? I realized—with much surprise—that I was a lot like my mother. This encouraged me to look more closely in my research at the relationship of mothers and daughters and how knowledge about appropriate body shape and dieting is transmitted from one generation to the next.

I could certainly rationalize my concern with my weight as motivated by my heightened health consciousness. But I had to admit to myself that although my weight has always been slightly less than average for my height, I have often thought that I would be more attractive if I were five to ten pounds thinner. This troubled me. Despite all I had read on the tyranny of slenderness, the extensive interviews I had conducted with girls and women about body image, as well as my awareness of the pain caused by body dissatisfaction, why was I unable to shirk the idea that being thin would somehow render me more attractive and more in control of my life? If *I* couldn't let go of this embodied sense of beauty after so much reflection, who could? I pondered the extent to which these concerns affected my everyday life. Although I did not diet with any frequency or regularity, I often watched what I ate. Looking back on my life, it was clear that my sense of appropriate body weight was internalized at an early age. What was more, this sense was tenaciously clinging to me even as I grew older.

As I listened to fat talk among teen-aged girls, I could identify with their concerns about their developing bodies. Although I am no longer as bothered by these concerns as were the teens I interviewed, I acknowledge with a degree of humility that such thinking has not faded completely from my consciousness.

Although many articles and books have been written on women, the body, and dieting as a cultural institution, this book is different. In these pages I strive to look beyond the oft-cited pathology of teen-aged girls in relation to their bodies, identifying not only their dissatisfaction with themselves, but also many of their positive attitudes and behaviors. If we as researchers look for what is pathological in girls, that is what we will find.

I also pay particular attention to the interactive nature of the female socialization process. From the outset of the project it was clear to me that girls do not single-handedly adopt the thin beauty ideal; indeed, they internalize an ideal that is reinforced by their peers at school and by their families at home. Nor is this ideal uniform across all age groups or ethnic groups. Thus in documenting girls' struggles to meet a cultural ideal of beauty, I explore how developmental age and ethnic identity influence this process.

fat talk

Introduction: Barbie and Beyond

"WHAT'S A MOTHER to do?" my friend Sally bemoaned while discussing her fourteen-year-old daughter's dissatisfaction with her body. "She's always complaining that she hates her thighs. She looks in the mirror, grabs hold of them as if they're a piece of meat, and asks me how she can get rid of them. I try to help her accept herself. I tell her that everyone has a part of their body that they dislike and that people don't just look at her thighs . . . they see her as a whole person. But she doesn't seem to hear what I say." After a momentary pause she asks, "Do you think her feelings of dissatisfaction with her body are just a stage that she'll outgrow, or will they persist for some years? What can I do to help her through this difficult time when her body seems so out of control?"

Sally's frustration with her daughter's concerns about her body is common among parents of teen-aged girls. Like her own mother, Sally has been a devout dieter for many years, though she hopes that the cycle of dieting and dissatisfaction will not be reproduced into the next generation. As a friend and a researcher in the area of body image and dieting among teens, I silently wonder whether Sally can teach her daughter to accept her body when she has not come to terms with her own shape. What message does Sally send to her daughter when she eats small portions of food and abstains from dessert for weeks at a time?

At first glance, Sally's daughter may appear to fit the general profile of a teen-aged girl growing up in the United States to-day. Study after study reports that dissatisfaction with weight and inappropriate dieting behaviors are pervasive—at least among white middle-class girls. This situation is considered to be so serious that it is sometimes referred to as an epidemic; indeed, some estimates claim that as many as 60 percent of white girls are dieting at any given time.[1] Researchers warn that the use of extreme weight-loss methods such as fasting, binging, and purging are escalating and that we may soon see a higher incidence of eating disorders.

The concern that many teen-aged girls are "at risk" for eating disorders reflects the increasing tendency to view the behavior of adolescents as pathological.[2] One need only glance at the morning newspaper to confirm that adolescents are portrayed as major players in the multiple "epidemics" that beset the country. Much of what is written about girls is derived from a youth-at-risk perspective that details the losses in self-esteem and self-confidence that girls experience across adolescence and that often lead to a host of other problems, including negative body image, eating disorders, teen pregnancy, sexually transmitted diseases, and drug abuse. This propensity to pathologize youth has led some social scientists to refer to adolescence as a culture-bound syndrome.[3] As a result, many parents live in fear of the dreaded teen-age years. The mere mention that one's child is about to enter adolescence can evoke deep sighs and sympathetic looks from others. Parents swap stories about the inherent dangers of having teenagers and discuss strategies for controlling them. As a result, parents have come to expect the worst.

Concern with eating disorders in particular is so widespread that when I mention to people that I conduct research on body image and dieting among teens, I am inevitably asked, "Is it really that bad? Are so many girls suffering from eating disorders?" In response, I explain that though 1–3 percent of females do suffer from eating disorders, the other 97 percent demonstrate a wide range of attitudes and behaviors toward their bodies. People are often surprised at this response because they have been led by the media to believe that eating disorders are far more common than they actually are. Some of the women I have spoken to assumed that eating disorders affect as many as one in four girls—and not just aspiring ballerinas!

These misperceptions are not surprising, given that in the past decade slimness as a beauty ideal has been the subject of countless magazine articles and books, constituting a cultural phenomenon in its own right. Much of this literature focuses on anorexia nervosa and bulimia, which are typically presented as culturally induced illnesses; cultural forms of rebellion or withdrawal; or addictions. Feminist writers describe the political and societal environments that contribute to women's struggle to discipline themselves, control their appetites, and achieve social status and a moral identity in the form of the "right look."[4] Some popular accounts of women and the body draw on therapeutic encounters with eating-disordered and obese women, giving voice to those at the extremes of weight-related behavior.[5] Although there are many in-depth studies of why adult women have attempted to discipline their bodies, we have mostly survey statistics about teen-aged girls and their eating habits.

Most of these statistics are derived from a series of standard survey questions presented to high school and college-aged females. The young women are asked to gauge their level of satisfaction with their weight and body shape, as well as to reveal their current dieting and exercising practices. While such statistics provide important baseline information on females, they fail to capture adequately the complexity of their behaviors.

Despite the claims that there is an epidemic of dieting among teen-aged girls, a number of questions remain unanswered, and indeed, unasked. What do survey statistics claiming that 60 percent of teen-aged girls are dieting actually mean? What do girls really do when they're on a diet? How long does a typical teen-ager's diet last, and when does she consider it successful? Do girls actually lose weight from their diets? Given the cultural imperative to be thin, are girls *overreporting* their dieting on surveys because they feel they *should be* dieting? As a culture, why do we focus so much attention on the 1–3 percent of girls who suffer from eating disorders to the exclusion of an in-depth understanding of what the other 97 percent of girls are doing? And finally, if "everyone" is dieting, why do studies continually report that American youth are becoming increasingly overweight?[6]

What is missing from the literature on body image and dieting are the voices of teens and the reality of what "being on a diet" actually means to them. Looking beyond those who suffer from eating disorders, I focus on what constitutes "normal" behavior among teen-aged girls and examine the extent to which body image and dieting play a role in female gender socialization. Is there an image of the "perfect girl" in mainstream American society? If so, what impact does comparing herself with this ideal have on a girl as she grows up? How consistent are beauty ideals across different ethnic or social groups? Do some girls resist popular images of beauty and body shape, and, if so, how is their resistance expressed? How central a role do dieting and diet talk play in girls' lives? Do some girls reject dieting and adopt healthier eating practices as a means of watching their weight?

As an anthropologist, I have focused upon the difference between what girls *say* they do and what they *actually* do. Beyond survey statistics, I examine how peers, parents, and the media contribute to girls' body image, dieting practices, and sense of self. I explore cultural meanings of the "I'm so fat" discourse—what I call "fat talk"—examining how this pervasive speech performance facilitates social relations among girls. Before describing the study upon which this book is based, it is important to provide a brief background and context for girls' concerns about their bodies.

◆　　◆　　◆

The Allure of Advertising

For many Americans, the "mirror, mirror on the wall" telling them who is the fairest of them all—or at least how they stack up—is television. Television programs present slender women as the dominant image of popularity, success, and happiness. Particularly in programs favored by teen-aged girls, female characters are almost always well below average weight.[7] This skew toward slenderness distorts the actual diversity of female shapes and erases overweight women from our vision.[8]

Advertisements, including the 400–600 we scan in the morning newspaper and observe on billboards and television on a daily basis, reinforce the slender image.[9] Indeed, one in every eleven television commercials includes a direct message about beauty, and these messages are almost exclusively directed toward women.[10] Similar messages about beauty and perfection are disseminated to girls in the guise of self-improvement features in teen magazines. Both articles and advertisements in these publications convey the message that "the road to happiness is attracting males . . . by way of physical beautification."[11] At least 50 percent of teen-aged girls are regular readers of fashion magazines such as *Seventeen* and *Glamour;* more disturbing still, they form their ideas of what constitutes ideal beauty for women from the images they view in these magazines.[12]

Even before girls reach adolescence, many have embodied the thin beauty ideal through play. Barbie, the most popular fashion doll in America, accounting for 1.9 billion dollars in annual sales, has a body that can rarely be achieved in real life. Ninety percent of all American girls ages three to eleven own one or more Barbies, and more than one billion have been sold since manufacturing began in 1959. It has been calculated that if all the Barbies in the world were laid out head to foot around the earth, they would circle it three and a half times.[13] As they dress their Barbies during their formative years, many girls engage in fantasy play of their grown-up life as thin, blond females. Barbie's one hundred new seasonal outfits are created by a team of nine full-time fashion designers and a roomful of hairstylists who gain inspiration by observing teen-aged girls at California malls. Barbie's designers do not attempt to create new fashions; they search for what signifies popularity among teens and then copy the look for Barbie. Teen fashion is capitalized upon and coopted. Whereas Barbie's outfits change continually, her body shape has been altered only minimally.

Television advertisements portray young girls happily playing with Barbie, declaring her attributes: "She's cool-time Barbie, she's rad, she's blond, she's beautiful." Irrespective of the outfit she dons, Barbie is the popular girl who conveys a subtle yet powerful message: If you get the body you can get the guy.[14] This same message is transmitted in advertisements in teen magazines. In a *Seventeen* ad for Weight Watchers, a handsome lifeguard is seated on a tower at the beach. The copy below reads: "We can help you get the body you've always dreamed of." Although the product is directed at adolescent girls, the message is that "getting a thin body" is the key to getting *his* body.

A growing number of American females cannot measure up to the image of beauty that pervades television and advertisements. More than half of teen-aged girls are size thirteen or larger. Paradoxically, injunctions to look thin and be "in control" of one's appetite are juxtaposed with directives to indulge, release, and enjoy a well-deserved break, be it in the form of a Big Mac, a Snickers bar, or a shopping spree. Such paradoxes promote the new American dream of having one's cake and eating it too![15] An advertisement for a low-fat chocolate pudding, for example, features an ultraslim model who holds a spoon to her pouting lips while exclaiming, "Dessert is always on the tip of my tongue!" Such ads suggest that we can indulge while still maintaining our sense of "being good." The miracle of olestra is that we can eat what we want and forget about the calories.

In addition to messages about what we should eat, we are bombarded with advertisements that tell us how we should look. "Making up and making over" have become prominent components of everyday life. Girls are led to believe that they should adopt beauty practices at younger and younger ages as "preventive care" and that makeup is an essential ingredient in achieving the "natural" look. Through the wonders of science, females have an ever-growing arsenal of products available to them that promise to maintain their youth and transform, camouflage, or mask their imperfect bodies. Frustration with one's body, from hair and skin to weight and its distribution, sells products because we are taught that our bodies are transformable objects, part by part.

In order to sell products, advertised messages offer hope after undermining self-confidence. This pattern of advertising reflects the American ideal of individual success through self-improvement, free will, and personal destiny. Beauty has, at once, become a symbol of moral self-worth, as well as a commodity purchased at a cost. But then we are told we are worth it! One of the hidden costs of buying into beauty work is that females have come to feel increasingly responsible for transforming their appearance to meet an elusive cultural ideal.

Teen-aged girls undergoing rapid physical changes are especially susceptible to advertising. The average girl gains twenty-five pounds in body fat during puberty. Weight gain and fat accumulation, though necessary components of puberty, may be particularly distressing for girls who believe that a slender body is a prerequisite for popularity and success. As psychologist Rita Freedman has described, adolescents' search for a personal identity has become distorted into a search for a packaged image.[16] A growing girl is directed to her mirror to discover who she is.

Exposure to advertisements with highly attractive models contributes to a tendency among teen-aged girls to be increasingly critical of their own physical attractiveness as well as that of others. As girls move from childhood to adolescence, they compare themselves more and more with models in advertisements—a tendency that is greater for those with lower self-perceptions of physical attractiveness and lower self-esteem.[17] Marketing messages directed toward adolescents promote the latest style built around images of bodily perfection embedded in a broader directive promoting consumption as a primary value of life.[18] Advertisers create the illusion of a community of consumption whose membership requirement is possession of popular brands and styles.

I do not mean to imply that advertising is the root of body dissatisfaction among teen-aged girls; indeed, to do so would be to oversimplify a complex cultural problem. In fact, fashion magazines *do* commonly address the issue of weight obsession among females. Unfortunately, rather than alleviating the problem, they perpetuate it by producing a steady stream of hype about weight. Articles in the popular media that address teen-aged girls' obsession with their weight often perpetuate stereotypes. The very articles which contend that women and girls must move beyond concerns about their bodies are sandwiched between ads of near-anorexic models clad in the latest body-revealing fashions.

Anthropologist and psychohistorian Howard Stein has argued that the trend toward dieting and physical fitness in middle-class America demonstrates a return of the "survival of the fittest" mentality. The wellness syndrome, which includes dieting, has emerged as an unconscious ritualistic solution to a sense of loss of control over the societal body. Forces of good (slimness) and evil (fatness) are pitted against each other in a morality play that takes the form of getting in shape.[19] Evidence for this is found in dieting discourse that is replete with references to dieting as "being good" and "doing right," and pigging out as "being so bad," leading one to "feel so guilty." Stein identifies the body as a battleground of magical control where fitness provides a personal path to salvation at a time when the specter of a nuclear, if not a viral, holocaust hovers close at hand, yet is denied.

Acts of control that center on the body, such as dieting and exercise, can also be interpreted as a social response to risk and uncertainty. As individuals have less control over their outer environments (be they social, socioeconomic, or natural), they tend to focus more intently on an immediate environment where they can reaffirm boundaries and exercise control.[20] This type of reasoning might help explain why going on a diet, redoing one's hair, or "getting in shape" often follows the breakup of a relationship as a form of coping. Extending the logic, the appeal of getting in shape or going on a diet may index feelings of insecurity and risk at the societal level. In a high-performance world in which the metaphor of trimming off "excess fat" and "streamlining" operations is incorporated into the discourse of business layoffs, a means of reducing feelings of powerlessness may involve working within the same metaphor at the site of the body.

◆   ◆   ◆

The Teen Lifestyle Project

But do ideas such as these, which link attempted control of the body to more generalized feelings of powerlessness, apply to teen populations? As a result of a growing theoretical interest in the "body" among social scientists and a sustained popular interest in dieting and body work, I became interested in exploring how issues concerning body image and control in the form of dieting played out in the everyday lives of girls. Were teen-aged girls, as media accounts and other researchers have suggested, really obsessed with their bodies, or was this true of only a small but highly visible group? In order to move beyond a snapshot account of girls' lives, my colleagues Mark Nichter and Cheryl Ritenbaugh and I reasoned that we would need to follow girls over several years to see how they changed as they got older and were exposed to different social influences. Rather than study body image and dieting as isolated behaviors, we felt it was important to view these as embedded within the lifeworld of teens. The name of the study, the Teen Lifestyle Project, was specifically chosen to reflect this broader perspective.

In order to interest girls in participating in the Teen Lifestyle Project, we spoke before physical education classes for eighth- and ninth-grade girls in four urban schools in Tucson, Arizona. I introduced myself as an anthropologist from the University of Arizona and told the girls about the purpose of the study. Many expressed surprise that an anthropologist, a title that conjured up images of old bones and past civilizations, would want to talk to them. I explained that my interest was in teen culture and that I considered them to be experts in this field. By talking with each of them alone and in groups with their friends, I hoped to understand what it was like to be a teen-age girl today.

As an introduction to the types of questions that would be asked of them if they joined the project, I presented the girls with advertisements featuring beautiful models from commonly read magazines (*Seventeen, Glamour*) and asked them how they felt about themselves when they saw those types of ads. I then raised some general questions about how they felt about their own appearance. "When you look in the mirror in the morning," I asked, "do you like what you see?" Girls immediately started moaning, groaning, and giggling among themselves. After a few moments, they began to call out what they perceived to be their "problem areas," which included being too fat, too short, too tall, too thin, having too many pimples, or having "bad" hair. Each girl had her own reason to be dissatisfied with her appearance. It was disconcerting to see how quickly the girls judged themselves by their external appearance, but from a research perspective, it confirmed the salience of the topic. I explained that if they joined the project, they would be asked about the pressures they experienced to look certain ways, what their ideal girl was like, and what if anything they did to change how they looked.

More than three-quarters of the girls addressed decided to participate. In total, 240 girls in the eighth and ninth grades joined the study. Reflective of the schools' populations, about 70 percent of the girls were white, 10 percent were Latina, and about 5 percent were African American, Asian American, or Native American. Interestingly, 15 percent of the girls did not identify themselves with any ethnic group. The girls' backgrounds ranged from lower to upper middle-class. Those who participated in the project were involved for 3 full school years.

Each participant in the Teen Lifestyle Project was interviewed for fifty minutes once each year at school. Interviewers included a team of anthropology graduate students and myself. Interviews were conducted in a private area of the school and were tape recorded. Each girl was also interviewed two times a year by telephone (in the fall and spring) and filled out a survey questionnaire each spring at school. In total, we conducted almost 700 in-person interviews. When girls changed schools, moved out of town, or dropped out of school, we made every effort to keep in contact with them by telephone. The attrition over the three years of the study was quite low (12 percent), with 211 girls remaining in the study at the end of the third year. (For more details on project methodology, see Appendix A.)

It seemed simplistic to us to assume that all teen-aged girls experienced and responded to representations of the dominant American beauty ideal in the same way. In previous studies, insufficient attention had been paid to issues of age and ethnicity as they influenced aesthetic appreciation of the body and beauty work. Although a few academic studies had found ethnic differences in body-image ideals and dieting practices, particularly between African-American and white teens, explanations for these discrepancies usually implicated "cultural differences." As an anthropologist, I hoped to examine further the reasons for these cultural differences. In the third year of the project, nutritionist Sheila Parker and anthropologist Colette Sims worked with our team to enlist an additional 50 African-American high school girls to enable us to compare issues of body image and dieting across cultures. These girls were interviewed over the course of one year and participated in focus groups. The majority of data presented in this book (Chapters 1–5) are drawn from the predominately white (70 percent) and Latina (10 percent) girls who participated in the longitudinal study. Findings of the study on African-American girls are presented in Chapter 6.

It is important to note at the outset that the use of the terms "white," "Latina," and "African American" is heuristic. It is not an attempt to essentialize particular groups or to infer that a monolithic white, Latina, or African-American culture exists. The depiction of cultural ideals related to body image and dieting discussed throughout this book is purposely drawn in broad strokes so that differences in orientation may be discussed.

In addition to ethnicity, we were also interested in youth

subculture and how it affected the way girls wanted to look. Did being a "prep," a "mod," a "skater," or a "stoner," members of four radically different social groups in the schools in which we worked, affect girls' ideal body shape? Following the work of other adolescent researchers, we initially looked at distinctions and markers of different subcultures and explored notions of ideal body shape among these groups.[21] Our early findings suggested a fair degree of homogeneity among the different groups in relation to preferred body shape. Although there was considerable intercultural variability, it was expressed less in terms of ideal body shape and more in terms of dress, style, hair, and music.

My colleagues and I were also interested in understanding what teen-age girls were eating, regardless of whether they were dieting. Because of the paucity of information on what constituted the normal, everyday eating habits of teens, we collected detailed information on food intake as well as on dieting from each of the girls in the study. Although we explored patterns of tobacco use, particularly the relationship between dieting and smoking, they are not discussed in detail in this book.[22]

In addition to individual interviews, many girls took part in focus groups, which consisted of self-selected groups of four to seven girls who were friends and members of the same social group. Early in the project we learned that placing girls from different cliques together made it less likely that they would disclose personal opinions. Whereas the individual interviews focused on personal ideas and behaviors regarding body image, dieting, and smoking, the focus groups tended to elicit generalized attitudes about these issues as well as notions of appropriate subgroup behavior. Focus group interviews proved to be an extremely important means by which to observe discussions among girls, and in particular to see how weight-control issues emerged in conversations among friends.

During the first year of the project, our focus was on girls' attitudes and behaviors in their peer groups, both in and out of school. As we became increasingly familiar with the girls, it became clear that their perceptions of self were influenced by their parents and siblings. Rather than focus on the girls as individuals, we expanded our questions to better situate them within the context of their homes, thus enabling us to explore the range of messages they received about their bodies and eating from other family members.

Conducting this research was sometimes heart-wrenching. As might be expected, asking girls questions about their lives—and in particular their bodies—generated a wide range of responses. Whereas some girls expressed satisfaction with their appearance, the majority did not. It was sometimes difficult, when faced with a litany of complaints from an attractive young girl who disliked how she looked, to refrain from blurting out comments like "you're not fat" or "you look great." As the girls described the painful comparisons they made between themselves and the airbrushed, picture-perfect models they saw in magazines, I was tempted to drop my researcher persona and blurt out, "Can't you see how ads manipulate you? Don't you know those women aren't real?" But as a social scientist in the early stages of a project, I felt that it was inappropriate to interject my own values into the discussion. After all, I was there to learn from them, not to influence them to think in ways that I thought appropriate. As my research progressed, however, I learned that many of the girls were aware that ads attempted to manipulate them, though they were also quick to discount the efficacy of such strategies.

Throughout the project, I was impressed with the honesty, willingness to share, and indeed the eagerness that many of the girls brought to our discussions. While body image and dieting were common topics of discussion among friends, before our project came along few of the girls had an opportunity to talk about themselves with adult women in a non-threatening environment. Although we had not conceptualized our research project as an intervention, we found that the process of asking questions allowed girls to articulate their opinions and "try out" their ideas. By listening as girls spoke, we provided them with a space to explore their own voices. They sometimes paused for a moment before answering a question, commenting, "Well, I never really thought about that before." They would then go on to detail their thoughts. Many girls commented that when they joined in focus-group discussions with girls their own age, they realized that others shared the same feelings they had. Learning that the way they viewed themselves and their appearance was culturally mediated allowed the girls to see beyond their own experience.

Despite widespread evidence of girls' dissatisfaction with themselves and extensive documentation of the lowering of self-esteem among girls during early adolescence, we were surprised to find how few school resources were being directed toward cultivating healthy body images. Inspired by girls' comments about our project, our research team designed and implemented an intervention for healthy body image, nutrition, and physical activity for girls following the completion of our study. In Chapter 7, I describe the intervention that we implemented to foster a critical awareness of the dominant construction of female beauty. I also raise questions about future steps that parents and schools can take to help girls move beyond narrow and rigid definitions of what constitutes beauty.

1

In the Presence of the Perfect Girl

You see all these models and these really perfect
people on TV and they're all perfectly thin and they
have all these guys after them. And you just can't
help saying, "I want to be that thin, that's how *I*
want to look!" It's like . . . you just know that if you
did, your life would be so much better.

KATE, *AGE 15*

IN ONE-ON-ONE interviews and in focus
groups, I asked the girls to describe their
image of an ideal girl. This "perfect" girl was often portrayed
as being 5'7" and between 100 and 110 pounds. She was usually a blonde with long, flowing hair, "the kind you could
throw over your shoulder." Descriptions mirrored those of
fashion models: "I think of her as tall—5'7", 5'8", with long
legs. She's naturally pretty with a model's face and high
cheekbones." She also had a flat stomach, a clear complexion,
straight teeth, and "good" clothes.

Listening to girls speak about their ideal and watching
them select silhouettes of her body type, I was continually
struck by the uniformity of their descriptions, regardless of
what the speaker herself looked like. This sense of ideal
beauty was rigid and fixed: fixed on the pages of magazines,
on the airbrushed faces of models, and in the minds of these
teen-aged girls.

For many of the white girls, "being perfect" was an unattainable dream that led to a devaluing of their own looks and a sense of personal dissatisfaction and frustration. This was particularly striking in middle school, when girls' bodies were changing so rapidly. During early adolescence physical growth occurs more quickly than at any other point in the life cycle except for the prenatal period and early infancy. Walking through the halls of any middle school, we can observe teens of the same age in different stages of physical development. While one girl may be barely 5'0 and weigh 85 pounds, her classmate may already have reached 5'6" and weigh 125 pounds. An early maturer (a girl who has attained menarche before the age of 12) may feel that she is fat and that her body is out of control.

Julie, an early maturer who was taller and more broadly built than her friends, expressed frustration with her changing body: "I just want to look like one of those models in a swimsuit when they walk on the beach—like a flat stomach, little hips, little waist, and skinny thighs, so you don't, like me, have to put on shorts and a shirt and sunglasses." Each time I saw Julie loping around the school, she was wearing oversized blue jeans and a huge, untucked tee shirt. Julie's desire to conceal her body in loose clothes was in part a fashion statement. But it was also a response to her belief that she could not measure up to media-generated standards of beauty.

Being the right weight was often perceived as a ticket to the good life. The girl with the perfect body who can "eat and eat and eat and not gain anything" was described as being "perfect in every way." By extension, she has a perfect life: she gets the boy of every girl's dreams. As Julie explained:

> Most girls buy *Seventeen* magazine and see all the models and they're really, really skinny and they see lots of girls in real life that look like that. They have the cutest guy in the school and they seem to have life so perfect.

"Perfect" was a catch-all expression that the teens used to describe a wide range of characteristics. The word itself evoked an image of "the chosen one," the girl with the body every girl wanted and wished she had been born with or had enough will power to obtain through beauty work. The designation "perfect" also appears prominently in advertisements and feature articles in teen and women's magazines. Articles entitled "Pretty Future Perfect" are sandwiched between ads for foundation promising a "perfect finish" and swimsuits assuring a "perfect line." Though we are led to believe that we are inadequate as we are, never fear! A wide range of products is available to mask imperfection in a way that appears natural.

In focus groups we asked the middle school girls if they thought magazines and television had an impact on how they wanted to look. Girls were eager to jump in with their responses, indicating that they had thought about this topic before and perhaps discussed it with friends. Tara, a fourteen-year-old redhead with freckles and a mouthful of braces, remarked: "On the front cover of magazines they always say things like, 'How to lose weight, how to look skinnier.' I think that's good because they give you tips on how you can manage your weight and lose it. But it's also bad because then it's like, 'Am I fat?' And then I start saying, 'Hmm, maybe I can lose weight.'" Her best friend, Amber, a late maturer with the body of a pre-pubescent girl, quickly chimed in: "In middle school," she began in an authoritative voice, "what you see on TV has like a really big influence on you. I think it's mostly due to the fact that dieting commercials, you know like for Dexatrim and stuff, show these very thin people eating the product. So then people who are like me look at that ad and go, 'Hey, wait a minute, they're thin, and they're dieting! I have to diet, I have to be thinner!'"

It was frustrating to hear girls like Tara and Amber talk about dieting when neither one of them needed to do so. To be clear, not all the girls commented on the influence of the media on body image, and of those who did, not all shared Tara and Amber's opinion. Indeed, we heard a range of responses about media influences on youth self-image from the girls we interviewed.

Depending on the medium in which we asked the question, we obtained different answers. For example, on the survey we asked the question, "Who most influences your look?" The responses were as follows: "Only I do" (37 percent), "looking at others" (28 percent), "my friends" (14 percent), "magazines, movies, and television" (11 percent), and "my boyfriend" (10 percent). What did this disparity mean? Why did almost 40 percent of girls report on the survey that nothing really influenced them, whereas in interviews they talked so strongly about the media?

Disparities such as these were also noted *within* interviews. The same girl who would claim that she wished she were thinner and thus more popular would at another point in the interview say that she really didn't care what others thought about her. She would then describe what she did to stand out and be different, such as mismatching her clothes or dyeing her hair. These seemingly contradictory statements about caring and not caring coexisted in girls' narratives about themselves. They seemed to be an intricate part of the developmental process of adolescence. I noticed the same inconsistencies of voice in my own reading of teen magazines. *Jump,* a magazine targeted at girls aged thirteen to fifteen, advertises itself in the following way: "Be singular in a plural world. Dare to be different! Dare to be you! Read *Jump!*" Marketers who target a youth population clearly understand that the idea of being an individual sells. The girl who becomes a reader also becomes an individual.

Developmental differences among girls affected not just their body size and height but also their ability to reflect upon and discuss their opinions. Kamie, a sixteen-year-old tenth-grader, remarked during an interview that she thought and acted differently from other people her age. She told me that she was her own person and didn't really care what others thought about her. In response to the question about the impact of the media on her self-image, Kamie remarked:

> Sure it affects me. You see somebody, and they're tan and beautiful and you naturally want to be just like them. Me, I used to be that way. But now, I just

look at those people and I ask myself, "Well, what kind of life do they have?" It can't be any better than mine, you know. Not if I let it. You know, some of the richest people in the world and the most beautiful people in the world are the saddest people. So I'm pretty blessed with what I have already, and if someone doesn't like me, I'm just like, "Well, I don't need them."

Although Kamie was not alone in her self-assertiveness, this was not an attribute that was reinforced in school. Within school curricula there was little opportunity to explore issues related to self-identity or to develop critical thinking skills about the media. Much later in the study, we learned that many of the girls valued their interviews as opportunities to discuss sensitive topics such as body image and perceived gender differences, a topic to which I return in Chapter 7.

◆   ◆   ◆

Competition and Social Comparison

Ironically, girls who were closest to the image of the ideal were admired, but at the same time envied and disliked by other girls. The perfect girl makes those around her feel frustrated and insecure because they just don't measure up to her embodiment of the ideal. These feelings were aptly captured in Susie's comment: "You just see all these older girls, like when you go to the mall, and it's like, 'Why was I born?' because they're so perfect."

Some girls explained that whenever they would see a beautiful girl at school, in the mall, or even on television, they would label her a "bitch." Not uncommonly, they would state that they hated the girl, despite the fact that they didn't know her. Some girls reacted with seething comments like "I want to hurt her" or "I could just kill her." Others looked for a flaw. Since the perfect girl's flaw is not immediately evident, it is often assumed to exist in her personality. As Cathy, a ninth-grader, explained:

> Girls, they completely stare at another girl. If a new girl would walk in, I would like notice every single flaw and then I'd wait for her to try to be my friend—I mean, show me that she is really okay . . . and then I kind of blow off her flaw, but until then I'm like, "God, do you see that big thing between her teeth? Do you see how much makeup she's wearing?" I like have to know everything . . . If she is really pretty, then I want to see her flaw . . . all of it, all of it. I want to know every single part of her flaw.

Many of the white girls in the study revealed that this intensive comparison was a behavior they regularly practiced. Kim, a petite ninth-grader who was on the cheerleading squad, had a particularly insightful description of how social comparison works:

> You know, I think that the main problem of society is that girls from when they are little are trying to be competitive with every other girl . . . There is like constantly a competition between who can have the best thighs. It's just not that way with guys, and that's why they don't have as many friend problems. Like for girls, we have to compete to get where we are. And I mean we're always sizing each other up in terms of how we look. It's like one day, me and my sister were talking and we said like when a girl comes up to you that you don't know, then after you'll be totally talking about her, trying to find faults with her. I mean, when we don't like a girl, we won't be like, "She's a bad person," or "She's mean," or "She's a liar," we'll say, "Oh, she's ugly," or "She's fat," or "Did you see her thighs?" I mean it's all about competition about how we look.

While much has been written about the importance of social connection to girls and women, Kim's observations speak to a politics of separation among girls played out through discourse about appearance and personality. She insightfully notes the insidious nature of girls' comparisons to one another. Girls actively search for a new student's flaws. They reach consensus about her limitations and thereby neutralize the threat she poses. By identifying and naming the flaws and by talking loudly about them, girls strengthen their sense of self-worth in opposition to that of others in a world marked by competition.

Kim's discussion also provides a sobering note about the nature of girls' comparisons. Girls do not simply engage in general comparisons; they target specific body parts and zero in on others' vulnerability. For many girls, the thighs are the most troubling area during adolescence. Not only do the media and boys reinforce an image of girls and women as body parts rather than as whole people, but girls engage in verbally dismembering one another and themselves. As we will see in Chapter 2, by participating in "fat talk" girls call attention to their own flaws as well as those of others.

As we continued talking, Kim contrasted the relationships that girls had with one another with the friendships of boys:

> I mean it's weird . . . guys can have friends, but they're not caught up in "you're my best friend" . . . Girls, I think we can have better relationships, because we can talk and we say stuff to each other like, "We know how you feel" . . . and we like to do hair and do makeup, just to bond. Guys, I don't even know if they have the capacity for that. But in some ways I wish I could act like a guy with some people, just like, you know, "I don't like you, let's not be friends" . . . it just seems easier. Instead girls get caught up in "well she said this, you said that" . . . just stupid stuff like that. I mean, I just don't know why girls are like that.

Despite the benefits of girls' capacity for closeness, as Kim notes, there is danger in this connection—in particular, the belief that they must share the same opinions in order to fit in.

While closeness can ostensibly be maintained through beauty projects, such bonding activities have their limitations.

In one-on-one interviews, we asked the girls if they thought they could be friends with someone their own age who was beautiful or "perfect." Something about the directness of the question made it difficult for them to come right out and say "no." Instead, they hedged their response by initially answering, "I don't know," and then explained that they probably wouldn't be friends with such a girl because she would probably be stuck-up and self-absorbed.

The phrase "I don't know" in response to this question commonly preceded a lucid answer which indicated that, in fact, the girl *did know* what she felt. Psychologist Carol Gilligan has explained that in early adolescence girls struggle to voice their opinions, particularly if they run counter to commonly held beliefs. Peppering their speech with the phrase "I don't know" allows girls to distance themselves from knowledge that involves strong feelings—knowledge that may be too dangerous to express because it could isolate them from their friends. Unlike the *physically* perfect girl described by the girls with whom I spoke, the perfect girl depicted by Gilligan's informants is "nice," "never causes any problems," and "has no bad thoughts."[1] She goes along with the crowd and doesn't speak out against what others think.

Lyn Brown, in her book about girls' anger in middle school, aptly describes this process of silencing one's voice:

> What begins as boldness and an ability to express a plurality of feelings and thoughts in young girls seems to narrow over time as girls become increasingly pressured at the edge of adolescence to fall in line with the dominant social construction of reality . . . In other words, girls' experiences, strong feelings, and opinions come up against a relational impasse that constrains possibilities and shuts down their loud voices, a wall of "shoulds" in which approval is associated with their silence, love with selflessness, relationship with subordination and

lack of conflict, and anger or strong feelings with danger and disruption.[2]

The knowledge of how a girl "should" look and act is a haunting presence in the lives of many teen-aged girls. Awareness of the importance of acting nice coexists with jealousy and anger at the girl who appears to have it all. Fourteen-year-old Jen, her face drawn taut and troubled, speaks to her inner rage in the presence of the perfect girl:

> I know this one girl, my brother likes her. It's so disgusting. Her name's Elena. Oh, oh, she's so perfect! She's got long hair and a perfect figure. It's so gross. It makes me ill. And everyone like falls at her feet, and it's disgusting. It just makes me sick. And she's nice! That's the killer—she has to be nice. Why couldn't she just be mean? It drives me crazy.

Finding a fault in an attractive girl like Elena would provide a rationale for Jen's disliking her and would also give her an excuse not to be friendly toward her. Despite how nice she was, Elena could not be accepted as a friend because she was too attractive and thus posed a threat to Jen's sense of self.

When asked if she could be friends with a beautiful girl, Stephanie, a tall, willowy girl, thought for a moment before she responded. I recalled from our previous conversations that Stephanie's goal was to be a model. At 5'6" and 122 pounds, Stephanie lamented the fact that she needed to lose at least ten pounds before she could even be considered for a modeling position. She had been told this by an agent who had interviewed her for a photo shoot. She felt that it would be especially hard for her to be friends with a perfect girl, because she would feel so competitive with her. She knew that she would look at the beautiful girl's physical attributes her long legs, her height, her weight—and would feel resentment: "I'd be like, oh my God, why can't I look like that? Why aren't my legs that nice? That's my problem, my legs. I hate them but I mean I'm not obsessed with them or anything." Uncomfortable with her disclosure, Stephanie shifted positions and gazed into the distance as she continued. Her voice lost its resentment and took on a tone of tacit acceptance: "It's very hard to deal with that . . . when you see someone else that's got something that you don't. But," she quickly added, "I usually don't let those kind of feelings show. I mean I try to be friendly. After all, it's not her fault." Stephanie was caught between her feelings of jealousy toward the perfect girl and her simultaneous desire to suppress those feelings and act in accordance with cultural dictates of appropriate behavior. Mature and articulate beyond her sixteen years, Stephanie was able to pull the reins in on herself. She was able to silence her voice.

Patty, a dark-haired, thin, and very attractive tenth-grader who had recently transferred into the school, told me that she was continually shunned by her female classmates. According to her assessment, the middle- and upper-middle-class girls in her new school had taken an immediate dislike to her because of her good looks and had avoided getting to know her. Because Patty wore a lot of makeup and tight jeans, other girls labeled her a slut, which served to further impede her potential entry into female social groups.

Sociologist Donna Eder has explained that middle school girls often criticize others who stand out in some way, either by dressing in an unusual fashion or by making themselves "too attractive" or "too sexy."[3] At the schools at which I worked, commentary about other girls often included statements like "Well look at how high her shorts are! What a slut!" Critical discourse reinforced the importance of looking like everyone else and served as an important means of social control. Although girls are expected to express concern about their appearance, there are rules to follow as they do so. Linguist Penelope Eckert contends that gossip and "girl talk" serve as measures of where girls stand in relation to group norms.[4]

Gossiping about other girls also served to level the playing field—it provided an opportunity to lessen the advantage an attractive girl may have over other girls. According to Eder in her description of middle-schoolers, a girl who achieves the perfect, "ideal" look of a model is "likely to be accused of portraying false images or wanton sexuality."[5] This aptly describes the experience Patty encountered when she changed schools.

Competition and envy are byproducts of advertisements which convey a message that we, too, can be beautiful if only we are willing to purchase and use a new product. This message was clear in a popular shampoo advertisement that appeared several years ago depicting a beautiful woman with vibrant, bouncy hair. The copy read: "Don't hate me because I'm beautiful." The subtext was that she would share her secret (the product) and the jealous viewer could "have it all" in just a few days.

◆　　◆　　◆

What about the Boys?

Relatively little has been written about teen-aged boys in relation to body image. What research there is indicates that physical appearance is perceived to be a more salient issue among girls than among boys. Girls consider physical attractiveness more important for popularity than do boys and experience more dissatisfaction with their appearance than do their male counterparts.[6] Whereas there is a striking disparity between self-perception of obesity and actual weight for height among girls, this is less true for boys. In one study in which 270 adolescents were surveyed, almost half of the girls thought they were overweight, although 80 percent were actually normal weight for their height.[7] In contrast, boys in the study who thought they were fat tended to be overweight. Overweight adolescent boys in general do not internalize their weight problem as a personal failure, as do girls, and they are much less likely to suffer from low self-esteem as a result of their obesity.[8] Further, while negative body image is associated with suicide risk for girls, it is not for boys.[9]

But could this topic really be that cut and dry? As I was conducting the research for this project, my son was the same age as many of the girls I was interviewing. Although the research about adolescent boys told me otherwise, the boy I watched at home was extremely concerned with his appearance. When he gained weight as he entered puberty, he was fretful. When a pimple appeared on his generally clear complexion, he complained that his day was ruined. Although dieting efforts may have been supplanted by sit-ups and push-ups, his concern with his body shape was evident. His focus was not on being thin so much as on being physically strong and tall. Discerning whether his abdomen was increasing in definition was almost a nightly ritual in our household. My son's attention, if not obsession, with his body led me to consider whether the continued attention on girls' body image was eclipsing a more in-depth understanding of boys' preoccupation.

Recognizing that possibility, however, does not minimize the continued findings about girls and body image. It has been well documented that a girl's sense of self-esteem and emotional well-being is closely related to how she feels about her body.[10] The study *Shortchanging Girls, Shortchanging America,* which documents the plummeting of girls' self-esteem during adolescence, identifies confidence in "the way I look" as the single most important determinant of self-worth for white middle school girls. In contrast, boys in the study were more likely to cite their abilities as a measure of self-worth.[11] Journalist Peggy Orenstein reports that the middle school girls she interviewed had difficulty describing the advantages of being a girl but found it easy to identify the disadvantages.[12]

Differences between males and females continue across the life span. Adult women are more involved in self-checks on "physical presentation" and vigilant monitoring of their body weight and shape than are men.[13] Although weight and shape are important issues for men, they are not as central to their self-perceptions of attractiveness.[14] Some researchers have noted that for women a positive self-image hinges on perceived physical *attractiveness,* whereas for men, it hinges on perceived physical *effectiveness.*[15] As psychologist Judith Rodin and her colleagues have noted, "women primarily see their bodies as commodities, their physical appearance serving as an interpersonal currency."[16] Not only does having a nice body facilitate getting a relationship with a man, but once that connection is secured, women can exchange their relative attractiveness for good treatment within the relationship.[17]

In response to the interview question, "Is there more pressure for girls to look a certain way than for guys?" most girls were quick to agree that there was. In general, girls believed that they were under far more pressure than boys with respect to "their hair, their looks, their body, their clothes . . . and stuff like that." Whereas boys could "just put on a hat" and come to school, girls had to "put on makeup for three hours and look just right." Girls believed that standards for boys were non-existent; they could "even come to school with their pajamas on, and no one would even care." By contrast, girls were expected to wear makeup to look "natural." "Girls are supposed to have rosy cheeks and bright lips. Because I don't look like that," one fourteen-year-old explained, "I need to wear makeup." For many of her friends, the face in the magazine ad had become the face of comparison—the so-called natural look to achieve through the purchase of products. With repeated exposure to the many external pressures to enhance physical appearance, girls come to experience their efforts to improve how they look as freely chosen and natural.[18]

Beyond appearance, many girls agreed that there were more constraints on their behavior than on boys'. In a focus group with tenth-graders, Melissa, who struggled with her weight, explained:

> A girl should look slim and have a good figure and be feminine and be, you know, be like a cheerleader type and do her hair and be smart. And a guy can be whatever he wants. And girls that have muscles and are jocks are less accepted, and girls that are a little overweight are less accepted than the ones that are cheerleader types that look perfect, that act perfect. Guys, they can do almost anything. Girls have to be more careful about what they do, who they do it

with, who they're seen with, because they don't want
to get a reputation for being like a slut or anything.

Melissa's response is insightful on gender issues of image
management. Another girl similarly explained:

> I think girls need to look more feminine and have a
> certain look. Guys, a lot of them, just throw on
> whatever, and it doesn't matter a lot. There are just
> so many rules: girls shouldn't sit with their legs
> crossed, they should sit up straight, eat little salads
> and stuff like that; they should just overall seem less
> active, like sit around and talk rather than go out
> and play football. Girls shouldn't be loud. Girls
> shouldn't spit a loogey on the sidewalk and run
> around and act wild. Girls are supposed to eat less.
> Most people consider a girl should sit down and
> have a little salad and a soft drink at lunch, and the
> guys should go and get a big humongous plate of
> food.

Her friend Shelley jumped in at this point, returning again to
the importance of appearance:

> We all talk a lot about this . . . I really do believe that
> girls have a lot more pressure than guys to look
> good. It's like if a girl really likes a guy, he can just
> look any way, you know, he could be wearing rags,
> his hair could be all messed up, he could be sweaty
> and smelly and she'll still think he's totally fine. But
> if a girl is not wearing makeup one day or her hair's
> messed up or she smells or something, he'll be,
> "Ugh, I gotta look at that other girl," you know. So I
> think it's easier for a guy to just do whatever, and
> he'll still be liked. But I think it puts more pressure
> on the girl because she feels she has to look better
> than the other girls.

Without prompting, she continued, explaining how girls
learned these rules for appropriate dress and behavior:

You don't really see people saying, "A guy shouldn't do that." You always hear, "A girl shouldn't do that, because it's not feminine," or something. You just never hear, "That's not masculine." Unfeminine things are to burp or to walk like a guy or to fight, you know, something that you would normally see a guy doing. Guys typically tell girls what is feminine or not. I mean other girls go, "Who cares?" you know and they all spit and stuff. You never hear another girl saying, "That's not feminine."

After a moment, Shelley added: "Well really, I can do anything I want to, but not if I want a guy to like me. You know, you can't do anything you want if you're trying to impress a guy!"

This litany of rules for appropriate dress and behavior was repeated across our interviews. Although not all the girls repeated the same rules, few were unaware of them.[19] One of the reasons they gave for following the rules, regardless of what they thought of them, was the fear that the boys would tease them if they acted differently. Some were also concerned about social censure from other girls. In *Schoolgirls,* Peggy Orenstein writes that girls in her middle school study who were harassed by boys either by being called names ("slut," "ho") or by being pinched or grabbed were too fearful of reprisal to confront their harassers.[20]

Despite the discouraging, centuries-old social control that continued to exert its influence on these girls, I was heartened to find that many of them could look to their future careers and lifestyles with a sense of freedom and opportunity. In terms of their relationships with boys, however, girls revealed a sense of being under their watchful gaze.

Christine, an overweight tenth-grader, was a perceptive observer of her peers and a good listener, a quality that her friends admired. In our interview, she explained why she thought it was so important for girls to work hard to maintain their best appearance:

> Guys are very visual and girls are more articulate and have analytical eyes, and I think they look more

into a person and that's why they attach sentiments to someone, you know. But guys are very visual. I mean, the biggest-selling magazine among guys, you know, is *Playboy*. So I think it weighs really a lot on them. Guys at this age are very often skinny and not very well built. But that doesn't seem to matter. If a girl is underweight or overweight, that's terrible, you know. And it doesn't matter that the guys are all skinny and scrawny, but it matters that the girl's like all skin and bones. And it's worse if she's fat. That's when it matters. It's like "hypocrites."

Christine's observations about developmental differences between girls and boys are accurate. Whereas the average girl reaches her full height by about age fifteen, boys enter puberty much later and continue to mature and grow until age twenty. In her narrative, it is evident that Christine was angered by boys' unchallenged power to critique girls' bodies, but she also felt singularly powerless to fight against it. She had been the brunt of much teasing throughout middle school, and these memories were fresh in her mind. Her friends agreed that if a boy was overweight, he would be teased far less than a girl who was overweight. From my own observations of my son and his friends, I knew that boys did get teased, particularly by other boys. But this was generally not something girls perceived.

Continuous critique by male classmates was one reason girls felt it was important to monitor their own eating behavior. "Guys say looks are everything, that's all they talk about. When you walk by, guys always comment on how you look, like, 'Oh, she's so fat,' 'Oh, she's ugly,' 'Oh she's so gross.' A lot of guys just make really nasty remarks about girls that are overweight . . . and what they think is overweight is not what I think is overweight!" Girls also explained that when boys made fun of them it hurt more than when the criticism came from another girl. It was also harder to get back at them.

We asked the girls how they responded to boys' comments, and several noted that when the comments were directed at them, they bore them silently. Others explained that when boys they were friendly with made teasing comments about other girls' bodies, they would tell them to stop acting so rude and insensitive. Unfortunately, the boys often ignored these comments.

Researchers have found that as students move through middle school from sixth grade to eighth grade, girls tend to reduce their overt ridicule of others, while boys continue with these behaviors.[21] Boys and girls tend to scrutinize each other differently with regard to perceived attractiveness. Whereas boys tend to discuss the flaws of all the girls in the grade, girls tend to target the boys they considered "real losers."[22] The girls I spoke with confirmed this finding, and complained that boys' comments were directed toward particular parts of their bodies, such as their breasts.

❖   ❖   ❖

Eating in the Presence of Boys

The table is one place where thinness as the ideal of beauty is embodied. As children and adolescents, females are taught to equate attractiveness with being delicate and petite.[23] In order to appear feminine, girls learn to limit their food intake in front of boys. Studies of school culture report a high degree of gender segregation during lunch, particularly in middle school. This is probably a result of girls' heightened self-consciousness in eating around boys.[24]

The cafeterias in the schools where I worked were raucous environments that provided opportunities for gossip and close scrutiny of others. Girls commonly described how they would just "eat a few fries or a bite from a salad" if they were with boys, so as not to appear "piggish." They believed that boys didn't like to see girls eat a lot of food, and that it was somehow impolite for them to do so. Christine, the overweight girl discussed earlier, complained that boys made comments about her eating or would call her a pig. They did this indirectly, "like, they'll tell their friends and by the end of the day every-one will know what I ate." Other girls reported that boys made indirect comments about the amount they were eating, such as, "Aren't you done yet?" One eighth-grader provided the fol-lowing description of eating around boys:

> Well Jill and I, we're not like on a diet or anything but her boyfriend sits with us now at lunch and we're both self-conscious about what we eat. We used to eat with a group of girls, and when her boy-friend started eating with us, we ate less. Just 'cause he was sitting at the table right next to us and he was in our group. We're eating a lot less and eating slow—we used to scarf down our food and get out 'cause we don't like the cafeteria, but now we eat a lot slower and he has to wait for us.

For purposes of image management, these two girls had re-duced their food intake so as to appear more feminine. Eating slowly so that "he has to wait for us" was a signal that they were in control of their appetites, that they knew "when to say when." Girls also described a fear of eating "messy" foods like pizza, spaghetti, or cheeseburgers in the presence of boys. At least for some girls, this fear of eating in front of boys per-sisted through high school. One eleventh-grader remarked that when she first started going out with her boyfriend she wouldn't eat anything in the movie theater even though she "totally loved popcorn." Finally she graduated to eating lico-rice in his presence!

Some girls did engage in a degree of resistance to ideals about appropriate eating behavior. Chloe, a rebellious fifteen-year-old whose black-and-purple dyed hair streamed down over her eyes, remarked:

> I guess girls are supposed to eat a little bit, but I don't know. I mean I'm not scared to eat around guys, unless it's something like spaghetti and then it's like totally embarrassing. But like guys get really irritated when girls like sit there and just nibble at

their food. I know some guys that just get so mad
when girls do that, but girls think they're supposed
to eat that way. I'm like, "give me a break."

In contrast to girls, boys were described as "inhaling" food
and eating whenever and whatever possible. Not only did they
themselves eat more, but in some instances, they even attempted to control their girlfriends' eating. At 5′6″ and 140
pounds, Lori was a high school junior who belonged to the
popular group and played on the girls' softball team. Like many
of her friends, Lori felt fat, a feeling that had intensified since
she began a relationship with her current boyfriend, Matt:

> Well, like I would be eating Doritos and then my
> boyfriend, he like makes these noises. He goes,
> "blub, blub" . . . [laughs] . . . you know like fat is
> supposed to sound . . . I don't know [laughs]. But
> then I'm just kind of like, "oh." You know, it's just so,
> I don't know, boys can be really mean about it. So I
> don't know. And I get mad at him about it too be-
> cause it's so insulting. I mean, he shouldn't go out
> with me if he feels that way . . . just because he
> might not like my appearance or whatever . . . so I
> really hate that.

Her boyfriend continually gave her "little hints" that she had
better be careful about what she eats. She thought that his
warning might be more for him than it was for her. "You know
like maybe he's like thinking, "Oh my God, she's gonna gain
weight and she's gonna like, plump out . . . and embarrass me."
Although Lori felt angry at her boyfriend for caring more
about her appearance than about her as a person, she continued to date him. In her narrative, laughter allowed her to distance her feelings of frustration at his attitude as well as to silence other voices that may have been sounding inside her.
She recognized that no matter who she was with, the pressure
to look good and be thin would still be there.

Pressure to maintain a "good" body shape was in part
predicated on the fear of losing a boyfriend to a girl with a

better body. Across high school, these pressures became increasingly pronounced as girls' social worlds expanded. Diane, a tenth-grader who was 5'6" and weighed 130 pounds, described how she changed her eating habits after she started going out with her most recent boyfriend:

> Well I diet more now, more because of my boyfriend than anything else, you know. 'Cause I don't care what they think [other girls], I don't want to impress anyone else but just because, you know, I don't think he wants to walk around with some gooch fat old girlfriend, you know. There are other skinny girls out there. I don't trust him.

Although Diane declares her autonomy from others' thinking, asserting that she doesn't want to impress anyone, she was still trying to lose weight, and her boyfriend was "helping" her by rationing her intake of foods. She had asked him for help because he was on the school wrestling team, where he had learned how to drop weight quickly. But she felt that she had limited will power to follow his suggestions. Although she sometimes "sneaked" chocolate when he was not with her, she usually confessed her transgressions to him later on. She described the following incident:

> I get rationed. Like we had Hershey's kisses one night. These guys brought two bags. I'm like the only girl and I'm like, "I won't eat any." So I sat there and watched and watched and I was like, "All right, I'll have some." So he takes this huge old handful of them and he puts them in front of himself and he flicks three of them over to me [laughs]. He goes, "That's it." I was like [sniffling noises]. I broke into tears. "I want more," I said.

Like Lori, Diane wants to be thin for her boyfriend so he will remain true to her. She also wants to be able to eat her share of chocolates, without worry or condemnation, just like the guys. The presence of conflicts such as these was continually reaffirmed during interviews with the girls.

Many researchers have described how males watch females with a controlling gaze, that is, by conducting a visual inspection of female bodies. This gaze carries with it the potential for sexual objectification, which occurs when a woman's body is separated from her person and regarded as if it were capable of representing her.[25] In other words, when women are objectified, they are treated as bodies—bodies that are there to be used for the pleasure of others. Socialized in this environment, some girls begin to view themselves as objects to be looked at and examined. Rosalind Coward has defined the different roles males and females play in this process:

> Men's bodies and sexuality are taken for granted, exempted from scrutiny, whereas women's bodies are extensively defined and overexposed. Sexual and social meanings are imposed on *women's* bodies, not men's. Controlling the look, men have left themselves out of the picture because a body defined is a body controlled.[26]

Teen-aged girls like Diane and Lori are already subjected to the controlling gaze of boyfriends who may only be important in their lives for a short time. Relationships such as these are a double-edged sword. In the process of developing opposite-sex relationships, girls move away from their primary relationships with their girlfriends. Gaining male approval often results in a lessening of intimacy with same-sex friendships because male interest is interpreted as the ultimate form of recognition.[27] Many girls I spoke with painfully described the loss of a close girlfriend who had shifted to a new relationship with a boy who monopolized her time and consumed her thoughts.

❖   ❖   ❖

Being Overweight

Stereotypes about fatness as "bad" are internalized at an early age. In one study, children ages six to nine were shown three body silhouettes and asked to ascribe behavioral characteristics to them. The children liked the thinner, "normal" figures best, describing them with positive attributes such as friendly, kind, happy, and polite. The overweight figures, by contrast, were seen most negatively and were described as lazy, lying, and cheating.[28] In another study, children aged ten and eleven were shown drawings of other children and were asked, "Which girl/boy do you like the most?" They consistently ranked drawings of obese children the lowest, preferring drawings of a child with missing limbs or a child in a wheelchair.[29]

Research indicates that obesity may also be a handicap in the educational system. One study of second- through fifth-grade students and their teachers found that in comparison with average-weight children, obese children were rated by teachers as having more conduct problems and were less well liked by their classmates.[30] These studies lend support to the notion that, from an early age, American children ascribe positive characteristics to thin people and negative qualities to heavy people.[31]

In one study in which overweight high school girls were asked how others viewed them, common stereotypes noted were that people thought they enjoyed fighting, that they were inactive or lazy, that they were tougher than others, and that they had no feelings if teased.[32] Similar judgments of overweight people were substantiated in our ethnographic interviews. Sarah, an extremely thin sophomore who was always surrounded by an entourage of girlfriends, remarked: "Who wants to be seen with a fat person? I mean I try to avoid really large people. I guess I feel uncomfortable around them. I'm just really quick to judge and assume. Like, 'Oh, that person's fat—they must be very hostile because of their weight.' So I just try and stay away from them."

Wendy, a curly-haired, heavy-set freshman, understood these attitudes from another perspective. At 5'7" and 180 pounds, Wendy had recently lost ten pounds and had as her long-term goal to lose forty more. She had been on a diet program for as long as she could remember, but her success was usually short-lived. When I asked her how she felt about her recent weight loss, Wendy remarked:

> Well when I lose a little more I think I'll probably start feeling better around people and stuff. Because I think, I mean, it's just like with smoking, society just prejudges people who are fat. Like they'll say, "Well, you know, she eats a lot," or "Don't go out with her, you'll never have a decent meal because she'll eat it all," or something like that. They think they're [fat people] really mean or something. And it's really not true. I know a lot of people prejudge people who are fat . . . but my friends seem to be very good . . . But there are certain people at school that just don't want to be with you, like if you're not a size six or you don't wear *these* kind of clothes or *that* kind of shoes. But *my* friends pretty much accept me 'cause I try to be nice.

Wendy was acutely aware of weight-related stereotypes even though she had a supportive group of friends who looked beyond her body size. Later that week, I interviewed Wendy's best friend, Lisa, who was tall for her age and of average weight. After some discussion, our conversation turned to the prejudice she had observed against Wendy. She plucked nervously at the grass as she shared her observations:

> There's like this group of girls at school who are really snobby and stuck-up. Kinda like the cheerleading crowd and stuff. Not a one of them is overweight—they're all *perfect*. You know, *perfect* hair, little designer clothes. And they make judgments. They would never be friends with someone like Wendy because she's a little bit overweight. She just doesn't look right for them. That's what I hate about groups like that.

Because of the airs they put on, Lisa opted to avoid the popular group. While discussing her social history, I learned that Lisa had, in fact, been in the popular crowd for a short time.

She was disturbed when another girl confronted her with the question, "How can you hang out with Wendy? She's so fat!" Wendy had been a friend of Lisa's since third grade, and joining the "in" group would have meant giving up her long-term friendship with her. Lisa felt that she didn't fit in with a group of people who, by virtue of their looks, sat in judgment of others. Wendy was a victim of that judgment and Lisa felt powerless to change the situation. The best she could do was to tell Wendy not to listen to their comments about her weight.

Stereotypes about being overweight abounded among the teens we interviewed. Overweight girls were commonly described as "very, very jealous—they don't like people that are a lot skinnier than they are." Fifteen-year-old Cathy related how her two former best friends, who were both overweight, began to exclude her from their social events. "I'm the smallest one of our group," she said, "and a lot of times they don't want me going out with them when they go out cruising because they think the guys are gonna come to me and talk to me more than they would them. My best friend, Tammie, well, I've been friends with her for ten years, she's kind of heavy . . . you know, overweight, and Carey, my other friend, she's also overweight." At that point, Cathy began to rummage through her backpack, retrieved her wallet, and showed me pictures of her friends posing in her bedroom: "I mean, like you can see, right . . . they're heavy but still attractive, you know. And Tammie she just throws a fit every weekend about my going out with them . . . I'm trying to stay away from them right now because I don't like how they treat me." Cathy's experience showed that some prejudices can work both ways: from thin girls to heavy ones and perhaps, as a form of self-preservation, from heavy girls to thin girls.

In one-on-one interviews we asked the girls, "If a person is overweight, do you think it's their responsibility to change?" We recorded a range of responses, often depending on the girl's own body shape, her personal experience with trying to lose weight, or her observation of family members. Many girls responded with a "whatever" comment that supported individual freedom and choice. Examples include: "If they want to change they should, but if they're happy then I'm happy"; "I'd rather see a girl who's fat try to lose weight, but if it doesn't bother her then it doesn't bother me"; and "If that's how she wants to live, then that's her choice." I was a bit perplexed by these responses. How could girls be so nonchalant when questioned about heaviness after having expressed such strong concern about the social risks of being fat?

Just as girls didn't want others, particularly parents or teachers, to tell them what *they* should do, they were reluctant to impose *their* opinions about body shape on others. I observed a similar phenomenon in discussions with girls about smoking. Even those who were adamantly opposed to smoking were reluctant to criticize other teens for their decision to smoke. After all, it was their choice, and if they wanted to do it, who were they to object? This double-think represents a fundamental paradox of adolescence—the struggle for autonomy and independence coexisting with social sanctions to appear to be like and accept one's peers.

Follow-up questions revealed a pervasive belief that if an overweight person "really wanted to" she could lose weight or could prevent herself from getting heavy in the first place. Although there was some recognition that obesity ran in families, girls were supposed to engage in a personal fight against fat. To do so constituted responsible action. Failure to do so was a blatant indication that the girl did not care enough about her appearance and, worse yet, that she was lazy. This same attitude has been reported among adults. As psychologist Esther Rothblum has written, "Weight is thought to be under voluntary control, so that fat people are held responsible for their condition and for changing it."[33]

Nina, a fourteen-year-old who had been on self-imposed diets for the past year, felt that she needed to lose about 25 pounds (she was 5′5″ and weighed 165 pounds). When asked how she felt about overweight girls, she remarked, "I look at them and I say, well, how could you do that to yourself? I mean how could you really not care for yourself so much as to let yourself look like that?" Nina had internalized this message and saw it as her responsibility to try to lose weight. This was being responsible, what a girl *should* do. Even if she was unsuccessful at her attempts, "then that's too bad, you know, but I should at least try." One way in which Nina demonstrated her commitment to losing weight was through her public eating behavior: no one ever saw *her* eating foods like pizza or french fries in the cafeteria. By letting others know that she was trying to lose weight, she enhanced her moral identity. She was heroically fighting the good fight.

Kate, a tenth-grade, self-described Type A personality, had successfully managed to lose about 30 pounds through a variety of strategies, including smoking cigarettes and fasting. At the time of our interview, she was 5′6″ and weighed 140 pounds. Though she was painfully aware that smoking was bad for her health (her grandmother had died of lung cancer), she also recognized that being fat was bad for her self-image and her popularity. Smoking cigarettes seemed like the lesser of two evils. She remarked:

> I know it's sad but the first thing that comes to my mind when I think about a fat person is "ugh." How much self-respect they have to lose every time they look in the mirror. I know I did. People have a tendency to kind of look down on overweight people. Especially people like me, who were fat and lost a lot of weight, you know. Because you look at them and you think, "There's got to be something they can do!" You know . . . even if it's just pick clothes that play it down.

Kate saw herself as a fat person who now fit into a skinny body through a lot of hard work. By suggesting that overweight girls dress in such a way as to minimize their fatness, she was identifying what she considered a socially responsible action. Dressing right entailed hiding one's "cottage cheese," or dimpley thighs, in baggy pants, sticking to big blouses, and never wearing spandex or miniskirts.

The absence of self-respect in overweight girls was a

theme that emerged repeatedly in our discussions. Stephanie, the girl who wanted to be a model, had been socialized by her father, a long-distance runner, to have a heightened consciousness of her food consumption, particularly how many grams of fat she ingested. She openly asserted that she had little respect for any girl who was overweight, unless she had evidence that the girl was dieting. During our interview, she described a girl in her geometry class who was "like super overweight." She recalled, "One day she was like sitting back in a chair, all slouched over, eating Reese's Peanut Butter Cups. I have no respect for her. She has no respect for herself." Stephanie's lack of respect for the girl stemmed in part from the fact that she had heard her complain about her weight. From Stephanie's perspective, the girl had no right to complain about her weight problem so long as she ate candy instead of taking responsible action. Dieting would at least buy her some social acceptability—but no, this girl wasn't even trying!

The ideal of responsible action is reminiscent of the Protestant work ethic. In today's society it is complemented by an equally pervasive message to enjoy, or what Robert Crawford has referred to as "the ethic of control and release."[34] This ethic fuels capitalism by causing us to be dissatisfied with ourselves and thus consume products.[35] In order to "progress," we need to produce and also to consume. One obvious source of this ethic is the anonymous voice of advertising that tells us it is both natural and desirable to participate in control (dieting) and release (indulging in one's senses or fantasies). Products have been crafted to bridge the paradox of working toward the ever-thinner body (an icon of success) and pleasurable consumption. Weight Watcher's promises that "dieting is a piece of cake," while Nutri/System tongue sprays "allow you to taste it," to have your cake without eating it! Whatever the product, the message is clear: there is a fix for your fatness, even if you are low on will power. But if you succumb to the sins of fat-rich temptation instead of opting for the fat-free SnackWell brownies, then you must bear the responsibility!

Many of the girls in the study perceived obesity as a kind of sickness. Just as some people were addicted to alcohol, others were "addicted to food." As one girl explained:

> I have a friend that's overweight and I feel that she should—I mean, I don't have anything against her 'cause she's overweight—but I guess it makes me mad that she doesn't do anything about it. She could do something about it and she doesn't. It's like her responsibility . . . like, last night I went over there and right when I walked in she had a bag of Doritos—she was just, I mean, it's just like she's constantly eating. She's addicted to food. She just can't stop.

Another girl commented that when she saw a fat person eating, she wondered why that person still needed to consume food. Eating when you already had an excess of fat was a clear indication that you were addicted to food. After all, fat people had plenty of reserves and should just be able to draw on them. After this girl had gained some weight—and still continued to eat—she realized how foolish her thinking had been and how "you're hungry whether you're fat or not." This feeling of anger toward a girl who was fat and who "dared" to continue to eat was expressed by many of the teens we interviewed.

Not being able to control a food addiction was a sign of personal weakness. Interestingly, similar ideas emerged in interviews with teens about smoking. Whereas it was cool and "kinda fun" to smoke, it was *not* cool to be addicted to cigarettes. In keeping with notions of adolescent independence, girls projected the image that they should be able to control their smoking, rather than have their smoking control them. Similarly, a girl shouldn't let her desire for food control her. Being overweight was a clear signal that she was out of control.

In interviews, I found myself reluctant to question overweight girls about their perception of obesity. Not unlike the girls I spoke with, I felt it was culturally inappropriate to call attention to another person's weight problem. I was a lot more comfortable talking to girls about weight-related issues when they were not overweight. I was uncertain how to talk with Jennifer, who at 15 was 5′6″ and weighed about 240 pounds. What were the appropriate questions to ask to tap into her feelings about weight? Would it be insensitive to ask her and other large girls direct questions about their body image?

To my relief, at the onset of the interview Jennifer began talking about her body size without prompting. She seemed comfortable discussing the issue. About half way into the hour-long interview, she spoke about how other ninth-graders felt about overweight people at her school:

> They turn away from them. So I don't know. Do you understand? It's like they don't talk to them as much . . . I don't know . . . It's like we're like outcasts. But that's changing now. 'Cause I mean that's how it used to be . . . like you would walk by and they would like totally tease you . . . I guess it just depends on the person. Because sometimes, you know, they can be nice and they don't even say anything, and sometimes they can be like total jerks.

Her question to me, "Do you understand?" was repeated often during the interview as she spoke about body image. In her discussion about weight issues in relation to her mother (see Chapter 5), Jennifer explained that her mother, who was of normal weight, "just couldn't understand" what it was like to be fat. Similarly, Jennifer seemed to doubt my ability to understand the problems of someone who was very overweight when I myself was not.

As I listened to the girls speak about their frustrations with their bodies and how they felt they needed to look, I was both saddened and troubled by their definitions of appropriate femininity. When so much had changed in the world of women, how could so much have remained the same? How could the litany of rules that girls feel pressured to follow be so reminiscent of the rules of the 1960s, when I was their age?

I wondered whether it was just the rhetoric that had remained the same, or whether girls' behaviors had changed. Were girls really doing something about their obsession with thinness, or were they just talking about it?

Discussing their bodies opens a floodgate of emotions in young girls, including jealousy, envy, rage, and alienation. Such feelings are silenced by some, whispered by others, and shouted by a few. By age fourteen and probably much, much earlier, many white middle-class girls have surmised that social competence comes with conformity, with striving toward an elusive ideal of perfection. As we will see in Chapters 2 and 3, some girls do resist, parody, and reappropriate culturally prescribed ideals for female body shape. But the image of the ideal is always close by, lurking like an inescapable shadow in the background of girls' lives.

2

Fat Talk

All the girls are always saying, "I'm *so* fat," like that. Then I'm like, "No, you're not." Then they're like, "Yes, I am." Some girls I know that say that . . . they're really skinny and they just wannabe . . . they just want people to say that they're skinny so that they'll feel better about themselves. I go, "No, you're not," but they keep on saying, "I'm so fat," so they can hear me saying that they're *not* fat.

HEATHER, *AGE 14*

URING ONE of the first focus-group discussions with eighth-grade girls I asked, "Do you think that a lot of girls your age are concerned about their weight?" Whereas some of the previous questions I had asked had evoked little response, this one caught their attention. The girls replied quickly, enthusiastically nodding their heads and giggling, leading me to ask, "How do you know that?" Within moments, they began to reenact a common scene from their lives, using a dialogue that revolved around the expression "I'm so fat." Delighting in their own performance, they all but forgot my presence for the moment. The opening statement "I'm so fat" prompted the same response each time: "Oh no you're not!"

As I listened to normal-weight girls engage in what seemed like ritualistic speech, several questions popped into my mind: What was their purpose in talking this way? Who used the expression "I'm so fat"? Was it just the "popular" girls, or was it also girls on the fringe who rebelled against convention in their dress and hairstyles? As I began to unravel the multiple layers of meanings behind such exchanges, I came to label them "fat talk."

No sooner had I given this phenomenon a name than I began hearing fat talk everywhere, even among women my own age. At restaurants, at parties, and even at work, I would hear women initiate fat talk. It seemed so pervasive that I wondered why I hadn't really noticed it before. My most memorable encounter with fat talk took place thousands of miles from my home, at the sculpture garden on the mall of the Smithsonian Institution. I was sitting on a bench in the garden, enjoying a peaceful moment, trying to decompress from an intensive adolescent health workshop I had just attended. The peace was suddenly shattered when a group of teen-aged girls arrived, obviously on a school trip. As they looked at the Rubinesque statues of naked women, they shrieked, almost in unison, "Oh my god, they're so fat!" "I'd die if I looked like that!" Shouts, elbow jabs, and gales of laughter accompanied their critiques, which quickly turned to specific body parts of several statues. The most caustic comments were directed toward oversized thighs and buttocks. "Even *my* butt looks small compared to hers," an average-weight blond girl said. Her friend immediately replied, "Oh shut up, you know you're not fat! There's nothing wrong with *your* butt!"

So it seemed that females of all ages saw the world in terms of thin and fat. But the question was, why did they talk about it so much? Did "talking the talk" have distinct meanings at different points in women's lives? I myself was certainly not exempt from commenting on feeling fat. When I put on a pair of jeans that were suddenly too tight (had I left them in the dryer for too long, again?), I would grumble to my husband, "I'm so fat." I was not fishing for a compliment, but merely stating a fact! From observations of what I myself did, and from conversations with friends, I had some sense of how fat talk was used by adult women, but I wanted to understand what it meant in the lives of girls.

Discussions with girls about weight and body image inevitably led to comments on fat talk. Many girls told us that fat talk occurs frequently among friends during the course of a day. By the time a white middle-class girl reaches adolescence, she has become a competent participant in this discourse, whether or not she actually practices weight control. Talking the talk doesn't necessarily reflect actual behavior; rather, it indexes important personal and cultural concerns. But there is more to it than that.

Girls engage in fat talk for a variety of purposes. At times, the statement "I'm so fat" can be used as an idiom of distress, allowing a girl to allude to widely diffuse feelings. In this sense, announcing that you feel fat is like stating that you are very stressed or feel out of control. Saying "I'm so fat" allows a girl to be ambiguous about what she feels. One ninth-grader remarked that among her female family members, the saying "I'm having a fat day" indicated that things in general were not going well. For another girl, saying she was fat meant she was really depressed. "Like sad is in my head," she said, "but feeling fat means I feel bad all over."

The statement "I'm so fat" is actually much more than an observation about how a girl looks or feels. It is a call for support from her peers. The response she receives from her friends is an affirmation that she is, in fact, *not* fat, and that things aren't as bad as they seem. In addition, fat talk serves other purposes related to group identity. It allows a girl to call attention to her imperfections before others do (that is, beating them to the punch just in case that's what they were thinking). Girls read cues provided by the speaker and the situation to derive the meaning of their "I'm so fat" statement. For example, when "I'm so fat" is uttered by a girl who is changing her clothes in the locker room, the impetus for the statement may come from the vulnerability of exposing her body to the sight of others. It is then appropriate for another girl to respond in a way that mitigates the speaker's discomfort. When the statement comes before eating, it provides an apology or excuse for the indulgence at hand (in effect, a secular "grace" before eating). When examining the "I'm so fat" interchange, it is important to look beyond the content of the message to the social relations of the discourse as a performance in which group solidarity and personal identity are negotiated.

A main goal of conversation in general during adolescence is understanding the self in relation to others. Being vulnerable and being able to talk about oneself are mechanisms for achieving this goal. Saying "I'm so fat" performs the function of disclosing vulnerability and may give other girls the impression that the speaker is "withholding nothing." Through the sharing of thoughts and feelings, girls bond around shared problems and increase one another's self-esteem by providing positive feedback and social support.[1] Girls are socialized to rely heavily on external acceptance and feedback to inform their identity.[2]

Research has found that girls are more social than boys before adolescence and become even more social during adolescence.[3] That is, they spend more time talking than boys do, spend more time grooming in front of friends, and spend more time doing homework in the company of their friends. Psychologists Reed Larson and Maryse Richards found that the amount of time girls spend talking with their friends nearly *triples* between fifth and ninth grade.[4] In part, this may be because at an age when their sense of self is fragile, girls are both reassured and gratified to know that friends understand how they feel. In contrast to girls, who achieve closeness through a sharing of private thoughts, boys experience closeness through shared activities. Indeed, intimacy, emotional closeness, and trust are generally more characteristic of girls' relationships than of boys' at all ages.[5] Through interactions with their friends, girls learn and practice social skills such as the ability to empathize with and understand the point of view of others.[6]

Linguist Deborah Tannen has shown that the language of conversation among women is primarily a language of rapport, that is, a means of establishing connections and negotiating relationships. To this end, emphasis in female conversation is placed on showing similarities and matching experiences.[7] Fat talk, the sharing of one's thoughts about the inadequacies of one's body shape, serves this rapport-building function well.

What follows is an excerpt from a discussion with three high school freshmen that typifies the kind of exchange I often heard among the girls. The conversation began as a response to a question I posed about the reasons for weight control. These three fifteen-year-olds, Colleen, Nicole, and Kelley, had been best friends since seventh grade:

COLLEEN: I remember this so clearly . . . in third grade we had to fill out these forms . . . like how tall you were, what color your eyes were, what color your hair was, and your weight. And I remember in third grade thinking, "I'm so fat." Seriously. That's really young, but I remember just being *so* ashamed of my weight.

NICOLE: Oh yeah! I remember filling those out!

MIMI: Do you talk about it a lot among your friends? About weight and feeling fat?

NICOLE: About weight? All the time.

KELLEY: Who doesn't say, "Oh, God, I'm so fat!"

NICOLE: Yeah, or "I hate my hair" or something.

KELLEY: Yeah. I don't think anyone really takes anyone seriously.

COLLEEN: It's so true.

KELLEY: I mean, because you just, you say that and . . .

NICOLE: I have one friend . . . she's little and she doesn't . . . I mean, okay, I'll say it [laughs] . . . okay, it's Jennifer . . . I don't think, she has like an ounce of fat on her. But her friends—like me—um . . . we'll be like, "Oh God, I'm so fat," or "Look at my thighs," and she'll just say the same thing. And I have a feeling she does it just because everyone else does it. I mean, if I was skinny *I* wouldn't do it. I'd be like, "ha, ha, ha" to everyone else.

KELLEY: But I don't think anyone really takes anyone seriously. And when I say, "I'm so fat," people just go, "Shut up," but I'm really saying what I mean. I don't want people to go, "Oh no, Kelley. You look great." I don't want that. I just want people to know how *I* feel.

Although Nicole reluctantly questions why their mutual friend Jennifer bothers to engage in fat talk and claims that she herself would flaunt her thinness to her friends, she does not recognize an important fact: by participating in fat talk, Jennifer negotiates her sameness and shows she is no better than her friends.

Fat talk is not entirely satisfying for Kelley, who uses it but is frustrated with the curt responses of her friends. By talking about how fat she feels, Kelley is giving voice to how she sees herself. She wants her friends to listen, to attend to what she has to say, not to silence her quickly. She feels as though her friends "bandaid" her feelings, trying to cover up the places where she doesn't feel good about herself.

Why is there so much concern with talking about one's self, particularly one's body? According to psychologist David Elkind, adolescents believe that others are even more preoccupied with their appearance and behavior than they themselves are.[8] He explains:

> The adolescent takes the other person's point of view to an extreme degree. S/he is so concerned with the point of view of others and how they regard her that s/he often loses sight of her own point of view.[9]

From Elkind's perspective, the adolescent is always on stage as the main actor, and his or her peers are an imaginary audience. Girls are particularly involved with this audience, and put on an ever-changing performance.[10]

"I'm so fat" is also used as a marker of group affiliation. Group identification is a central developmental task of early adolescence, with a more autonomous sense of identity achieved in late adolescence.[11] Fat talk offers the opportunity for all group members to obtain affirmation that they look good. It becomes a way for friends to share positive comments as well as to build group solidarity. Beyond one's immediate group of friends, fat talk also serves the purpose of consensus building in the larger community of girls. As Colleen described at another point in the interview: "I don't know, like somebody will make a comment in the girls' locker room or something and everybody adds, 'Oh my God, look at these legs of mine' or something, you know. 'You think you're fat! Look at me!'" Pausing for a moment, Colleen continued, "It's fun, though. I mean, it's not really fun, but . . . you get input on what everybody else thinks."

The creation and maintenance of group affiliation also take place in conversations before meals. "I'm so fat" is sometimes stated by a girl waiting in the cafeteria line, particularly if she is about to make a fattening or calorie-laden food choice. Stating that she knows that she is already fat is an admission that she knows she shouldn't be eating, that she knows she should be on a diet. It is a public presentation of responsibility and concern for her appearance.[12] The confession of a little guilt forestalls further scrutiny and frees the speaker to do as she pleases.[13] This statement also puts her in control of the situation. She has announced that she knows the true state of her body, and has therefore precluded anyone else from telling her what it might be.

Girls generally agreed that those who say "I'm so fat" are not significantly overweight and do not attempt to change their weight for sustained periods of time. Rather, for many girls, the motivation in saying "I'm so fat" is to gauge what other girls think of them. In response to fifteen-year-old Shari's discussion of feeling fat, I asked: "Do you tell your friends that you feel that way?" She answered, "Yeah, and they sit there going, 'No, you're not,' but I don't know really if they're telling me the truth, and I *really* would like to know. Even if I say, 'Tell me the honest to God truth,' they'll probably say, 'No, you're not.' And inside their heads . . . I mean, they're probably saying, 'Yes, you are,' but . . . I mean, I don't really know that but I would like to." Despite her frustration with the politics of fat talk and the fact that she sees through its veneer, Shari still continues to use it.

Girls in our study who were significantly overweight would not say, "I'm so fat" because that would call attention to their problem. It is also considered inappropriate for one girl to call attention to another's fatness. In one study of junior high school students, it was found that given the option of "talking with a friend about eating concerns," only a few girls who actually were over- or underweight expressed interest in doing so.[14] Girls who *felt* they were overweight (but were actually normal weight) were more likely to want to talk about such concerns than were girls who actually *were* overweight.

Tacit cultural sanctions seem to prevent females from commenting on another's fatness or recent weight gain. The presence of certain phrases and the conspicuous absence of others in everyday conversation provide examples of how these sanctions operate. In some circles, there is no better compliment than "Gee, you look great. Have you lost weight?" Yet few woman in the United States would approach another female— even a close friend—with the comment, "You look like you've gained some weight." To do so would be considered rude and hurtful.[15]

◆   ◆   ◆

To Participate or Not?

So was there peer pressure to engage in fat talk? Girls we spoke with were hesitant to use the term "peer pressure." In fact, most denied that they experienced pressure to do anything! For example, when we asked if there was peer pressure to smoke, the vast majority of girls stated that there really wasn't any, that it was a girl's own choice. This directly contradicts the literature, which has concluded that peer pressure is one of the main reasons for smoking initiation among youth. In contrast to the notion of peer pressure, girls described "self-pressure"—a need to adopt behaviors similar to those of their friends that was internally, not externally, motivated. The term "self-pressure" may more adequately capture the experience of adolescents, who are keenly aware of what they "should" do and yet are adamant that their decisions and actions are totally independent of anyone else, including their best friends. Thus, although most girls agreed that they needed to engage in fat talk, from their perspective, they were not "pressured" to do so.[16]

In one-on-one interviews we asked the girls if they heard many of their friends saying "I'm so fat" and if they said it themselves. Robin, a fair, red-haired fifteen-year-old, explained that even though she didn't really think she was too fat (and at 5′5″ and 125 pounds she wasn't), she felt she *had* to say it when she was with her friends. In fact, she was "fed up" with fat talk and diet talk. She knew, however, that if she did not acknowledge that she shared those feelings, she would separate herself from the group by implying that she was perfect. In other words, saying that she didn't diet or watch what she ate would be an admission that she didn't need to work on herself—that she was satisfied with how she looked. Being satisfied with one's appearance displaces the goal of working toward a more perfect future.

Shortly after I spoke with Robin, I interviewed Karen, who was a freshman at the same high school. Despite being tall and thin, Karen told me that she "sometimes" felt like she needed to lose ten pounds. When I asked her if she said "I'm so fat" to her friends, she answered:

> Well, I don't know, it's just like I feel stupid if all my friends are like, "Oh, I'm fat," and I don't say it, I feel like I'm bragging about myself, so I automatically say it anyway . . . so I don't know . . . Sometimes I *do*

{ 53 }

feel fat, but other times I don't really feel that I'm fat
but I still say it. I mean, it's not like I'm looking for a
compliment, it's just I don't want to feel like I'm
bragging about myself by not saying it.

Talking about her bodily imperfections establishes and
maintains a girl's position as part of the group and makes it
known that she doesn't consider herself better than any of the
other girls. Like what Robin had told me, Karen's comment
implies that a girl's failure to complain about her body may
elicit an indignant response from other girls, something along
the lines of, "Well who do you think *you* are?".

Is there something wrong with being satisfied with how
you look? Yes! In many of my conversations, what was striking
was the degree to which girls qualified their positive thoughts
about themselves. For example, girls who were generally considered to be very pretty (as assessed by their classmates)
were hesitant to refer to themselves in that way. The comments of Jody, a very attractive tenth-grader, seemed to typify
this: "Well I'm not bad, I mean, I wouldn't call myself pretty,
but I guess I'm okay." This was true not only about looks, but
about getting good grades, being an athlete, or excelling in
any way. On one level this humility made sense, because
clearly it is not appropriate to brag, but I sensed that there was
something deeper in the girls' aversion to speaking highly of
themselves.

The need to downplay one's positive attributes struck a
chord deep within me. When I was growing up, my mother
had repeatedly told me, "Self-praise is of no recommendation." I heard this whenever I spoke highly of myself, and it effectively silenced me. It also led me to believe that I should
look for praise from external sources. I hated that saying, but
years later when my son would come home from school
speaking of his successes, I would change the tone of my voice
into an authoritative one and say, "Remember what Grandma
used to tell me: 'Self-praise is of no recommendation.'" That
made us both laugh. Somehow parodying the saying in that
way mitigated the influence it once had in my life. Though I

no longer use those words, they have left an indelible impression on my sense of appropriate presentation of self. Perhaps the reason I was so sensitive to the absence of positive talk in many girls' self-narratives was that I had been trained to be that way myself.

Just as a girl needs to participate in fat talk, she also needs to be careful not to speak of herself in a way that might lead others to characterize her as being "stuck up"—a label that would cause her to be shunned by her peers. In her study of pre-teen and teen-aged girls and boys, anthropologist Marjorie Goodwin found that girls' behavior was subject to heavier sanctions than was boys.[17] Girls who seemed too sure of themselves or who set themselves apart from the crowd were ostracized. Self-deprecation and self-effacement are common devices to downplay one's achievements and natural attributes.[18] From childhood, girls learn to temper what they have to say so as not to appear too self-assured or overly aggressive. The use of the term "I don't know" allowed girls to offer their opinions and at the same time qualify them with a cloud of uncertainty.

I observed that attractive girls couldn't accept compliments easily from their peers and often added disclaimers. Girls recognized this pattern themselves. As Vicky, a tenth-grader, explained, "Like I'll say you look nice today to a girl who's real pretty and she'll go, 'No, no, I don't' and start complaining about something, her hair or something. It's just so annoying!" Expressing imperfection or revealing one's dissatisfaction with oneself may operate in dominant American culture in the same way that a protective device (such as a talisman) is used to avert harm from the evil eye in other cultures. Both serve to deflect the jealous thoughts of another.

Although it is not acceptable for a girl to speak highly of herself, it is acceptable for her to say self-deprecating things and have others correct her. Consider for a moment the ramifications of this practice. If one of the only appropriate avenues for a girl to gain praise from her peers is to criticize herself (specifically, to comment on how fat she is or how she hates her hair or her thighs), what effect might this linguistic strategy have on an already fragile sense of self? Putting one-self down reinforces, rather than corrects, what one already feels is wrong with oneself. In effect, it makes it worse. It is important to consider that "I'm so fat," a seemingly innocuous phrase, has potentially far-reaching implications.

Fat talk was not just an external dialogue that emerged in conversations with friends but also an internal dialogue that many girls carried on with themselves each time they looked in the mirror. Tracy, an attractive, petite (5′1″) high school junior who was on the track team, remarked:

> I hate to admit it but I'm chubby. I may not look like it, but I feel that I've got excess, you know, cellulite and stuff [laughs]. I want to put it nice. Um, well, uh, I don't know. My boyfriend, I mean like he looks like he should be with a nice, slender, trim, well-toned girl. And I mean I'm not trim. My legs might be muscular from track but now they're going flabby. Of course, I'm tiny, well, other people say I'm tiny. I'm proud to say that I weigh 113 pounds . . . but I'd still like to be trim, lean, and slender.

Tracy "admits" that she's tiny but qualifies her statement by explaining that this is what "others" have told her. Again, it's more acceptable to comment positively on your own body if you're repeating what others have told you. Yet Tracy is still dissatisfied with her body because it is not well-toned—despite the fact that she practices with the team for two hours each day. In Tracy's case, fat talk is not just shared among friends but is also part of her inner dialogue.

This internal dialogue is not uncommon. Even if a girl looks good on the "outside" and others tell her so, she may still be aware of areas of her body that do not meet her notions of culturally appropriate standards of beauty. Increasingly revealing advertisements that focus on particular body parts and promote specific products (such as cellulite creams and thigh-firming lotions) to reduce or remove "unsightly imperfections" promote dissatisfaction with the parts of ourselves that are largely hidden from public view. These products offer hope that we can change and become more perfect.

◆   ◆   ◆

The Dangers of Being Thin

Although girls who were very thin did not participate in fat talk, they were often the target of comments about weight. Janelle, at 5'2" and barely 100 pounds, described how her friends practically "accused" her of being thin, "as if it were my fault or something." The fact that she could eat with abandon and never gain weight made her friends jealous. Her resentment about this surfaced in a focus group in which her friends were talking about feeling fat and she suddenly lashed out at her friend Tina, demanding to know why she always said, "Oh, you're so skinny" to her. At first, Tina did not respond, so Janelle continued with her questioning: "Well, how do you think that makes me feel? Good or bad?" Tina remarked, "Well, I think it would make you . . . like totally happy." Janelle continued, "Well, it makes me feel bad. It's like, 'Oh you're *so* skinny,' what is that supposed to mean, you know? Do I have a problem? . . . I don't know, it just makes me feel uncomfortable." Janelle euphemistically refers to an eating disorder as "having a problem" because she is afraid to speak openly about it.

For some thin girls like Janelle, the statement "you're so thin" was easier to transform into a fault than to accept as a compliment. Denial becomes the appropriate counter to the compliment. Such girls often single out what they consider an imperfect body part and identify it as a flaw.

Another girl I interviewed, Gina, was a small and skinny ninth-grader who often wore a wide-brimmed floppy hat that hid half her face and almost all her lovely curly hair. We spoke on a lawn outside the school on a sunny spring day. I was initially hesitant about asking her questions about feeling fat given that she was so small in stature. But I had learned many times over that it was hard to read teens, especially in relation to body image. So I asked Gina in a rather casual way if she had felt fat in the past week. She brought her face, which had been largely hidden from sight, in closely to her chest and replied:

> Well yes, I have felt fat . . . I've been like . . . like having these dreams. I've had this same dream three times already. In my dream, I look in the mirror and I'm really fat. And the next morning, like as soon as I wake up, I'm like, "Oh my God, I'm fat!" I mean I just couldn't help it . . . there I was just fat . . . and I remember in the dream, that when I like looked down at myself, I looked skinny but when I looked in the mirror the reflection was of a girl who was really fat!

Gina's dream troubled me for days after our interview because it seemed to confirm my worst fears about girls' body image. Gina denied her thin self, at least in her dream, and had to confront the fear that lurking inside her was a fat girl, just waiting to be seen. This fat person could appear at any time, leaving her with feelings of shame. Such self-image problems were common among anorexics, I knew, but Gina was not anorexic!

Another petite girl, Laura, had a sister who was anorexic. Being small herself and living in a household where weight was an issue, she was particularly sensitive to the topic:

> Yeah, I hate it when everyone's like, all my friends, it's like, "You're so thin, you're like . . . anorexic." It's like . . . "I guess I am kinda anorexic," and they like joke how they're kinda anorexic or how they're gonna be anorexic. And when they say that, when they say, "Laura, you're so anorexic," I just wanna say like, "Come to my house," you know what I mean? I guess . . . it's just 'cause they're kind of ignorant about what the real thing is. It really upsets me when girls decide to starve themselves for five

days and think that's gonna be good. I mean if
they're gonna lose weight first they should find out
if they really need to and then they should learn
how to do it right.

Although Laura knows all too well how an anorexic be-
haves, she goes along with her friends when they question
whether her thinness is the result of an eating disorder. She
thinks, "Maybe I am kind of anorexic" and joins in the joke. At
the same time, she is angered by her friends' ignorance about
the disease. She doesn't reveal to them that she understands
the reality of the disorder or how many times her own sister
has been hospitalized. But during an interview, she discussed
how her family's focus on her sister's illness had deprived her
of a "normal" life and how frustrated she was that all her parents' emotional energy had been directed toward her sister.

Given that so many girls are talking about being fat, what is
the potential impact of such dialogue on girls who are at risk
for eating disorders? Girls who are anorexic or bulimic also
participate in this discourse. The difference is that they mean it
literally and are speaking out loud to themselves, not to others.
When friends respond, "No you're not" to their complaints of
being fat, they do not believe them. How could their friends
not see how fat they are? For such girls, the impact of fat talk
may not be transient. Indeed, this discourse may serve to legit-
imize a position that is potentially dangerous.

◆   ◆   ◆

Misuse of Fat Talk

While a girl may need to engage in fat talk in order to maintain
group affiliation, it is important that she not overuse it. To complain continually about body dissatisfaction can provoke the
anger of her friends. Several girls described having friends
whose constant body complaints led them to respond that they
really were too fat. They noted, "When she says, 'I'm so fat,' we

just say, 'Yeah, you are' to shut her up." Vanessa, a fifteen-year-old, described her strategy for dealing with her classmates:

> I think they just say it so they can hear other girls say, "Oh no you're not, you're skinny." It kind of makes me mad. My friend in eighth grade said that every day, so when she'd say it, I'd just say, "Oh." She'd get mad and say, "Well aren't you going to say something?" After a while, she stopped doing it. She just wanted attention. Now when I meet people like that, I just stare at them until they shut up.

Kathleen, a fifteen-year-old whose family had moved frequently, also remarked that she continually heard girls saying, "I'm so fat" at each of the schools she had attended. She explained:

> Most of the people who need to lose weight don't really say it, and most of the people who say it don't really mean it. You know they do it [say "I'm so fat"] for attention. I just tell them, "Yeah, so am I." I'm not going to give them a whole bunch of sympathy for something that they know is not true.

Kathleen's strategy entailed agreeing with the girl and at the same time implicating herself. She was not fat and would respond in a sarcastic voice. By not feeding into another girl's attempt to receive compliments from fat talk, she thwarted the discourse before it developed further.

Girls I talked to who were slightly overweight were offended by thin or normal-weight girls who referred to themselves as fat. Cyndie, a sixteen-year-old, explained:

> Even the thin people, they'll walk around saying, "I'm so fat." I just want to hit them on the head. Maybe their idea of gaining weight is like one or two pounds and they like weigh 100. I just want to say, "Shut up, you don't even know what being fat is."

Cyndie went on to note that if those thin girls *really did* think they were fat, what must they think of someone like her? They must think she was humongous! Their fat talk made her feel more self-conscious.

I asked the girls if they ever used fat talk in front of guys. While some said that they did, there was a general consensus that boys were intolerant of girls' talk about weight. As one tenth-grader explained:

> My friend Brian and I, we're like really close. So I can say most things to him. When I say, "I'm so fat," at first . . . he was always like, "Shut up! Oh no you're not!" . . . Now, he's just like, "I'm not going to say it again." Guys get sick of hearing it after a while, so I try not to say it in front of them. I feel like guys have less patience with it. But I *have* to say it if all my girlfriends are there!

◆　　◆　　◆

Fat Talk and Social Groups

Membership in a peer group or a crowd is particularly important for one's identity during early adolescence because of its perceived ability to facilitate friendships and social interaction as well as to provide emotional support.[19] For girls, group identity is especially critical since their status is achieved more through social networks—that is, the friends they are seen with—than through personal achievement. Peer groups or crowds are differentiated by dress, hair, music, and behaviors that can have potentially negative health consequences, such as smoking, drug and alcohol use, and sexual activity.[20] Taking into account the importance of the peer group, we must consider the extent to which girls' desires to be thin and their use of fat talk were mediated by social-group influences. Did fat talk take place regardless of the social group to which a girl belonged?

Girls in our Tucson study identified the following dominant crowds: preps, jocks, nerds, mods, skaters, and stoners.

Preps were characterized as very involved in school activities and often came from wealthier families. Their style of dress, hair, and makeup followed the latest mainstream fashion dictates, and some felt that "they walk around with their noses up in the air." Jocks were the more athletically oriented preps, while the nerds were the students who "got really good grades." Stoners were characterized as smokers and drug users who were indifferent toward school. Their wardrobe consisted largely of jeans and tee shirts advertising heavy metal rock bands. As one girl explained, "Stoners, they don't care much about anything, it's like, be free." Mods were another fringe group, often students involved in drama or the arts. Their style was an amalgam of fashion from previous eras. Mod girls often wore black and made their faces pale, highlighted their eyes with dark makeup, and wore bright red lipstick. Although the term "skater" generally referred to boys who skateboarded, girls who hung out with skater guys also said they were part of this group. Reference was also made to other groups, such as punk rockers, with the differentiation between groups often attributed to their choice of music. Not all adolescents belonged to a social group, but even nonmembers were aware of what was appropriate in particular social settings.

Over the course of our study, we found that membership in a group changed frequently and that girls often resisted self-classification. When we asked the following question on our survey: "Most of the time, what social group do you think you're in?" girls' responses were "no group, I'm just me" (44 percent); jock/prep (41 percent); stoner (8 percent); mod/punk (4 percent); and Mexican (3 percent). Many girls wrote in comments like "My group can't be classified—I'm friends with everyone" or "I'm just normal." Others made comments like "I don't believe in groups . . . I'm just myself" or "I'm an individual." Clearly, there was a lot of fluidity to social groups and it was often easier for others to label a girl than for her to label herself.

Did girls who considered themselves to be "stoners" or "mods" engage in fat talk as much as girls who were "preps"?

Through dress, stoner and mod girls adopted counterculture values, and part of their identity as a group was that they "didn't really care." Did these girls also reject mainstream notions of preferred body size, resulting in less fat talk? From interviews with girls from a variety of social groups, I found that desire for thinness crosscut all groups. I asked Stacy, a self-identified stoner, whether she thought there was pressure among girls in her group to be thin. She replied, "Well I think there's pressure to be thin in all groups. I think with stoners it's not as bad, but it's still there." Her response surprised me because I assumed from her appearance that she really was not into mainstream values. "Stoners," I began, "seem to be against other things—like adopting dress that preps are wearing. So why do you think the importance of being thin still holds?" She paused for a moment and then commented, "Well, everyone loves to be thin [laughs]. I mean just every girl wants to be thin. Well, the guys are still after thin girls."

Stacy's comments were confirmed by other girls in her crowd. Leslie, a stoner who often hung out with her friends smoking cigarettes in front of the local convenience store, told me that her boyfriend—who was also a stoner—had said that if she ever got fat, he'd dump her. Although she doubted that he really meant it, his comment heightened her insecurity about her weight.

A few days later I pursued these questions with Christina, a slightly overweight sophomore who fit the classic description of a "mod." Her face was plastered with pasty white makeup, she had dyed black hair drooping over her eyes, and she wore oversized black clothes. When I asked her what group she thought she belonged to, she replied, "People always call me a mod. I guess, that's kinda what I fall in, but I don't really consider myself like that. But most of my friends are mods and punks, so I can see why people *might* call me that." I then asked her to help me understand the difference between these two social groups. She replied:

> Mod people, they always seem to think that the world is coming to an end, like every minute. And

they write all this black poetry. And they're just weird. I mean they're not weird, they're just like depressing. Everything is like blackness to them. It's just sad and the punkers are like really burned. They're like, "ahhh." And they listen to punk rock music and are wild.

When I asked her if being thin was important to the girls in these two groups, she commented, "Yeah, it is. The mod chicks and the punker girls that I know, they all, I think it's the same with every girl . . . 'cause all my friends, no matter how skinny they are they think they're fat. And no matter what they are, they think they're fat, even if they're not." I responded, "Well, mods, if they're into death and everything, then what difference does weight make?" Her pasty white face broke into a smile and she said:

> Well, yeah . . . that is something to think about . . . I think it's because, I think like the mods sometimes, deep inside they're happy, they just don't want people to know it because they're just insecure about something. Or else sometimes I think they're just doing it because it seems to be what everybody else who they want to be with is doing. So a lot of times I think that's it. But I think that *everyone*, every girl no matter how down they are, wants to be attractive. And being attractive means being thin.

Christina's observations of the importance of being thin despite social-group differences are insightful. She speaks of a resistance to some mainstream values and yet an acceptance of others. Not caring and concern about being thin may seem paradoxical, but teens do live in a paradoxical world where they are asked to act responsible and yet are treated as dependent. In opposition to the control imposed on them, teens often act out through behaviors that defy norms or blow them out of proportion.[21]

Popular resistance is an important factor influencing teen fashion and body-related behavior.[22] This brings to mind the novel hairdos and clothing combinations some teen subgroups adopt as alternatives to prevailing fashion. Given the flexibility to create one's own style and to affiliate with a group that appreciates novelty and variation, one might expect a more flexible and fluid concept of beauty across groups. However, my research suggests that while hair and clothing are commonly areas of resistance or invention, ideals of body shape remain fairly constant and conventional. Irrespective of social-group affiliation or fashion statement, the white girls we interviewed predominantly strove for a common ideal of beauty associated with thinness.

As I interviewed these girls, I could not help wondering whether fat talk changed as they got older. Was it something that was used more by middle school girls, who were experiencing bodily changes as they moved through puberty, than by high school girls? I continued to collect data as the girls in the study aged and went through high school. The prevalence of fat talk appeared to vary with a girl's social group and the friends she hung out with at a given time. It continued as strong as ever in some groups, but in others, girls seemed to age out of it.

One mature ninth-grader told me that "it's something girls go through—like a stage of thinking. Like when you're in middle school and you're real insecure with how you look, you're more apt to do it." Now that she and her friends were in high school, they were "more secure" and "you just feel better about yourself." She told me that she was glad things had changed because "it's hard to be insecure about the way you look and always talk about it like that." Another girl, a tenth-grader, provided a similarly positive response, while noting at the same time that pressures to look good increased as adolescence progressed:

> I think, well, I don't know, I think a lot of freshmen are self-conscious of themselves because they have all the new guys around them that are so much older, but I think, I don't know, I just don't hear it as much this year . . . I mean I hear it once in a while,

but it's not like an every-single-day thing like last year it was . . . and this year it's not . . . and like I've noticed that most senior girls don't say anything about it, so I think it just wears off after a while.

Many of the eleventh-graders in the study felt that the level of concern about weight remained the same throughout high school, although girls stopped "announcing" their feelings about their bodies in public. As girls become older, the large social groups they belonged to in middle school become smaller, more intense friendship units. In addition, there may be fewer opportunities for the group sharing of fat talk, which found its natural home in places where girls gathered, like the locker room.

In the classes I teach on adolescence at the University of Arizona, I generally ask my students (who are juniors) whether they hear fat talk among their friends. Those who are vocal and willing to speak out in class have told me that the pressures to be thin are worse in college than they were in middle school or high school. Many of them do hear fat talk spoken among friends. In part, they believe that because they are now living on their own, they are more responsible for their own body shape and can "take care" of themselves in ways they previously could not. What this says to me is that just as weight concerns are tenacious across a woman's life span, so fat talk persists as a means of communication between women.

Girls and women are encouraged on a daily basis to subject themselves to ever-increasing examination and to engage in self-correction. A female needs to identify herself as both the spectator and the spectacle, one who sees and is seen. Teenaged girls keenly sense the gaze of others and engage in frequent self-assessment. By taking part in fat talk, they actively adopt a strategy for reproducing a model as well as a plan for achieving a more perfect life. Even if they're not actually working on themselves, they must at least *talk* about it. Talking about weight control in itself constitutes action in that it serves to create and project an image of self. Adopting the "I'm so fat" discourse allows girls to present themselves to others as responsible beings concerned about their appearance. By sharing their concerns about their weight and appearance with girlfriends, they make it clear that they do not think they are better than their peers. Because white middle-class culture promotes an unattainably thin female as the beauty ideal, and thus creates widespread discontent with weight, the girl who presents herself as dissatisfied with her weight resembles rather than deviates from her peers.[23]

Although media reports have tended to exaggerate the pervasiveness of dieting among teen-aged girls, it is important to recognize that fat talk is not an accurate barometer of dieting behavior or weight obsession. Fat talk is particularly prevalent during adolescence, when concern about appearance and group affiliation needs are high and appetite and bodily development are hard to control. The litany of fat talk and its importance in peer-group social activity indicate that teen-aged girls are greatly concerned about body size. Regardless of what girls actually do to achieve their body goals, they are attempting to reproduce the cultural ideal of beauty through fat talk.

3

Are Girls Really Dieting?

I'm always on a diet. But then I'll end up like, you
know, eating something when I'm really hungry.
You know, something *really* gross and then I'll feel
really guilty about it. Then I'll still be on that diet.
I'm always *trying* to be on a diet.

LORI, *AGE 14*

DESPITE INTENSE pressures to be thin
and media portrayals of an epidemic
of dieting, teen-aged girls live in a world saturated with junk
food. The typical dietary choices offered in middle and high
school lunchrooms are a variety of high-fat foods such as
pizza and french fries, served together as a luncheon special.
Ice cream and candy are readily available for dessert. How do
girls deal with the opposition between ever-present junk food
and the pervasive desire to be thin? One way the girls re-
solved this paradox was to reach for a candy bar and a Diet
Coke, a combination that some jokingly referred to as a "balanced diet"!

Given the food dished out in schools, it is not hard to understand why the Centers for Disease Control continue to
report increasing obesity among youth. The widespread availability of high-fat food in lunchrooms and in fast-food restaurants, coupled with a decrease in physical activity, is one reason kids are getting fatter. One in five adolescents between

the ages of twelve and nineteen is obese, and the trend is predicted to continue.[1] Although these findings are sobering, the academic literature on girls' dieting and body image provides a very different picture. Numerous studies have concluded that as many as 60 percent of white middle-class girls are dieting, using a variety of weight-reducing strategies including purging, fasting, and excessive exercising.[2] Such dieting practices, researchers warn, may lead to eating disorders.[3]

How can two such contradictory pictures exist? Who is getting fatter and who is getting thinner? By what means? Have definitions of what constitutes obesity and what constitutes a diet changed? What exactly does dieting mean? As my colleagues and I were planning this study, questions such as these were paramount in our minds. From our review of the existing studies, we were concerned that the details of dieting among teens were not adequately understood. What were teens doing when they said they were on a diet? How long did their diets last? Were their attempts at weight loss successful?

We were wary of surveys that asked girls to report whether they had "dieted" in the last week, month, or year. Teen-aged girls who say they are trying to lose weight *may or may not* actually be dieting. Social desirability may cause them to either overreport their dieting or underreport unusual or extreme weight-loss methods.[4] Reports of dieting may reflect intention or token gestures (for example, skipping a meal) rather than sustained dieting over time. We wondered whether girls felt a need to report that they were trying to lose weight, just as they felt a need to engage in "fat talk." Did some girls resist dieting, and, if so, what alternatives exist to this behavior? Considering how little is known about normative eating patterns among teens, we found it difficult to assess what constitutes a "diet."[5]

What emerges from our ethnographic study and detailed collection of food records runs contrary to the usual findings of survey questionnaires that have emphasized the negative, if not pathological, behaviors of teen-aged girls. Although girls are active participants in both "fat talk" and "diet talk," their behaviors largely reflect health-oriented strategies. Actual dieting episodes as recorded on food records were much less frequent than suggested by surveys, and were less severe in their structure. Analysis of food records showed that the group of girls who reported on the survey that they ate health- fully were in fact doing so, as demonstrated by higher micro- nutrient intakes on their food records.[6] These findings concur with recent data on American adults which reveal that while two out of three of those surveyed are trying to control their weight, the majority state that they are not "on a diet."[7]

Nonetheless, on the surveys we administered, the girls' re- sponses appeared similar to those reported on national ques- tionnaires on dieting. For example, on the survey given in the second year of the study, we asked, "Are you trying to change your weight *now?*" One hundred and thirty-five girls (56 per- cent) said, "No," ninety-six girls (40 percent) said, "Yes, I'm try- ing to *lose* weight," and ten girls (4 percent) said, "I'm trying to *gain* weight." These percentages concur very closely with the findings of the Youth Risk Behavior Survey, which involved more than twelve thousand teens in grades nine through twelve nationwide.[8] Other attempts at weight loss, such as the use of diet pills and induced vomiting, were reported consid- erably less often by girls in the Teen Lifestyle Project when compared with the nationwide survey.

During follow-up telephone interviews, we engaged in a more detailed discussion of dieting. First we asked, "Have you dieted to lose weight recently?" More than 60 percent of the girls reported that they had dieted. We then asked, "How long do your diets usually last?" Of the girls who reported dieting, the duration of their diets were as follows: a couple of days or less (thirty-five girls; 25 percent); a week (thirty girls; 21 per- cent); a couple of weeks (thirty-seven girls; 26 percent); about a month (twenty-three girls; 16 percent); and more than a month (seventeen girls; 12 percent).

We also asked girls to complete the statement, "The most I've ever lost on a diet is ___ pounds." Of the girls who re- ported dieting, forty-five (32 percent) had lost five or less pounds; fifty-three (39 percent) had lost six to ten pounds; twenty-seven (19 percent) had lost eleven to twenty pounds; and thirteen (10 percent) had lost more than twenty-one pounds. Thus, almost one-half of the girls who had dieted had done so for less than one week, and more than two-thirds of those who dieted had lost ten pounds or less.

Weight-loss efforts were not confined to dieting. A majority of girls used multiple strategies while trying to lose weight, including watching what they ate, eating healthfully, increasing the amount they exercised, and eating less. Watching what they ate and eating healthfully were differentiated from dieting. Girls were able to maintain these two strategies for longer periods of time than dieting and increased exercise, which were generally adopted short-term. Seven percent of the girls used diet aids (diet gum, Slim-Fast, and so on) or diet pills. Interestingly, the girls who took diet pills admitted that they stole them from their mothers! Taking diet aids or pills was generally a short-term strategy.

Experience with surveys and phone interviews about weight loss confirmed our concerns about teens' interpretation of words commonly used on questionnaires. During the phone interviews, we found that girls were confused about words such as "fasting" and "binging." When we read off a list of weight-loss strategies and asked if they had tried them, many girls paused when we asked, "Did you fast?" and responded, "What does that mean?" When we explained that it meant "you didn't eat," girls asked, "For how long?" before answering. On the survey, several girls who did not circle that they had "fasted" to lose weight wrote in the margin "I stopped eating." But what did "stopped eating" mean—stopped for a few hours or a few days? Surveys that ask questions such as "Have you fasted?" or "Have you starved yourself?" generally do not ask how long this was practiced and in what context. There is a difference between skipping breakfast because you're in a rush and purposely not eating. It seems plausible that a girl may fast to fit into a dress for a particular event (for example, the prom). This behavior is episodic and event-oriented. Given the apparent ambiguity of the meaning of "fasting" even when girls *are* allowed to ask questions, I cannot help wondering what it means when a girl silently reports on a survey that she has fasted.

"Binging" is another term that may be misunderstood by teens. Girls overreported their binging because they often confused it with overeating or "pigging out." But even "pigging out" is subject to personal interpretation. For teens, an admission of binging on a survey may not be a report of an abnormal behavior so much as an admission that they ate more than they should have. Researchers may interpret such self-reports in a much more serious or even pathological light than is warranted. In order to increase the validity of self-report on questions such as these, relevant examples from girls' lives need to be provided in the form of case scenarios that ground a behavior like binging in a context teens can understand. In this way, girls can be clear about what they are answering and researchers can be more certain of how they should interpret girls' responses.

Misinterpretation of survey questions by respondents is important because findings of studies reporting a high prevalence of dieting, binging, and fasting receive widespread attention in the media. If girls believe that "everyone else is dieting" and that binging and fasting are common, they may be more likely to engage in such behavior themselves. Misinformation can affect behavior when it makes extreme forms of attempted weight control appear normal. This has been the case with teen smoking. Teens who believe that smoking is more prevalent than it actually is are far more likely to smoke than are their peers.[9] In fact, one of the recommendations of tobacco-prevention programs is that youths learn the actual prevalence of smoking in their community to combat directly the notion that almost all kids smoke.[10]

But what numbers should be presented? If teens are given data on "ever-smokers," including those who have experimented with one or two cigarettes, the behavior appears more normative than when they are presented with data on routine smokers. When attempting to make the problem visible to policy makers and funding agencies, researchers would do well to present numbers of "ever-users," but is this the best figure to present to youth? We need to remember that adolescence is a period of experimentation, and many girls attempt a fast just as they may try smoking a cigarette. This indicates not pathology but rather normal experimentation.[11]

◆   ◆   ◆

What Does "Dieting" Really Mean?

Although the girls in our study appeared to match the national profile in terms of their self-report of dieting, interviews generated a far more complex picture than is currently given. We found that talk and action about dieting are as varied as talk and action about feeling fat. When a girl says she is on a diet, she may mean not that she is actively trying to lose weight, but rather that she wishes to gain control over her life. However, the need for control or the ability to control is often short-lived among teens. The same girls who "talk fat" often do not engage in sustained weight-reducing activity. Erin, a short, average-weight tenth-grader, explained what dieting meant to her:

> Well, I mean, everybody thinks they're fat. Well not
> everybody, but, you know, most people . . . I guess . . .
> well . . . I mean, I don't know. If you see people your
> age that look skinny but weigh more than you, you
> know, it feels good, right? But sometimes I think I'm
> fat or something. After usually I get weighed. You
> know, but . . . I never really do anything about it. I
> just say, "I'm going on a diet," you know.

For Erin, diet talk was a way of making herself feel better. It was a means of boosting her morale, not a plan that she was ready to implement. Saying "I'm going on a diet" temporarily assuaged her worries about her weight.

Just as fat talk was a pervasive conversational strategy, so was diet talk. It signaled to others that a girl was appropriately concerned with her appearance. Diet talk didn't commit a girl to sustained action, as Melissa, a tenth-grader, explained:

It's like people talk about it but there's not that much conviction about losing it, as I see it. I mean, they say they want to lose weight, but—and maybe they really do—but I don't see people really doing anything about it. Like they'll go on a diet, well like I do [laughs]. I go on a diet for a little while and exercise and stuff and then just stop.

Diets have a short life but a recurrent presence. Drew, a ninth-grader, complained to me on several occasions that she felt fat, though she was clearly *not* overweight. Her answers on each of her surveys made it appear that she dieted. In reality she thought about it more than she actually did it:

I always say I'm going to go on a diet and then I never do. I'm always like, "I'm gonna diet next week," or yeah like, "I have to start dieting," and I usually last for like a day or two if I *do* actually go on a diet and then it's like, "forget it."

Like Drew, some girls said a diet just lasted a day or two. Other girls just dieted for a few hours, from breakfast until lunch, when temptation in the cafeteria or boredom with the diet would compel them to have something to eat. When they would see their friends with french fries or candy bars, they would say, "Nah, forget that diet!" However, eating the candy bar was often accompanied by the rhetoric of dieting: "I know I shouldn't be eating this! Now I've *got* to go back on my diet." Several girls told me that if they managed to "be good" for a few days during the week, then they didn't feel so bad about indulging with their friends. In fact, dieting for a few days made food look and taste all that much better! On the weekends their diets would disappear. "As soon as I lay my eyes on that pizza, I have to gobble it up . . . and then it's like, 'Okay, I'll diet on Monday!'"

Teens live in a social world in which injunctions to eat abound. Girls socialize over food, and vending machines with soda and candy are centrally located in each school, providing the resources for snack breaks. Selling candy to classmates at school is one of the most common ways that teams and clubs raise money for their activities, and once you buy a candy bar, you had better share it! In such an environment, talk about future diets seems more feasible than not participating in a shared food event.

Dieting can also be a shared social event. Some girls described their experiences with short-lived group diets, which I interpreted as a dieting ritual. First, they would talk about their need to diet, and then they would plan, commit, and try. There was a common pattern to this group activity: as soon as one girl went off the diet, the others joined her as an act of solidarity! In this case, *attempting* to diet together was a bonding experience. Two best friends who were not overweight described their joint dieting experience:

> Well, we both thought we were fat, so we thought we'd go on a diet together. And we kept saying, "Oh, we'll do it tomorrow," and the next day, "Oh, we'll do it tomorrow." And it kept going on and finally we did it for a couple of days but then one of us went off so it was like, "Oh well." So we just ate whatever we wanted again!

Overweight girls appeared to put more thought into planning their dieting attempts. Melanie, a slightly overweight tenth-grader, described how she and her best friend, Holly, had planned their diet:

> We like, we would be over at Holly's house and we went through all the diet books and all of the magazine articles and everything, and we like planned out what we would eat each day. What we would eat every day, and how many calories they had and what exercises we'd do. And everything. That didn't last for too long [laughs]. That lasted about a week!

When I asked her why they had stopped, Melanie broke into laughter and said, "Well, it wasn't me, it was Holly. She went off it at lunch, and so I was like, 'OK, well she's off, then I'll go off too,' and I just ate this huge old dinner. I mean if she was-n't going to diet anymore, why should I?"

Although the diet books and magazines that Holly's mother kept on hand were helpful in crafting their diet, their joint venture was thwarted by the temptations of the lunchroom and the lack of healthier choices. In contrast to the widespread availability of candy, salads are rare and costly commodities in the cafeteria. Several girls complained that they would like to eat better at school but that the healthier foods like salads were more expensive than the high-fat foods like pizza and french fries. As one girl explained:

> *Everything* is fries here. They should try and push a little more nutrition, but they don't. I mean, like before going to buy your fries and stuff, I think they should have, like a No Smoking sign that warns you that it's dangerous. They should have what fries can do and how much fat they have and stuff. I mean, it probably won't stop very many people here, but it might make them take a second look at it . . . Well, I don't know. I mean, all the bad food tastes good, and all the good food can be like so nasty. Food that's good for you costs more too.

On their limited budgets, girls faced the same problem when they went out for lunch at fast-food restaurants. Although they could always bring a healthier lunch from home, some girls did not consider this a viable alternative once they were in high school, because it seemed "like something you did when you were younger."

On our survey we asked girls to respond to the question, "What do you usually have for lunch?" Responses indicate that 50 percent of the girls ate the school lunch; 20 percent ate french fries or chips; 20 percent had nothing to eat (just something to drink); 8 percent had ice cream or a candy bar; and 6 percent had a salad.[12] In interviews some girls said that they didn't eat much at lunchtime because they preferred to save their lunch money for the weekend, when they could put it to better use.

✦   ✦   ✦

Smoking as a Dieting Strategy

One of the main objectives of our study was to determine the extent to which girls began to smoke as a means of controlling their weight. Although several studies had suggested a strong correlation between smoking and attempts at weight control, only one girl out of the sixty smokers in our study had *begun* smoking for this reason.[13] For most of the eighth- and ninth-graders we interviewed, smoking as a dieting strategy was not an idea they had ever considered. Even girls who had mothers who were diet conscious and were smokers failed to make an association between the two behaviors. Although 30 percent of the girls in our study were smokers, they did not have the option of lighting a cigarette at times when it might have provided them with an alternative to eating (for example, before or after meals) because their parent(s) would not allow it.[14]

As girls became more established smokers and had more freedom to smoke when they chose (especially once they began to drive and get jobs), a clearer association was made between smoking and weight control. One girl remarked that smoking "makes you not want to eat," while another girl who had recently quit noted, "When I used to smoke, I hardly ate. As soon as I stopped smoking, I ate all the time." Smoking does increase the metabolic rate by about 10 percent and decreases the desire for sweet foods.[15]

Several girls who smoked heavily had experienced weight gain after they had tried to quit. As one girl noted:

> Well, I'd like to quit smoking but I just can't do it now. It's like I'm gonna go on a diet, and I know I'll wanna have a cigarette. Because instead of eating I'll have a cigarette, you know, that kind of thing. Like when I smoke I don't think I eat as much as I do when I don't smoke.

Significantly, this pattern of association was described by a few girls in our study who were the heaviest smokers. Although the girls we interviewed did not *start* to smoke as a dieting strategy, once they became smokers, it was harder for them to quit for fear of gaining weight. This same pattern is found among adult women.

◆   ◆   ◆

Commercial Weight-Loss Programs

What about commercial weight-loss programs such as Jenny Craig, or products such as Slim-Fast? While some girls did "buy in" to commercial programs, the majority of girls had little or no experience with them. Because these programs tend to be costly, they were not an option unless a girl's parents were willing to pay for them. More commonly, it was the heavy girls who used these programs, not those who were of average weight.

As the girls became older and got jobs, they had more decision-making power over how they would lose weight. Andrea, for example, was an eleventh-grader who was 5′5″ and weighed 130 pounds. During our interview, she expressed frustration that she had regained almost all of the thirteen pounds she had lost over the summer. When I asked her how she had lost the weight, she told me that she had bought herself Slim-Fast from money she had made from her summer job. Although she didn't relish the taste, she preferred it to "those other diets where you have to measure a gram of meat or eat a hard-boiled egg or raw tuna fish with no mayonnaise." The latter kind of diet was "really gross" to her. She had been initiated into the wonders of Slim-Fast by her mother, who told her it was easier to stick to than other diets. When I asked her if her mother knew of or approved of her purchasing Slim-Fast with her own money, she replied, "Well even if she didn't like it, she couldn't complain because I wasn't using *her* Slim-Fast." Andrea finally stopped purchasing Slim-Fast when she ran out of money.

Although all the girls had heard of commercial products,

several were suspicious of whether they really worked. One girl commented that on the commercials you see "those really fat people who say they lost thirty pounds in three weeks after taking Slim-Fast, but it doesn't happen like that in real life." "Even Dexatrim," one seasoned dieter told me, "never really works because it's supposed to help you control what you eat, but then you end up getting addicted to it! You just keep hoping it's gonna work, so you keep taking it all the time." Diet drinks and weight-loss pills were not conducive to the highly visible lives that most girls led. Because they were surrounded by other teens for most of their day, there was little opportunity to do anything alone—particularly around lunchtime. As one girl observed, "It's real hard to eat that kind of stuff at school . . . you have to sneak around with all those pills and special foods and stuff."

◆　　◆　　◆

Resistance to Dieting

While "diet talk" was common, many girls who were not on formalized programs like Weight Watchers or Jenny Craig were reluctant to say they were on a "diet" because the word itself connoted participation in one of these plans. For example Nina, a bubbly tenth-grader who was an avid soccer player, spoke to me about wanting to lose the ten pounds she had gained from her acne medicine. When I asked her if she had dieted in the past three months, she laughed and said, "I haven't *really* dieted." Later on, however, she told me that she had changed how she ate in order to lose weight. Realizing that I might be onto an important distinction, I asked her to describe the difference in her two responses. She replied, "Well, when I think about dieting it's more like, you know, you think of commercial diets, like you have to take this or take that. And I guess by losing weight, like I think that's just me, doing exercises and eating healthier."

Talking with other girls, I soon realized that many were reluctant to label their attempts at weight loss as a diet. In some cases, this response was related to a reluctance to be controlled. "Being on a diet" constituted "being controlled" by an imposed structure. In a group discussion about dieting with self-defined preps, Keri, an eleventh-grader, explained:

> I think I'm always conscious of what I'm eating. Whether it's good or bad I'm always thinking, "What's this gonna do?" Especially, I mean, if I'm eating like candy or something, I go, "I shouldn't be doing this." But I don't really consider it being . . . I don't like saying I'm on a diet. I hate that when I'm at home and say, "I'm on a diet," and then for the rest of the week my mom's pestering me and saying, "You shouldn't be eating that." And I'm like "OK, I'm not on a diet, I'm just eating carefully." You know, I just don't like to phrase it that way.

By declaring that she was on a diet, Keri called attention to her behavior. This resulted both in the need to control herself more rigorously and in close scrutiny from her mother. Her friend chimed in with a similar observation: "If you consider it a diet, then you're in trouble because then you'll *have* to lose weight. If you don't lose weight, then, you know, you realize you've failed. Then, you know, you get upset and you'll eat more." For these girls, saying they were on a diet established a set of personal, if not public, expectations. With expectations came the possibility of failure. Furthermore, if a girl didn't announce that she was dieting, a little cheating would be no big thing.

Girls' reluctance to define themselves in terms of a routine cut across several other domains of life. For example, in a discussion about physical activity, Allison, a regular exerciser, remarked, "Well, I really don't like to say, 'Oh I have to exercise this many times a week,' 'cause if you do that you're setting yourself up *not* to meet your goal and then you get discouraged and you don't exercise. I think you should just exercise when you feel like it . . . you know, like it shouldn't be a 'have to' thing. Do it because you want to." Another girl had a similar philosophy that she related to both her studies and dieting:

> If you don't try, like with school, you'll do better. Of course, you have to try but I mean, if you don't really think about it too much, like you're not conscious of it all the time, it works better . . . 'cause if you think about something too much it's gonna blow all out of proportion. And it's the same thing with dieting. If you call what you do a diet, you'll think about all the foods you're missing out on, and you'll really wanna eat them.

The notion of not setting oneself up for failure was also evident in the girls' narratives about smoking. When girls who smoked were asked about their quitting attempts, some of them explained that they had tried to quit but had not announced to anyone that they were formally trying to stop smoking. To do so was risky and placed too much pressure on them, amounting to a test of their will power. By not acknowledging that they were trying to quit, a day without cigarettes was a "moral boost"—something that made them feel good about themselves, a positive incentive to keep up the good work. Conversely, to say that she was trying to quit smoking and then to give in and have a cigarette would be an acknowledgment that a girl had failed. Similar ideas about not wanting to fail surfaced in discussions with female college students about their contraceptive use. When asked what methods of contraception they used, many of the women were often reluctant to "admit" that they regularly utilized a particular method, for fear that by defining themselves in that way they might somehow set themselves up for failure in the future.[16] By not speaking about contraceptive use overtly, they would not be committed to it. They felt it was better not to make too many rules for themselves.

✦   ✦   ✦

Watching What You Eat

In conversations with each other and with me, girls discussed "watching what they ate" far more than they talked about dieting. I recognized this as a behavior that I myself practiced, but "watching" was not a word I had ever come across in the dieting literature.[17] What did watching their weight mean to girls? How did they practice it, and how did they differentiate it from dieting?

Like dieting, watching proved to be multifaceted. Girls identified several reasons for watching their weight, including a desire to be healthy, to maintain their weight, to lose weight, and to gain control over their environment. Girls who watched to be healthy often described avoiding candy, chips, soda, and fatty foods and eating more vegetables and fruits. Becky, a quiet fourteen-year-old who was 5'5" and weighed 145 pounds, explained what watching meant to her:

> When I watch, I try not to eat as much candy and sweets and I try to eat more vegetables and stuff, but I don't eat less, I just eat better . . . better for my body, healthier, and I don't consider that really dieting. I just make sure that my body gets better things than it was.

Becky's emphasis on making healthier choices rather than dieting allowed her the option of having a candy bar every now and then if she really wanted it.

Both watching and dieting involved a consciousness of what one ate. The difference was the matter of degree. Susie, a tenth-grader who was 5'4" and weighed 150 pounds, told me that she was trying to lose weight because she had "gotten really huge." She was particularly frustrated because she could barely squeeze into the new school clothes she had purchased at the end of the summer. When I asked her how she had gained weight, she told me that over the summer she had hung out at a pool with her best friend, her boyfriend, and his brother. She and her girlfriend hadn't eaten much because they were self-conscious about eating in front of the boys and because "the guys kinda scarfed down whatever there was to eat." Now that she was back in an environment where food was readily available, she had gained back all her weight. When I asked her what she was doing to lose weight, she told me that she was watching what she ate. Without prompting, she told me that she didn't like to diet. "If you're dieting," she explained, "I think you're more strict about things, like you can't have this and you can't have that. If you're just watching you can say, 'I can have a little bit of that' but just don't get over excessive, you know, stuff like that."

Like Susie, other girls explained that watching involved eating in moderation rather than stuffing themselves when the opportunity allowed. When asked if she dieted to lose weight, Paige replied, "I try and watch what I eat. I mean, I don't like totally gorge myself on a bag of potato chips and have fifteen Cokes with it, but I mean I do eat, like a handful of chips every day." Adopting the rhetoric of watching allowed Paige to enjoy within limits.

Whereas dieting was associated with rigid behavior that set a girl up for personal failure and frustration, watching was a positive action that she was able to manage on her own. Watching what she ate afforded a girl greater agency by permitting her to negotiate her eating behavior in different situations. Her behavior was flexible. If at one time she ate more than what she thought was acceptable, it could be balanced out over time. As one girl noted, "It's based on me, you know, and what I'm like right now and whether I should eat this much, you know." In other words, watching entailed *exerting* control instead of *being* controlled by an imposed structure. Rather than evaluating her behavior in terms of "calorie counts" or "weigh-ins," a girl evaluated herself contextually—how she behaved in a particular situation given the options available.[18] Watching was less threatening than dieting and entailed the broader concept of eating *more healthfully* as distinct from eating *less*. Watching made girls feel better about themselves than dieting did because they had a better chance of success with it.

The connection between eating healthfully and increased self-esteem is captured in a recently launched ad campaign for SnackWell crackers.[19] As described in the *Wall Street Journal:*

> One new spot opens with a shot of a beaming mom putting her arm around her pigtailed daughter, who holds a box of SnackWell Zesty Cheese crackers. As a gust of wind whirls the blades of grass where they stand, a woman's voice chimes: "At SnackWell's we like to think that snacking shouldn't be just about feeding yourself, but in some small way, about feeding your self-esteem" . . . A few seconds later, there is a close-up of a middle-aged woman with her teenage daughter, and the white-haired grandmother, all nuzzling together. The message: Snacking is not about "filling yourself," but "fulfilling yourself."

In this ad, females of all ages enhance their self-esteem by choosing a low-fat cracker. This is a multigenerational message in which older, more knowing women pass down the knowledge of healthful eating to the next generation. Snacking is transformed from a mere act of filling one's belly to an act of fulfilling one's self.

In addition to boosting their self-esteem, some girls watched what they ate as a maintenance strategy once they had lost weight. At 5′2″ and 146 pounds, Erica wanted to lose about 25 pounds. She knew that she would have to diet to lose all that weight, but once she got down to her ideal, she would become a watcher. "After I lose all my weight," she remarked, "I'll definitely have to keep myself there by watching, you know, eating healthy and stuff, 'cause otherwise I probably would just put it back on just as fast, or faster than I had lost it."

Watching also implied paying attention to the nutrient content of foods, primarily by reading nutritional labels. During interviews, however, it became evident that labels were often read after the fact and did not necessarily help a girl decide whether or not to eat a particular food at a given time. For these girls, saying that they watched indicated that they had a heightened awareness about what to put in their mouths in the future and could evaluate how good or bad they had been in the present. Mandy, an eleventh-grader, aptly explained this position: "Sometimes I look at candy bars to see how much fat I'm eating. I just want to see how bad they really are, so I'll feel even more guilty. Then maybe the next time I want one I won't eat it!" She laughed and added, "But it doesn't stop me this time!"

When I asked Mandy what eating healthfully meant to her, she seemed to find it easier to list what was bad for her than what was good. Watching to her meant eating fewer chips and drinking lots of water. After a few moments of thinking, Mandy replied, "Well, my mother says she's healthy. She doesn't eat at Burger King every day. I guess that's a definition of healthy eating!" Another girl told me that eating healthfully meant eating foods labeled as lite because that meant there was less "fat or calories or cholesterol or something."

I knew from my discussions with girls that there was a great deal of confusion about how to read labels such as lite, low-fat, fat-free, low-calorie, low-cholesterol, healthy, and so on. Reading nutritional labels does not imply understanding what is written in a scientific sense. Numerous surveys have shown that Americans have become increasingly aware of the health risks associated with sodium, fats, and cholesterol, and as a result, they report reduced consumption of salt, red meat, butter, whole milk, and eggs.[20] However, while awareness of the relationship between diet and risk of disease seems to be better recognized among adults than it was in the past, actual dietary behavior has not shifted dramatically. For example, after examining dietary changes of adult women over a seven-year period, the U.S. Department of Agriculture (USDA) reported that although consumption of red meat had declined substantially, "the overall fat intake of these women had not declined because women had correspondingly increased their intake of salad dressings, table spreads, and rich desserts."[21] Most likely, women had given up "token" foods (like red meat), which had become symbolic of making healthier choices.

One tenth-grader who was an avid watcher described how she tried to read labels but found them very confusing:

> I look at how many calories there are . . . not that I'm *that* concerned . . . but just to know, to see . . . to get a grasp. Sometimes I look for fats, but not really, just calories. Like with calories, like, you know, to see if it's bad or not. But like with fat, it will say 3 grams and I have no idea whether that's a lot or not . . . so I usually look for things that have zero fat, 'cause I really don't know what I'm looking for!

Just as adolescent girls experiment with what they wear, they experiment with how and what they eat. Consider Stacey, a lean fifteen-year-old who never thought of dieting. A few weeks before one of our interviews she had sworn off junk food. As she explained, "Lately I just think about what's in the food I'm eating and what's going through my bloodstream and it just grosses me out. And so I've switched to vegetables and fruit because I know it's pure and good for me." Two months later she was living on pizza and burgers again. Between interviews, it was not uncommon for a girl to move quickly in and out of these "pure" stages, swearing off all meat in one interview and eating it again by the next.

In one-on-one interviews, girls tended to identify themselves along a continuum, as a "dieter," a "watcher," someone who did both, or someone who did neither. In follow-up phone interviews, we asked girls how often they practiced each of these behaviors through a series of three questions. Each girl was asked: "Would you call yourself a dieter?"; "Would you call yourself someone who watches what she eats?"; and "Would you call yourself someone who does nothing at all?" Response options for each question were: always; most of the time; sometimes; or never. Each girl was asked to respond to each of the three questions.

To analyze the responses, we defined "dieters" as girls who said they dieted *always* or *most of the time*. We defined "watcher-dieters" as girls who said they watched *always, most of the time,* or *sometimes,* and *sometimes* dieted. "Watchers" were those girls who *never* dieted but did watch. "Neithers" were those girls who said they didn't diet or watch.[22] Using these categories, only nineteen girls (8 percent) were "dieters," ninety-eight girls (42 percent) were "watcher-dieters," and eighty-four girls (36 percent) were "watchers." Thirty girls (13 percent) reported that they neither dieted nor watched what they ate.

Next, we compared girls in these categories in terms of the frequency and duration of their weight loss. To do this, we analyzed responses to two survey questions: "How often did you try to lose weight last year?" and "How long do your diets usually last?" Although there was a range of answers to this question, more than one-half of the girls who were "dieters" said that they tried to lose weight once a month or more and that their diets lasted "more than a month." Thus, the small group of nineteen girls who self-reported that they were dieters did seem to be trying to lose weight very frequently. By contrast, the most common response of girls who were "watcher-dieters" was that they attempted to lose weight approximately one to three times each year, with each episode lasting one to three weeks. Girls who were "watchers" or "neithers" predominantly reported not dieting at all. Thus, it appeared that the girls who claimed to be dieting did in fact do so, although the percentage of girls who did so was much smaller than reported on our initial survey.

We also explored whether differences might exist in the physical characteristics and exercise levels of these girls. We found that in general girls who were "dieters" and "watcher-dieters" were heavier than girls in the other categories and had higher body mass indexes, or BMIs (see Appendix B, Table 1).[23] "Dieters" gave higher responses than girls in any other group to our question about physical activity ("How many times did you exercise at least thirty minutes in the past week?"). "Dieters" exercised four to five times a week, as compared with girls in the other categories, who exercised an average of two to three times a week.

Why would the "dieters" be heavier than their peers if they ate less and exercised more? How could that be? One of my colleagues on this project, the nutritional anthropologist

Cheryl Ritenbaugh, believed that some of these girls might already be caught in a cycle of "yo-yo dieting," that is, their repeated attempts at dieting had disrupted their normal metabolism and increased the likelihood that they would gain weight when they went off their diets. Thus, they were dieting with increasing frequency yet it was becoming more and more difficult for them to lose weight.

Dieting frequently sets the stage for craving and binging, which usually involve foods laden with fats and sugar. It is not known precisely why dieting intensifies preferences for high-fat and sugar-loaded foods. Some believe that it is largely cultural, related to the ever-present advertisements for junk food and the concomitant feeling that one is being denied. Exercise physiologist Glenn Gaesser suggests that it may also have a strong biological component. He notes that the fact that laboratory rats develop strong preferences for fatty foods during the re-feeding stage of a yo-yo cycle hints that the longing may be in our nature.[24]

In an effort to understand what girls were eating, we asked them to complete food records for six days of each year of the project: two weekdays and one weekend day both in the fall and in the spring. The girls were instructed to write down everything they ate and drank during a twenty-four-hour period, the quantity of food they consumed, and whether they were dieting to lose weight that day. This information provided us with background data on what girls were eating every day and how they changed their eating habits when they tried to lose weight. Few attempts have been made to collect this type of data among teens because it is an extremely arduous task.[25]

Analysis of one year of food records (we collected 756 that year) showed that only 33 girls (14 percent) reported at least one dieting day on their food records. The total number of dieting days indicated on food records was 65 (see Appendix B, Table 2), indicating that only 9 percent (65 of 756) of all food records contained "dieting days." Notably, food records *failed to confirm* the high prevalence of dieting suggested by our survey data, in which 40 percent of the girls reported dieting on the day of the survey. Some of the 33 girls who reported dieting on their food records did so on several recorded days, not just one. Thus, even in the food records, there emerges a small core of girls who self-report to be dieters and actually are.

How did the food habits of girls labeled as "watchers" and "dieters" differ? Girls who labeled themselves as "watchers" were more likely to report on surveys and during interviews that they ate more fruits and vegetables and consumed less junk food. An analysis of the girls' micronutrient intake from their food records confirms their self-reports (see Appendix B, Table 3). As a group, "watchers" tended to report higher micronutrient intakes of vitamin A, calcium, and iron than "dieters" or "watcher-dieters," whereas "dieters" reported significantly lower micronutrient intakes than girls in all the other groups. "Watchers" and "watcher-dieters" had nearly the same caloric intake and were making healthier choices, consistent with their reports on the survey. Girls who fell under "Neither" had the highest caloric intake and the highest intake of iron and vitamin E. Intake of vitamin C did not differ among groups. Interestingly, although dieters had the lowest caloric intake, fat intake did not differ across groups. This was partly because girls who were dieting ate salads with calorie-rich dressings. Using consumption of less than two-thirds of the Recommended Daily Allowance (RDA) as the criterion for nutritional risk, the average intake for those girls who were "dieters" was at a level low enough to suggest real concern.

I began this chapter by posing a question about what girls do to reconcile wanting to be thin with wanting to consume in an environment replete with injunctions to control and release. The answer appears to be "watching what you eat." This makes the girls themselves responsible for coping in an environment permeated with high-fat foods promising instant gratification. "Watching what you eat" and "eating healthfully" are lifestyle strategies that afford girls a sense of control, as opposed to dieting, which girls tend to find oppressive.

Previous studies on adolescent weight-control have concluded that girls are involved in excessive dieting. However, our interviews and analysis of food records found more evidence of health-promoting behaviors than of pathology among a majority of girls. Although 40 percent of the girls we surveyed reported trying to lose weight on the day of the survey, only 9 percent of the food records were designated as dieting days. The large discrepancy between these two data sources hints that previous research which reports that 60 percent of girls were dieting to lose weight on the day of the survey may overstate actual dieting. Further, with regard to the duration of dieting and actual weight loss, almost one-half of the girls who said they had dieted had done so for less than a week and more than two-thirds had lost ten pounds or less on their diet.

It is important to understand that the results of surveys on dieting interpreted alone are misleading. Data from our own survey would have led us to the conclusion that 40 percent of the girls in our study were dieters. However, when we listened to girls describe what they did in their everyday lives, the picture that emerged looked quite different. The dichotomy between dieter and non-dieter found in the literature is too simplistic because it fails to capture a continuum of health-oriented behaviors adopted by many teen-aged girls who occasionally diet. The term "dieter" as usually found in surveys encompasses girls who diet all or most of the time—as the term might lead us to believe—and also girls who *sometimes* diet but *mostly* watch what they eat. Findings from our interviews suggest that among girls who consider themselves "non-dieters" there are girls who *don't* diet or watch what they eat, as well as girls who *do* watch what they eat but *don't* diet. The latter group of girls ("watchers") claim to be making conscious choices to maintain healthy bodies rather than remaining passive. The gloss term "non-dieter" does not accurately portray the complexity and range of behavior patterns adopted by teen-aged girls.

As suggested earlier, when girls self-report that they are dieting, these responses may tap key cultural concerns about weight rather than reflect actual sustained weight-loss behavior.[26] Many teen-aged girls experience cultural pressures to engage in fat talk and diet talk, even when they are not actively trying to lose weight.

Research on teen dieting has paid far more attention to describing negative behaviors than to identifying positive health attitudes and behaviors. In fact, more attention has been directed toward factors that lead to sickness than toward describing successful coping or resilient behaviors.[27] Hype about weight control has dominated the media in the United States for many years and has been contributing to the very problem it addresses. By propagating the idea that dieting is pervasive, we fail to give equal attention to attempts at healthful weight control by a growing percentage of American youth.[28]

While some girls I interviewed valued dieting as an expression of control some of the time, many others did not. Most girls saw dieting as an imposed structure that constitutes a form of domination. In interviews, many girls resisted calling themselves dieters, just as they resisted calling themselves smokers.

Rather than focus on what is wrong with youth, we need to begin to identify and build upon their positive behaviors. Health-promotion efforts need to emphasize the idea of "watching what you eat" as a counter to dieting messages that dominate the media and are associated with diet programs and products. We need to listen carefully to girls who talk about and employ watching as a strategy for maintaining their health because they find it less open to failure than dieting and more conducive to long-term success.

4

Who Will I Look Like?

I hope how my mom looks doesn't affect how I look! A large butt and big thighs runs in our family . . . it's like all the women have that. It kind of worries me a lot 'cause I don't want to look like that when I grow up.

MAGGIE, *AGE 15*

DURING THE FIRST year of our study, we primarily talked with the girls about how they felt about their bodies, how they wanted to look, and what they did to look that way. We paid much less attention to what was going on in their homes. Although these girls were spending increasing amounts of time with their peers, we recognized that their parents remained important influences in their lives. We wondered what girls were learning at home about body image. Were family members talking to them about their bodies? Were girls observing older family members to determine how they might look one day? If so, what did these observations tell them and how did that knowledge influence their behavior? Did mothers engage in fat talk and, if so, how did their daughters respond?

Part of my burgeoning interest in girls and their families was based on my day-to-day observations of my teen-aged son. Because he was concerned with how tall he would eventually be, he would keenly observe and comment on the height of other family members, which served as a gauge for his own potential. His observations and comparisons were reinforced by family members who offered commentary on who he most resembled. Listening to these conversations at home, I began to feel that they were a missing dimension of my research, which had to that point focused on girls as individuals, to the neglect of their lives at home as daughters. To understand better how parents influenced their daughters with regard to body image and dieting, I added several new questions to our second-year interviews.

The open-ended question, "When you look at family members do you get ideas about how you might look when you're older?" evoked a resounding "yes!" from about half the girls in the study. For these girls, looking at other members of their family helped them gauge whether they needed to take precautionary measures, such as watching what they ate or dieting, to avoid becoming overweight.

When I posed this question to Angela, a thin fifteen-year-old, she nodded immediately and explained:

> I kind of watch what I eat because my mom's side of the family has a history of being overweight. My dad's side of the family is very thin and about my size, you know. And so, I could go either way. I could take after my dad's side of the family and be thin all my life or I could . . . you know, I could take after my mom's side of the family and be heavy, which, you know, I don't want to do. And so I kind of, I try and watch what I eat, I think, a little bit more than some people just because I know I have that in my history.

Angela went on to tell me that most of the women in her family, with the exception of one aunt, had problems with their weight. Although she was doubtful that she would turn out to be heavy given her present thinness, she just couldn't be sure. She felt "at risk" for becoming fat.

◆   ◆   ◆

Fighting the Curse

Several girls spoke of inheriting a "curse" that was passed down within their families. Yvonne, an animated sixteen-year-old whose body was hidden beneath oversized sweat pants on the chilly day we met, graphically described her "curse" to me. In response to my question about whether looking at family members gave her ideas about how she might look, Yvonne jumped up, grabbed at her sweat pants, and stretched them out inches from her hips. As she did this, she rolled her eyes and exclaimed, "Oh my God, all the women in my family have like hips out to here . . . just like me! That's our family curse!" Momentarily letting go of my researcher self, I told Yvonne that her hips were *not* big, nor was she. Seemingly unaffected by my words, she sat back down and shifted to a more serious voice: "Well, my sister and my cousin, we're all like trying to fight off this curse, but it's not easy. We want to try to do something about it, you know." Fighting the curse meant watching what she ate and trying to exercise whenever she got the chance. Yvonne had made her older sister promise her that if she ever got as fat as their mother, she would take her to Weight Watchers and sign her up for a lifetime membership. There was no way she was going to turn out like her mother, whom she described as being quite overweight.

Fifteen-year-old Karen also feared her family curse. At 4′11″ and 120 pounds, Karen was self-conscious about her height and her big breasts, which were the target of comments from both girls and guys. Even though she knew people didn't mean to stare—and sometimes they just looked for a moment—she was certain that *everyone always* noticed. While guys would tell her outright that "they" were big, girls would divulge their jealousy through statements like, "You're so lucky. I wish I had as much as you do." Karen confided in me that she would do anything to be flat-chested or to grow a few inches taller so "they wouldn't stand out as much."

Karen lived with her mother, her stepdad, and her twelve-year-old brother and saw her biological father infrequently. She knew that there was a history of obesity in his family, particularly among the women. From a young age, Karen had been alerted to the possibility that this could be her future. She explained:

> Yeah, we call it the Champlin Curse . . . that's my real dad's last name. It's like all the women in his family are huge, I mean I'm talking huge, fat ladies, and I'm really scared. And my dad's like, "You keep eating and you're going to get the Champlin Curse" . . . I mean one of my aunts just had liposuction. They're so huge, so huge, and it's scary.

The idea of the curse was powerful for Karen because she believed that she looked very much like her father. Although this curse had not affected her yet, the mere thought of it and her dad's cautionary comments led her to be "kinda conscious" of what she ate. Although many people had told her that she looked just like her mother, she didn't believe them. She was sure she looked like her dad and that his comments about how fat she'd turn out might be right.

Cyndie, an outgoing tenth-grader who was 5'1" and weighed 130 pounds, was a classic "wannabe" dieter, a girl who was always *trying* to be on a diet. She was amused by my question about family influences. "Well," she said with a laugh, "in some ways I'm just like my mom. And we have this curse in our family . . . we call it the Wilson Curse. We've all got hips out to here and you know, we just hate it!"

Although only a few girls referred directly to a "curse," it was clear that the specter of fat within the family loomed on the horizon and was of concern to many. Having an overweight parent, particularly a mother, served as a silent reminder for some girls to control their weight, while for others it resulted in worry more than action. The pervasive concerns about weight and bodily comparisons that I had documented in schools were also commonplace in girls' homes.

In discussing what it was like to have an overweight

mother, Robin, an average-weight, self-reflective tenth-grader, explained:

> I think it makes me worry about how I look more, 'cause I don't want to grow up and look that way. I don't want to be overweight. My mother's got like a big butt and big thighs and I'm like totally afraid of that. The whole family, they all have big butts and I'm like afraid. I'm like, "No, I don't want a big butt." I guess it's kind of late. I already do!

Robin told me that she "felt like a failure" because she had stopped exercising once soccer season had ended. She had gained weight but hoped that she would trim back when she started practicing soccer again. While talking about her mother, Robin told me that even though her mother was overweight and "kinda last century" in her choice of clothes, she admired her ability to problem solve and handle difficult situations. It was encouraging to hear her identify positive attributes of her mother following disparaging body-centered comments.

In addition to weight, height was another area of concern expressed by some girls. When I asked fourteen-year-old Dawn the question about family influences, she frowned as she told me that she avoided thinking about how she might look in the future because the possibilities were just too depressing. Her gaze became distant as she explained, "Both my parents are short and I don't want to be short. I have my dad's figure and he's kinda stout. So it makes me feel really awful."

Were girls really thinking about their appearance so much or were we getting a skewed picture because we were asking about it? In order to understand this issue, we asked girls to respond to the following question on our survey: "How often do you think about your body shape?" Responses were *all of the time* (fifty-seven girls; 24 percent); *a lot of the time* (seventy-six girls; 31 percent); *sometimes* (eighty-four girls; 35 percent); *hardly ever* (twenty-two girls; 9 percent); and *never* (three girls; 1 percent). In another survey that we conducted among six hundred high school girls (grades 9–12), we found almost identical responses to this question. In summary, more than half the girls we surveyed were thinking about their body shape *all* or *a lot of the time*. The limitation of a survey question such as this is that taken alone, it does not tell us *what* girls are thinking about their body shape. Good thoughts? Bad thoughts? On the basis of interview data, I would wager that they were rarely positive thoughts, and were more likely to be critical analyses of specific body parts.

◆　　◆　　◆

Concerns about Development

In addition to worrying about weight and height, some girls—particularly those who were late maturers—expressed concern over their own development. In discussing family issues Jodi, a petite fifteen-year-old who had only recently gotten her period for the first time, told me that her looks pretty much came from both her parents, "but then there are things about me that aren't either of them." Talking about her changing body, she related this concern:

> Sometimes I worried, like when I was younger and most of the people in my class had already started wearing bras. I was like in seventh grade and I hadn't. My mom is very flat, um, training bras are too big for her and I'm not exaggerating. She's very flat and so I used to kinda wonder, oh gee, 'cause I didn't want to look like that . . . I started looking at my mom going, well, if I don't start doing something soon, I'm gonna be in big trouble. But I never really thought that I was going to look like her when I grew up. Even though we look a lot alike in some ways, there are still a lot of differences. I have my dad's genes too. So I never really think about looking like her when I'm older.

Despite Jodi's concerns about her late development, she hadn't said much to her mother about the changes that were occurring in her body, partly because she was embarrassed and partly because she didn't want to dwell on potential similarities between them. The differences between them were more important, especially given what Jodi saw as appearance "deficits." She had inherited "some stuff" from both her parents as a legacy, but her own uniqueness was what mattered to her. She was gambling on her dad's genes coming through for her in the end.

Later on in my interview with Jodi, I returned to the question of whether either of her parents, who were divorced and remarried to other partners, had talked with her about puberty. Shrugging her shoulders and blushing, Jodi said, "Not really." There was a long pause before she continued:

> I mean my dad likes to joke a little. Like um, when I went back to Chicago at Christmas to see him . . . I got my first bra last year in the summer, so when I went back at Christmas I was kinda sneaking around, pulling it down when I had to 'cause, you know, I'm not really that close to my dad. Well, no I'm close but I don't know him all that well 'cause we don't spend that much time together anymore . . . And so, um, he caught me pulling at my bra once. I forget exactly what he said but he made some comment on my bra. He'd make jokes like, "Puberty? Oh, I didn't know that you started that!" or something like that. But I mean that's pretty much the only way he's commented. And then my mom, she's like, "Oh my little baby's growing up!" I mean, she'll come into the bathroom when I'm taking a bath 'cause our family's really free, I mean it's not the normal family, and she'll come in and say, "Your tits are shaped really nicely." I'm like, "Mom!" That's pretty much the only comments I've gotten so far.

Jodi's comments speak to the silence that exists in many families about sensitive topics like puberty. Not knowing what to say, many parents say little. The teasing remarks that Jodi received typify comments recalled by many of the girls I interviewed. In another study in which girls were asked if they had been teased about breast growth, the most frequently mentioned teasers were parents. Girls primarily expressed anger about this teasing, although they felt there was not much they could do about it.[1]

How should we interpret Jodi's father's joking remarks about her physical development? Research suggests that his behavior is quite typical. Studies have shown that for many fathers, being intimate with their teen-aged daughters consists not of sharing thoughts or feelings but rather of joking and teasing.[2] Considering the high premium that teen-aged girls place on personal understanding and sharing, their fathers' brusque manners and attempts at humor are usually not well received. In fact, many daughters report that their fathers do not understand them. One study of teen-aged girls found that only 35 percent felt that their fathers met their emotional needs, compared with 72 percent of mothers.[3]

Meeting a daughter's emotional needs and being able to talk about her emerging womanhood, however, may be two separate issues. It is one thing to discuss schoolwork and relationships with friends, and quite another to talk about budding breasts! Jodi's mother's comments about the shape of her daughter's breasts may have heightened her embarrassment and sensitivity to her changing body rather than provided her with support or an answer to her worries about how she'd turn out. Developmental changes, coupled with heightened self-consciousness and uncertainty of self, can make for a troubling period for girls, especially if they have little opportunity to discuss these issues with parents who are themselves uncomfortable with their daughter's growing up.

There is little research addressing parents' discomfort with discussing pubertal changes with their children.[4] Psychologists Diane Ruble and Jeanne Brooks-Gunn found that though mothers do discuss pubertal development and menarche with their daughters, these discussions are generally focused on practical concerns and symptoms, not on the girls' feelings about the experience.[5] These authors suggest that mothers may be prisoners of their own experiences, having been unprepared for the changes brought about when they themselves experienced puberty. In addition, some mothers and fathers may not be knowledgeable about what happens during puberty and thus are inadequately prepared to educate their children. Suffice it to say that the information that girls and boys garner at school is limited and given the context, asking questions may seem inappropriate. As one might expect, very few girls discuss bodily changes and menarche with their fathers. In fact, it is often not until several months after menarche that fathers and brothers come to know that it has occurred.[6]

So how do girls get information about the dramatic bodily changes they experience during early adolescence? In the absence of family members willing or able to explain to them the process of development and what they should anticipate next, girls take it upon themselves to study their environment, through close observation and scrutiny of others in their family. Friends serve as another source of information. Closeness and intimacy with same-sex friends increase during early adolescence. Girls gather together and pool the scraps of information they have collected from a variety of sources, including their sisters, mothers, magazines, books, TV, and movies.[7]

Puberty affects not only the maturing adolescent in the family, but all family members. Early adolescence is a realignment and redefinition period, a time marked by shifts in the power structure and the social relations of those in the household. Having a teen-aged daughter can act as a stimulus to change in other family members, particularly mothers. As Rita Freedman has observed:

> Many a mother tries to act out her unrealized dreams through her daughter. She may see her daughter as an extension of herself, and try to control the girl's looks as if she were managing her own body. In reaction, a daughter may rebel against the pressure in one way or another. The mother-daughter tug-of-war over beauty takes many forms. To get psychologically separated, a girl may concentrate on how not to look or be like her mother. At the same

time, mothers are caught between wanting their girls to grow into lovely women and hating to grow older themselves.[8]

Watching a daughter's development and being privy to the comments of others who are also observing her maturation can be a delicate matter for a mother. One obvious issue she must face is the contrast between her daughter's youthful body and the reality of her own aging. The complexity of the mother-daughter relationship will be further elucidated in the next chapter through discussion of their joint weight-control efforts.

◆　　◆　　◆

Teasing and Scrutiny

The potentially exciting appearance of breasts, hips, and thighs was tainted for some of the girls we talked to by toxic comments from family members. While such comments were more common from fathers and male siblings, mothers were not immune from teasing their daughters. Several girls described being teased by their mothers as they moved through puberty and recalled nicknames they had been given like "fat stuff," "chubbo," "big mix," and "fat cat," among others. One fourteen-year-old despairingly recalled how when she was ten years old, her mother had taunted her with the name "pigger-wiggers." "I guess it was like a joke," she said, her eyes swelling with tears, "but it hurt so much because I was a little chunky thing and I couldn't stand being called a name like that."

Girls were also teased for being too thin (for example, with the nickname "beanpole"). Several girls described being tormented about their weight by brothers and sisters, especially if their siblings knew it was a sensitive issue for them. Whereas some girls described acting defiant and impervious to this teasing, others ran into their rooms and cried. Teasing and disparaging nicknames remained poignant memories long after their bodies had changed. The image lived on as a painful, embodied identity. In our survey, almost one-third of the girls reported that family members had used comments about their body shape as a way to tease them or to get back at them after a fight.

Notably, few of the heaviest girls in our study described being teased, although I suspect that they might have had the experience but were reluctant to talk about it. More commonly, it was the girls who were now thin or of average weight who described these teasing incidents. These girls—who were no longer significantly overweight—referred to messages received several years earlier when they had been going through a "fat stage," or what one girl remembered with despair as her "Pillsbury dough boy stage."

Eleanor, a fifteen-year-old ninth-grader who was 5′5″ and 135 pounds, recalled the teasing she received from her sibling, coupled with scrutiny from a parent:

> Well my mom would like say stuff like, "Oh, you actually have a waist again," and I mean, you know, "Eleanor, this is great, you're finally losing *enough* weight. You're starting to look good." And you know my little brother would tell me stuff like, "You're fat" in a real mean way, but he's a little brother and he has absolutely no fat on his body, the little geek. The two of them just made me feel really bad.

In this and several other examples, I found little appreciation among family members for the biologically based changes that occur in females during early adolescence. Eleanor's mother's excitement over the reappearance of her waist and her brother's teasing over how fat she was both seem to fault Eleanor for the normal changes her body had been undergoing. What was particularly embarrassing for Eleanor was that everyone seemed to notice subtle and not-so-subtle changes in her body. She was already self-conscious about her burgeoning womanhood, and this public commentary by family members served only to heighten her concerns and embarrassment.

The following excerpt from an interview again depicts how a daughter can be subject to the scrutiny of her mother's critical gaze. Brenda, an attractive eleventh-grader with long, straight blond hair and an enthusiastic smile, noted:

> Like, I know my mother is obsessed with herself. I mean it's disgusting to the point where she loves herself more than anything. She works out four hours a day, she doesn't eat, all she cares about is how she looks, so she rubs off on me ... She knows when I've gained half a pound, I'm not kidding. She'll say, "You didn't work out this week, did you?" And I'll say, "How can you tell?" and she'll say, "I can tell." She like knows everything like that ... she like picks up my jeans and says, "These aren't going to fit you anymore." She knows, and it's because she's so obsessed with herself and she's like a twig—she's like 5′8 and 120 pounds. It's just like she wants me to be just like her and I'm six inches shorter than her and I'm almost the same weight as her.

Although Brenda recognized how unrealistic her mother's goals were for her, as she explained, her mother had "rubbed off on her" and she could not free herself of the desire to be thin.

Whereas many girls did feel that they got ideas about how they might look from family members, some explained that they did not currently resemble any members of their family and, therefore, certainly would not look like them in the future! For others, a reluctance to comment on their resemblance to family members resulted from a desire to be seen as individuals. This theme was expressed by Lisa, an independent-thinking sixteen-year-old with a "mind of her own":

> I don't look to anybody really for the way I look. I mean, I'm just me. My mom's taller than I am and more heavy-set than me. Some people say I kinda

look like my dad. But the only person I really see that remotely looks like me is my dad's sister, 'cause she's about the same height as me and weighs about the same as I do. But the similarity ends there. I don't really look at her and think that's how *I'll* look.

By stating that "I'm just me" and "I don't look to anybody for the way I'll look," Lisa plays up the differences in her appearance that complement her sense of independence from others in her family. Lisa was not interested in speculative thinking about herself in relation to her parents. This detracted from her sense of who she was now.

Other girls dismissed the possibility that they could look like an overweight family member by referring to their own level of physical activity. Sixteen-year-old Katrina, for example, told me that her mother needed to lose "about two dress sizes." When I asked her if she got ideas about her future from looking at her mother, she quickly remarked, "No, because I'm really different than her. I play sports all the time." Similarly, fifteen-year-old Brooke told me that even though her mother was "sort of chubby," she didn't think that it was going to affect her much "because I'm active and mom wasn't, even when she was in high school and stuff. So, I don't really worry about it that much." Physical activity conferred upon girls a level of immunity from becoming like their parents.

In several narratives it was apparent that the quality of the girl's relationship with her mother affected how she felt about looking like her. More specifically, if the girl was close to her mother, she was more willing to entertain the possibility that she might look like her. Conversely, girls who had conflictual relationships with their mothers were often adamant about defining themselves, both physically and mentally, as different from their mothers. For example, although fifteen-year-old Nora acknowledged that everyone said she looked exactly like her mother, she told me in no uncertain terms that she hoped she would *not* look like her when she got older. She felt this way not because she found anything wrong with her mother's physical appearance, but because she had negative feelings about her as a parent and as a person:

> She doesn't bother me by the way she looks, it's more like it bothers me that she's my mom and I might look like her when I get older . . . 'cause sometimes we fight and she really annoys me and stuff, so I think that's what bothers me, but I don't know, it's not like she's really ugly or fat or anything. It's just that I don't want to look like her.

From Nora's perspective, it was "seriously annoying" to be compared to her mother—the one person she didn't want to be like!

From her research with mothers and daughters during adolescence, Terri Apter has found that in relationships marked with conflict as opposed to positive interactions, the daughter is more capable of establishing boundaries in which she sees herself as distinctly separate from her mother. In contrast, writes Apter, "what a good relationship offered was something more diffuse, less well-defined; and yet these girls clearly turned to their mothers for self-definition and self-confirmation."[9] Nora's narrative reveals a distinct separation from her mother; indeed, she defines herself in opposition to her mother. Her sense of self-definition is strong, albeit negative.

At puberty and beyond, conflict in the family is more likely to surface between an adolescent and his or her mother than between the adolescent and his or her father, who more often commands unquestioned authority in the household. Because mothers spend more time with their children than fathers do, there is more opportunity for bickering and diminished levels of positive interaction. For the most part, however, these are temporary problems in family relations and do not result in long-term negative relationships. Girls feel a greater need than boys to separate themselves from their mothers, and increased conflict may facilitate this separation.[10]

Some teen-aged girls found it difficult to think of their

own bodies in relation to their mothers, because the standards they employed for evaluating older women were different from those they used when thinking about themselves and their peers. In describing their mothers, the girls often used comments like, "She's got the total mom figure"; or "She's just got a little extra weight on her, like most moms." Other comments, such as, "I guess she's okay for a mom," or "I just can't imagine her any other way," provide insights into why it was difficult for some girls to draw any meaningful comparisons between themselves and their mothers. Mothers were excused for having some fat on their bodies. But there was a limit, and some mothers were described as no longer caring about how they looked.

Gina, a sixteen-year-old, gestured with her hands at her sides as she described her mother as "all big and fat." Laughing as she spoke, she told me, "I'm telling you the truth, but she doesn't even think she's big and fat. She doesn't even care about her weight anymore because she just says, 'I'm too old to worry about that.'" Gina wished her mother would take better care of herself—that she would at least work on her body a little by "dieting or something at least sometimes." But her mother felt she was beyond the stage of life when such things mattered. She had been pretty in her youth, but looks were fleeting and now she was a mother. Anyway, she warned her daughter that even if you try, you can't fight age.

Most daughters had combed through family albums at one time or another and knew what their mothers had looked like when they were young. They commented on how different their body shapes in particular had been then, and sometimes remarked that their mothers were unrecognizable. To some extent, girls attributed their mothers' weight gain to having had children. For example, fifteen-year-old Connie described her mother as "short and fat," but, she quickly added, "that's probably my fault and my brother's and sister's fault because after she got pregnant she didn't lose weight very easily." Connie had listened to her mother reminisce about the days "before she had kids," when she felt she had been attractive and had a good figure. Observations of this type led some girls to say that they didn't want to have children because they were afraid they'd end up fat like their mothers and other women they knew.

◆   ◆   ◆

An Environment of Worry

After listening to the girls speak about weight and body shape in relation to their mothers, I wondered just how pervasive their mothers' concerns about their own bodies were. To what extent were girls growing up in a household environment where body image was a concern?

Although little empirical data address this question, the popular press has generated some impressions. One survey conducted by *Glamour* magazine found that among 33,000 female respondents, an overwhelming majority (87 percent) believed that their mothers were dissatisfied with their own bodies, whereas only 13 percent thought their mothers were satisfied.[11] A recent survey conducted by *Ladies Home Journal* reports that 70 percent of the magazine's readership worries about their weight "at least occasionally," and 30 percent dwell on it "most of the time." The survey found that women aged thirty to forty-nine are the most likely to worry about their weight almost constantly, as are women who work full-time.[12]

In our survey we asked girls to complete the following statement: "My mother (stepmother) worries about how her body looks . . ." Response choices were *all the time* (twenty-six girls; 11 percent); *a lot of the time* (fifty-eight girls; 25 percent); *sometimes* (ninety-one girls; 39 percent); *hardly ever* (thirty-four girls; 15 percent); and *never* (twenty-three girls; 10 percent). Collapsing three of the responses (*all the time; a lot of the time;* and *sometimes*), we find that the majority of mothers (76 percent) harbored some degree of worry about their own bodies, at least in their daughters' opinions.

In contrast to how their mothers perceived themselves, daughters reported the following when asked how often their fathers worried about how they looked: *all the time* (three girls; 1 percent); *a lot of the time* (fifteen girls; 7 percent); *sometimes* (forty-six girls; 23 percent); *hardly ever* (forty-nine girls; 24 percent); and *never* (ninety-three girls; 45 percent). Compared with mothers, fathers appeared to be far less concerned with their bodies. More than two-thirds of the fathers were *hardly ever* or *never worried* about their bodies, compared with only 25 percent of mothers in these categories. Whereas 36 percent of the mothers were reported to worry *all* or *a lot of the time* about how their body looked, only 8 percent of the fathers were believed to worry to this degree.

The girls were also asked the following question about their parents' body shape: "In my opinion, my mother (stepmother) is . . ." Responses were *too thin* (seven girls; 3 percent); *just about right* (sixty-five girls; 28 percent); *about the right weight but out of shape* (fifty-eight girls; 25 percent); *kind of fat* (eighty-nine girls; 39 percent); and *very fat* (twelve girls; 5 percent). In response to the same question about fathers, girls answered that they were *too thin* (eight girls; 4 percent); *just about right* (eighty-four girls, 40 percent); *about the right weight but out of shape* (forty-three girls; 20 percent); *kind of fat* (sixty-one girls; 29 percent); and *very fat* (fifteen girls; 7 percent).

The girls' reports of their parents' body shape show greater similarity between mothers and fathers compared with their reports about the extent to which their parents worried about weight. In terms of perceived body size, daughters were more likely to report that their mothers were "kind of fat" (39 percent) when compared with their descriptions of their fathers (26 percent). Without seeing their parents, it is difficult to assess whether daughters held different standards for body size for their mothers than for their fathers or whether this was an accurate description of their parents' appearance. It seems highly plausible that daughters maintained thinner standards for appropriate body weight for women than for men, and this may account for why they reported their mothers to be fatter than they believed their fathers to be. This was suggested in the interview data by several girls.

❖   ❖   ❖

Learning from Their Mothers

Whether or not girls got ideas about how *they* might turn out from looking at other family members, there were valuable lessons to be learned about body shape within the household. In particular, girls learned about the life consequences of excess weight from their mothers. Erin, a ninth-grader who did not identify with her mother's body shape, had a heightened concern about her weight because her mother and other female relatives were overweight. Attributing this to heredity, Erin explained to me how difficult it was for her mother to lose the forty pounds she wanted to take off: "It's just so hard for my mom because it's just in her blood, you know." Although Erin thought her mother looked good despite her extra pounds, she understood why she wanted to diet. From her mother's remarks about work, Erin had learned how being overweight can affect a woman's career. Her mother had been a victim of fat prejudice, which had taken the form of snide comments and career stagnation.

Erin noted the great difference her mother had experienced recently when there was a change in office staff:

> It's getting better for my mom at work now because she used to work with people that were all really thin but now her boss is overweight and her secretary is overweight, so they're all like the same. I think that's a big part of why it's better now. 'Cause they kind of tease each other about it, but they can, because they're all the same way. So I think it makes her feel more comfortable at work now. But I think when you're in the public eye, like she is, you feel a lot better if you're thin.

Erin learned about the consequences of being fat not only from her biological mother, but also from her stepmother, who jokingly referred to weight watching as a form of insurance. Although her stepmother did not overtly talk about feeling fat, Erin reported that "her strategy is just to work out and diet because her mom and sister are overweight and she doesn't want to have to deal with it." Her stepmother looked good and had a successful career, unlike her "fat relatives." She had worked hard for everything she had achieved, and there was "no way she was going to lose it all to fat!"

Sadly, empirical research substantiates Erin's observations about her mother. Obesity has been found to negatively affect women's, but not men's, social mobility.[13] Hostile work environments and job discrimination are more frequently reported by overweight women than by overweight men. Further, women who are considered unattractive by their coworkers are described in more negative terms than are unattractive men. In one study in which teens were followed into adulthood, it was found that being overweight had both social and economic consequences that were more severe for females than for males.[14] Such findings lend credence to the popular notion that physical beauty can translate into power for women, whereas being overweight can be a serious impediment to their career paths.

Another theme that emerged among girls whose mothers were significantly overweight was that their large body size was interpreted by some people as a sign that they were out of control. Julie, an articulate tenth-grader whose mother was about seventy-five pounds overweight, spoke passionately about how unfair this was, and how people judge women too quickly, "before really understanding their problem." She explained:

> Some people, like my mom, are genetically overweight but others just don't have much self-control. Even though they're large, they usually are nice people . . . well, just like anyone else. I think a lot of people look at women who are like my mom and think they're just fat slobs and that they're always eating everything in sight. But, you know, my mom, she just can't help it. She doesn't even eat that much.

Although Julie did not think that she resembled her mother, she confessed that she worried when she looked at her and silently prayed "that it doesn't happen to me."

Expressing sentiments similar to Julie's, fifteen-year-old Cassidy also told me that others could potentially see her mother's weight problem as resulting from an inability to control what she ate. As her daughter, however, she recognized that it was not her mother's fault:

> Well, some fat people have an eating problem while other people can't really help it because of their metabolism and some people just don't care and let themselves go. It depends on the person. Sometimes it's their fault, you know, but with my mom it wasn't really her fault, she just has a different metabolism and stuff. She had to get professional help to deal with her problem.

Cassidy distinguishes three possible causes of obesity: having an "eating problem," which she thought of as similar to an addiction; having a metabolic problem, which was something a doctor could help with; or just giving up and not caring about how you look. Cassidy classified her mother's problem as metabolic and thought of her as taking charge of her life when she sought help from a weight-loss center, where she had lost seventy pounds over the past year. She was very proud of her mother's accomplishment and felt that losing weight had made her mother happier, healthier, and more accepting of herself. When asked whether she was concerned about her own weight, Cassidy, who was average in size, remarked, "Well, anybody can get fat, so you have to care about what you eat . . . but I don't have a medical problem like my mother does."

Medicalizing the problem allowed Cassidy to establish distance from it. In her view, her mother's obesity was not exclusively her responsibility; it was beyond her control. By labeling her heaviness as an illness—a metabolic disorder—Cassidy allowed her mother to enter the sick role. Her perseverance at the weight-loss center provided a cure for her illness.

Girls had also witnessed the impact of becoming fat on a

woman's close relationships. Yvonne, who worried about the "curse of the hips," told me that her father had left her mother because she had gotten fat. While this seemed an over-simplification of what would lead a couple to separate, I had no way of knowing whether Yvonne's story was accurate. At best, it was her rendition of familial events—possibly what she had garnered from listening to her mother or father talking.

About a year before our interview, Yvonne told me, her dad had walked out, and since then her mother had battled to lose weight. Through daily exercise and vigilant dieting, she had successfully gone from 175 to 130 pounds over an eight-month period. What was Yvonne's response to her mother's predicament? She adamantly insisted that she was going to take better care of herself than her mother ever had. Echoing her father's words, Yvonne told me, "My mom gained a lot of weight after she got married. It was like she stopped caring. I don't plan to do that because then people lose respect for you." Notably, after her mother lost weight, her dad moved back in, and he was still living in the house at the time of our third-year interview.

In the four cases highlighted, the girls learned from their mothers about the difficulties of being overweight in the work-place and in the home and were able to articulate the kind of prejudice that their mothers experienced because of their weight. Their firsthand knowledge of the way weight gain influenced social relations had an impact on their lives, and was already a source of anxiety for both Yvonne and Julie. Three of these four girls had already begun watching their own eating as a precautionary measure to ensure that they would not experience prejudice and isolation as their mothers had.

What was particularly striking was how few of the girls discussed hardships or prejudice that their fathers faced because of their weight or other aspects of their appearance. Even in families where both parents were overweight, girls' discussions centered on their mothers and how excess weight affected their lives. This is not to say that men do not experience prejudice with regard to body size. It speaks, rather, to the issue of girls' limited understanding of their fathers' lives. The father-daughter relationship is often the most difficult and distant relationship in the family. Typically, it is marked by limited communication and few shared activities when compared with the mother-daughter relationship.[15] Fathers are more reticent about disclosing information about their everyday experience, and thus it may not be surprising that daughters know little about the prejudice they encounter as a result of being overweight.

Girls learn from their mothers the consequences of being overweight, but at the same time they learn that food can serve as a source of comfort and solace during times of stress. Vanessa, whose mother weighed more than two hundred pounds ("although she won't really tell me how much"), expressed sympathy for her mother's "problem." From photographs, she knew her mother had been quite thin at the time of her marriage. She attributed her mother's weight gain to financial worries. When worries plagued her, she turned to food:. "She eats a lot because we've had a rough life. See, my mom worries a lot about the bills piling up. She's had a lot of stress divorcing my stepdad. When her life gets crazy, she eats to calm down."

Vanessa's comments about eating as a coping strategy were reminiscent of some girls' descriptions of how their mothers smoked as a way to deal with stress in their lives. By watching when their mothers lit up, girls learned that smoking a cigarette was a form of self-medication that enabled their mothers to calm down and refocus. Particularly if a mother was going through a troubling period in her life (such as a divorce, an illness in the family, or a financial crisis), daughters would comment, "Cigarettes help her, like a friend," or "It's not a good time for her to quit." In their mothers' everyday lives, both smoking and overeating were seen paradoxically as enhancing their immediate well-being, while at the same time contributing to their long-term ill health.[16]

Sixteen-year-old Rachel also spoke of sweets as her mother's only source of relief. Recently divorced, her mother had always had a problem with her weight and was a chronic dieter. When asked about her mother's dieting, Rachel replied, "Right now, well since my dad's left . . . she wants to be . . . she's *trying* to be on a diet. But it's kind of hard when she's upset and depressed. When she gets that way, eating sweets, especially Snickers bars, cheers her up a little." Rachel felt that as a source of immediate comfort during times of emotional need, eating a candy bar was understandable. She also felt that her mother would have to make up for her transgressions later on. Penance would follow momentary solace.

Rachel's mother is not unusual in eating to ward off bad feelings. Furthermore, studies confirm that this practice is much more common among women than men; whereas women have been found to eat nearly twice as much sweet food and more bland food under stress, men consistently eat less.[17] Such eating patterns are learned at least partly in the family, where chocolate may be offered as a way to cope with stressful events. Particularly when their children are young, it is not unusual for parents to offer candy as a treat. One girl recalled how each time she did well at school, she was taken out for an ice cream cone. Although she had looked forward to this when she was young, it was frustrating when she got older, especially if she was trying hard to "be good" and avoid temptation. Several girls told me that when they were having a bad day, their mothers offered them sweets ("Here, have a candy bar") as a way to make them feel better.

Eating sweets was not only a coping mechanism but also a source of bonding between females in the household. Lorraine, a mature eleventh-grader, told me that she had a "real sweet tooth," which she attributed to her mother's eating habits. "We had these nights where my sisters were sleeping over at a friend's house or they'd be out at some school thing, and me and my mom would go out and have ice cream. We'd buy a half gallon and sit down and watch a movie and eat ice cream together. It was like a real bonding experience. It was lots of fun."

Beyond the need to bond, there may be biological variables influencing desires for calorie-rich foods. Physiological research has indicated that because of changes related to the menstrual cycle, women crave higher-calorie foods at different times of the month.[18] Such cravings, which we noted in the narratives of many girls, may explain sudden desires for calorie-rich foods like chocolate. Given that women who live together often have synchronized menstrual cycles, it is not unusual that these cravings often occur at similar times of the month.[19]

◆ ◆ ◆

Listening to Moms' Fat Talk

Was the fat talk that was so pervasive among teen-aged girls and their peers also a form of discourse that mothers engaged in routinely? If so, what kinds of responses did daughters provide to their mothers' "I'm so fat" comments? I found that the girls' responses were complex and dependent on the quality of the mother-daughter relationship, as well as on what the mother looked like and how expressive she was.

As I began to speak with girls about their mothers' fat talk, I became aware of the limitations of this line of questioning. As sixteen-year-old Tia succinctly explained to me, "I don't think that my mom has ever directly said that she was fat, but like indirectly for my entire life, you know, she's basically been saying that." Her mother's continual diet-hopping from one plan to another was an obvious testament to how she felt about her weight. Tia's observations of what her mother ate and didn't eat gave her insights into how her mother felt about her body, regardless of what she actually said.

Sixteen-year-old Jaime lived with her mother, her stepdad, and their two young children. In response to the question, "Does your mom say, "I'm so fat"? Jaime explained that her mother periodically complained to her about the weight she had gained during her pregnancies. In response Jaime, who was very close to her mother, tried to respond in a way that would mitigate her negative feelings about herself:

> Sometimes my mom will say, "Do I look fat?" you know, she'll just ask me that, and I'm like, "No, Mom, you look the same," and she's like, "Well what

does that mean? Tell me, do I look good or bad?"
And I'm like, "Mom, you look fine. You're not fat."
She asks me questions like that every once in a
while, then other times she's all right with her
weight. I mean sometimes I'll say, "I'm so fat" and
sometimes she'll say it. It just depends on how we're
feeling that day. We just say it to get like reassurance
from each other that we really look okay.

Among girls like Jaime who were close with their mothers,
complaints about being fat were used as an opportunity to re-
assure their mothers that they were *not* fat. In such instances,
"fat talk" serves a similar purpose among mothers and daughters as it does among girlfriends. As sixteen-year-old Karen
explained, "Yeah, my mother says it all the time and I just tell
her she's not . . . I mean she really isn't fat but she just thinks
she is. She thinks she's fat and ugly. I just want to let her know
that she's not. I want to support her and make her feel better
about herself."

A mother's fat talk can also serve as an opportunity for her
daughter to offer constructive criticism. In many ways the girls
found that there was less social risk in telling their mothers
what they thought about their bodies than in telling a friend.
Yvonne, whose mother was desperate to lose weight so she
could get her husband back, commonly engaged in fat talk.
When I asked Yvonne how she responded to her mother's
complaints about her body, she told me that she used the opportunity to give her mother honest advice.

When she says, "I'm so fat," I'm like, "Yeah, you are."
I mean I don't want to lie to her, especially after all
she's been through. I try to tell her the truth and
help her out. I mean, when I see her cheating on her
diet, I say like, "Mom, is that good for you?" and
she's like, "Well, no" . . . and then I say, "Then why
are you eating it?" She buys these little chocolates
and I'm like, "Mom!" and she's like, "Oh, Yvonne,
just one?" and I'm like, "It's just gonna be another
ounce of fat right on your hip, Mom."

In this mother-daughter relationship, a role reversal has occurred, and Yvonne assumes a position of authority. When her mother begs to be allowed to eat "just one" candy, Yvonne sternly reminds her of the consequences of "wrong" behavior. By adolescence, Yvonne has been socialized to be surveillant of her mother with regard to weight and eating behavior. In Chapter 5, I describe how surveillance extends to sibling relationships as well.

Being subjected to their mothers' fat talk proved problematic and uncomfortable for some girls. Sixteen-year-old Leslie, who was shy and withdrawn during our interview, told me that when her mother said, "I'm so fat," she didn't know how to respond so she didn't say anything. The problem, she explained, looking down and speaking in a small voice, was that she *did* think her mother needed to lose weight, but she thought that telling her would hurt her feelings. After all, even though she commonly heard fat talk spoken among friends, she had *never* heard anyone respond to the comment "I'm so fat" with a realistic appraisal—"Yes, you are." Leslie felt that she could *never* say that to her mother; nor could she feel comfortable lying by responding, "No, you're not." Silence seemed the appropriate solution to her dilemma.

Fifteen-year-old Mary also expressed discomfort with her mother's fat talk, which she practiced with great regularity. She described her mother as "real pretty with big blue eyes and long brown hair. But she's had three kids, so she's gotten a little big in the hip area and the inner thighs." When I asked if her mother complained about her own weight, Mary threw her head back and laughed. "My mom?" she asked. "Oh yeah, like every night!" She continued:

> Well, she like stands in front of the mirror without her clothes on, I mean she's not modest or anything, and she'll be like examining every part of herself and she'll just say, "I'm so fat, just look at this," and she'll grab hold of her thigh . . . and I have to listen to it! I mean she goes and works out a couple of times a week, which I think is really good because if

she does that, then she thinks she's firming up. She may not look it, but she thinks she is, so that makes her feel more self-confident. You know, she feels better about herself. I don't really say much to her when she says, "I'm so fat." I mean, she's talking out loud to herself, not really to me.

Let us consider for a moment what the impact might be of listening to a mother engage in fat talk every night as she looks in the mirror. What message might this send to a girl who is in the midst of adjusting to a body that she feels is out of control? Mary's lesson was that there was no end in sight for a woman's body work—dissatisfaction with weight persists, even as a woman gets older. In Mary's family, dissatisfaction with body shape is even of concern to her grandmother, who visits frequently and shares dieting tips with her mother. Having been divorced three times already, Mary's mother craved the confidence that she felt a slim body could provide.

As a late maturer, Mary was gangly and tried to cover up her bony limbs by "dressing big," even to the point of wearing big socks to hide her skinny ankles. Her mother encouraged her to take advantage of her thin body by showing it off in tight, short clothes, but Mary had no desire to do that. As she began to fill out, I wondered, would she share the dissatisfaction of self that so permeated her home environment? My question was answered later that year, when I again spoke with Mary. As I had suspected, she expressed concern over her recent weight gain and was exercising more vigorously and more frequently to fight off her "emerging fat."

The more stressful a girl's relationship with her mother, the less likely she was to offer supportive responses to her mother's fat talk. Fifteen-year-old Stephanie, who was in a very stressful relationship with her mother and was continually grounded, commented that when her mother said, "I'm so fat," she would reply in a sarcastic voice, "You're not fat, you're just my plump little mommy!" After a moment of reflection, Stephanie added, "I don't tell her she's *not* fat 'cause she is, but I do tell her to stop putting herself down." Although

Stephanie wasn't interested in engaging in supportive fat talk with her mother, she felt that her mother needed to get a grip on reality and overcome her negative feelings about her body weight. Other girls who had problematic relations with their mothers reported using negative responses to their mothers' fat talk as an opportunity to criticize them and put them down, rather than to provide support or offer affirmation that they looked good "for a mother."

Sixteen-year-old Sarah, who characterized her relationship with her mother as "fighting, fighting, fighting," complained about how annoying it was to be the recipient of her mother's fat talk. When asked if her mother ever said, "I'm so fat," she replied:

> Oh yeah, all the time! Like when we go shopping, she's like, "Do these make me look fat?" I go, "Mom!" She like walks into fat people stores, you know, where they have those really large clothes and she goes (changes voice to whisper), "Sarah, am I as large as her?" and she like looks over to some other fat woman. And I'm like, "No, Mom." I mean that woman was like shaking the floors as she walked. I'm like, "No, you're not *that bad,* Mom." It's like, gimme a break, you're a little self-conscious, dear.

Although Sarah's mother has invited her to become her confidante, Sarah shows little interest in her mother's comparison game. When asked if her mother actively tried to change her weight, Sarah responded with the following story:

> Oh yeah! She's like, "Oh, I can't wear these pants anymore. I'm going to save these pants." I mean they're like a size 3 and she goes, "When I get skinny I'm going to wear these." It's like, "Yeah, when you die, Mom, we'll dig you up and we'll put those pants on you after you lose a few pounds!"

Despite the sarcasm of her comment, Sarah is keenly aware of the futility of her mother's past weight-loss attempts. Her lack of patience with her mother is the result of a long history. Sarah characterizes her mother as extremely self-absorbed. Frustrated with her narcissistic behavior and her displays of insecurity, Sarah has little interest in placating her feelings.

As troubled as I had felt while listening to girls' self-deprecating comments about their own bodies, their stories of their family environment left me equally, or perhaps even more, disturbed. Both at school and at home, girls seemed to be surrounded by excessive concerns over physical appearance and talk of feeling fat. Was there no respite from dissatisfaction with one's body? Was the message of self-acceptance truly absent from girls' households, or was it spoken and did they fail to hear it?

I was surprised to find that in response to their complaints about their weight, only a handful of daughters had been told by their mothers that they didn't need to worry about it. As fifteen-year-old Mia explained:

> Sometimes I'll say to my mom, "Does my butt look big today?" and she'll say, "I hate when you say that. You're fine the way you are." She says, "You know, I would tell you, even though it would hurt you, I would tell you if I thought you needed to lose weight . . . if you had a problem or something." You know, my mom always tells us how cute we are and stuff like that.

This interchange between mother and daughter was impressive because it was so unusual in comparison with the other narratives. It is telling, not to mention depressing, how few white and Latino mothers in our study tried to foster positive self-image on the part of their daughters.

Talking to girls, and not to their parents, certainly colored my view of household dynamics and communication patterns. I heard what girls remembered. Who knew what other conversations had taken place, what else had been said? As a parent myself, I had often considered whether my efforts to bolster my son's faltering self-esteem fell on deaf ears. Even if he heard what I had to say (which I sometimes doubted), did he really care what his mother thought about him? How could I get him to understand that we as individuals are more than our weight, our height, or the label on our shoes? Having struggled with these issues, I had some grasp of the frustrations and difficulties parents face. I sensed that what was at issue was a reluctance on the part of parents to talk with their daughters because they were unsure of what to say or how to say it. If parents subscribe to the belief that puberty is "just a stage," there may be little need to spend time talking about it. Daughters who have been given the terse message that "they'll outgrow it" may assiduously study other family members for much-needed clues to the puzzle of their eventual size and shape.

As I continued to talk with girls about their home life during the second and third years of the study, I gained insights into how mothers and fathers attempted to help their daughters deal with this unsettling period of their lives. It is to this experience that I turn in the next chapter.

5

Mothers, Daughters, and Dieting

I was brought up to think being thin . . . like I'd say, "Mom, have a piece of pie," and she'd be like, "No, I'm on a diet." So I mean I've known diets since I was in kindergarten.

TINA, *AGE 14*

T HE QUOTE ABOVE reminds me of my own childhood, growing up with a mother who was always on a diet. During the brief periods of time when she wasn't dieting, my mother was actively searching for dieting tips in the pages of *Ladies Home Journal* or *Good Housekeeping.* She didn't impose her diets on me, despite the fact that by age twelve I was chubby. Although attentive to her own weight, she was not overly concerned that I had gained about twenty pounds during puberty. When I complained about my weight to her, she told me that it was a stage and that I would outgrow it. By age fifteen I had lost some weight and gained height, but I was still waiting impatiently for "it" to melt away. I knew that my older sister had gotten diet pills from our family doctor, and I asked my mother if I could get them, too. Her approval was clear; she called right away and made an appointment for me.

One month of taking amphetamines left me a bit on edge but very upbeat. Having lost fifteen pounds, I experienced a new-found pride in my appearance and the fact that I had tamed my previously ravenous appetite. I continued to take diet pills until I was thinner than I had ever been at 5'7" and 125 pounds. I stopped taking pills and, not surprisingly, as the weeks went by and my Twinkie habit resurfaced, my weight crept back up. The disparity between the girl I saw in the mirror and my recent memory of my svelte self made me depressed. Was I, like my mother, destined to diet for life? I wondered what shape my woman's body would take, and I actively studied my mother, my older sister, and other women in my family for answers. Though nothing was said to me overtly about my need to diet, I had received a message about women, weight, and their relationship to food that was to stay with me for many years to come.

◆　　◆　　◆

Like Mother, Like Daughter?

The mother-daughter relationship and maternal body concerns are central to the development of a girl's body image and her attitudes toward food.[1] Feminist writer Susie Orbach has stressed that on both conscious and unconscious levels, mothers transmit to their daughters cultural ideals and contradictions about gender and femininity.[2] The mother-daughter relationship is often characterized by high levels of closeness and discord and by a high level of shared activities.[3] Dieting may constitute one such shared activity. Whereas much has been written about the impact of family relations on the development of eating disorders, relatively little has been written about how mothers influence daughters who fall into the "normal" range of eating and dieting behavior.[4]

Ruth Striegel-Moore and Ann Kearney-Cooke found that both mothers and fathers who had recently dieted themselves were more likely to encourage their children, both male and female, to diet. Parents were generally very positive about their children's appearance, although as their children got older, they became increasingly less positive about how they looked. The authors note, "Adolescents consistently received the least positive evaluations, being the targets of the most criticism, the least praise and the most efforts to change physical appearance."[5] Importantly, parents were more likely to rate their daughters as fatter than their sons, even though the reported height and weight data for the same-age children suggested that the boys were actually heavier than the girls. Thus, even within the family, standards for appropriate body weight become more stringent as girls develop physically.

As gatekeepers of the home, mothers are more involved than fathers in monitoring and controlling their children's eating behavior and are more likely to be responsible for their children's physical appearance. It is usually the mother and not the father who experiences pressure from others to improve her child's appearance.[6] A mother may find herself in a precarious position with her adolescent daughter, who is upset with her ever-changing body. How is she to advise and guide her through this troubling time? If she encourages her to celebrate her weight gain as a sign of her womanhood, will she be accused by others of not properly monitoring her daughter's weight? If she invites her daughter to diet with her, will she inadvertently be encouraging her down a life-long path of dissatisfaction and frustration?

A mother's concern may be intensified if she and her teen-aged daughter both want to lose weight because they are experiencing biological transitions that result in weight gain. While the daughter's weight gain is generally related to puberty, her mother's may be related to subsequent pregnancies, to being in the later stages of menopause, or to side-effects of hormone replacement therapy.[7] Indeed, according to one study, the mother-daughter pairs who were most at risk for unhealthy eating attitudes and practices were those who were experiencing reproductive transitions at the same time.[8] In such cases, the mother's dieting practices seemed to be very influential on the daughter.

❖   ❖   ❖

Media Portrayals of Mothers and Daughters

An increasing number of advertisements portray images of youthful, glamorous mothers with pre-adolescent daughters, styled through makeup and dress to resemble their mothers and appear old beyond their years. The general subtext to be read in such ads is that youthful—seemingly ageless—mothers serve as powerful role models for their daughters in terms of beauty practices and secrets.

In a Danskin advertisement in which mother and young daughter are side by side on exercise bikes, the daughter looks up adoringly at her mother. They appear to have a loving relationship, with the five-year-old playfully mirroring her mother's behavior. The fact that they are dressed identically serves to reinforce the similarity in their bodies. The daughter learns at an early age that, like her mother, she too can remain young and slim forever, provided that she works hard (though this is not expressed).

In a Bain de Soleil advertisement for "elegant skincare for the sun," a mother and daughter are both dressed in identical black bikinis and are adorned with gold jewelry and lipstick. They share the same white beach chair, with the daughter sitting upright in a provocative pose, looking far older than her six or seven years. The mother looks down at her daughter, her face marked by a critical gaze, while the daughter looks off into the distance. This downward gaze from one to another is generally depicted in advertisements of a man looking at a woman, what the sociologist Erving Goffman has coined the "anchored drift."[9] To show this in the relationship between mother and daughter is to highlight the control the mother has over her daughter in the domain of appearance.

In the world of advertisements, not only do mothers teach their daughters how to be beautiful, but daughters in turn share this knowledge with their friends. Feminist researcher Susan Bordo describes the following:

In a television commercial, two little French girls are shown dressing up in the feathery finery of their mothers' clothes. They are exquisite little girls, flawless and innocent, and the scene emphasizes both their youth and the natural sense of style often associated with French women. (The ad is done in French, with subtitles.) One of the girls, spying a picture of the other girl's mother, exclaims breathlessly, "Your mother, she is so slim, so beautiful! Does she eat?" The daughter, giggling, replies: "Silly, just not so much," and displays her mother's helper, a bottle of FibreThin. "Aren't you jealous?" the friend asks. Dimpling, shy yet self-possessed, deeply knowing, the daughter answers, "Not if I know her secrets."[10]

This ad brings up another important component of the mother-daughter relationship: jealousy. The little girl's friend, wise beyond her years, recognizes the inevitability of jealousy between women. Jealousy is controlled, however, by sharing in her mother's dieting secrets. Like her mother, the little girl can stay beautiful and slim forever.

In the ads described, pre-pubescent girls are depicted as already having embodied the struggle for beauty, be it in the form of dieting, exercise, or physical beautification. Their mothers serve as role models for them, showing them how to exercise, how to control their weight, and how to enhance their physical attractiveness. This repository of beauty tips is transmitted across generations.[11]

❖   ❖   ❖

Messages from Parents

Parents can serve as important role models and transmitters of cultural norms and values for their children. How do parents make their values about appropriate body weight known to their children? To what extent are girls getting overt messages from their family members that they should lose weight? And if they are receiving such messages, who is telling them and what are they saying?

On our survey we asked, "Has your mother (stepmother) or father (stepfather) ever told you that you needed to lose weight?" Responses were: *yes, both my parents have* (34 girls; 14 percent); *just my mom has* (20 girls; 8 percent); *just my dad has* (12 girls; 5 percent); and *neither parent has* (176 girls; 73 percent). Combining these responses, we find that 27 percent of girls had been told by a parent to lose weight, compared with 73 percent who had not.

Were heavier girls more likely to receive weight-loss messages than average-weight or thin girls? Analysis revealed that heavier girls (as calculated by BMI) were significantly more likely to receive parental messages to lose weight when compared with girls who were in the mid or low BMI groups (see Appendix B, Table 4). More than one-half the girls in the high BMI range (that is, girls who were significantly overweight) had received messages to lose weight, compared with one-quarter of girls in the mid BMI range (average weight for height). Importantly, of those girls who were in the mid BMI range who received messages, about one-third were on the heavier end of this group. Thus it appears that, at least in some cases, when a parent expressed concern about his or her daughter's weight, it was because the daughter was overweight by biomedical standards.

In order to understand more about the content and delivery of parental messages, I asked girls to discuss what had been said to them. Mothers' comments to their daughters about losing weight usually came in response to concerns the daughters themselves had raised. Complaining "I'm so fat" was a common way for girls to solicit comments and feedback from their mothers, just as mothers did from their daughters. Leslie, a tenth-grader who at 5'5" was 135 pounds, reported that her mother had told her to lose weight, but qualified her statement by adding, "Well, she's not like pressuring me or

anything." After thinking for a few moments, Leslie continued:

> Well, before she said, "You're getting a little over-
> weight, you might want to start watching what you
> eat," or whatever, I think I might have brought it up,
> I might have said, "Help me," you know, and so she
> did help me. Nobody ever really told me, "Oh *you're*
> *fat,* lose weight," so I don't really know if I brought
> it up or if she brought it up, but then she kind of
> helped me like, "Do you really think you need that
> today?'"—ice cream, you know. And she'd say things
> like, "You need to eat more fruit." 'Cause last year
> I'd come home and eat ice cream when I got home
> . . . I was like addicted to ice cream and now I have
> ice cream like once every two weeks.

Leslie accepted her mother's advice because it was offered
with positive suggestions and encouragement on how to maintain her efforts to lose weight. Under her mother's watchful
eye, Leslie was learning to be "good" and to eat healthfully.

Brooke, an energetic ninth-grader, recalled how, in response to concerns she raised about her weight gain in the
summer before seventh grade, her parents had encouraged
her to lose weight. She remembered that it was her mother
who had indirectly talked to her about this: "One time I was
porking on a lot of food and my mom said, 'That's a lot of food
for you,' but she never said, 'You're fat,' she just commented on
the amount of food." Brooke remembered this comment as being more acceptable than a direct statement like, "Stop eating,"
or "Lose weight" might have been. Brooke's mother, herself a
member of Weight Watchers, had encouraged her daughter
to join the group. Although her mother later dropped out of
the program, Brooke had stuck with it and had successfully
lost 25 pounds over a five-month period, going from 160 to
135 pounds. Although Brooke spoke of her weight loss as her
own personal accomplishment, her mother's non-judgmental
attitude and support helped her reach her goal. It was her
mother who had encouraged her to join the weight-loss pro-

gram, had made low-calorie food choices available to her, and had supported her by taking her to the weekly meetings. At the time of the interview, Brooke was still going to meetings and considered herself a member for life.

The way a mother delivered a message about weight control was an important factor in her daughter's acceptance of it. Rather than forcing the issue, many mothers sensitively approached the topic of weight with their daughters. One overweight ninth-grader remarked, "My mom mentioned it and said she'd help me lose weight if I *wanted* to, but she didn't say that *I needed to* or *that I had to*." The message was easier for her to accept because "she's not *pushing* me to do it, she's just *asking* me to because it will make me feel better."

The communication style of these mothers reflects their desire to maintain a good rapport and connection with their daughters, a style particularly characteristic of women's speech. According to their daughters' reports, these mothers were not overtly critical of them and did not speak to them in a manner that was mean or unfeeling.

Some weight-loss messages from mothers were intricately linked with concern for the daughters' health. In households in which daughters went on yo-yo diets or skipped meals, parents sometimes told them that dieting was unhealthy and encouraged them to eat less of what they usually ate and more fruits and vegetables. By establishing rules for healthy eating, some mothers advocated a healthy lifestyle for their daughters, which might prevent them from needing to diet.

Some mothers warned their daughters about gaining weight because they themselves knew what it was like to be overweight and wanted their daughters to avoid it at all costs. Memories of being heavy haunted women, even if their bout with being overweight had occurred many years earlier and only for a brief period. Monitoring their daughters' food intake carefully, they attempted to control them with statements like, "Don't eat that, it has a lot of calories, you'll end up fat like I am," or "You'll get fat like I was in high school and was so miserable."

Sixteen-year-old Amy, a pensive young girl who was thin

and unconcerned about her own weight, told me about her best friend, Kelley, whose mother was "really, really over-weight." According to Amy, Kelley was an "okay weight" and had no reason to think about dieting. From spending time at her friend's house, Amy had surmised that her mother was "angry at what life did to her" and was determined not to let it happen to her daughter. Life had placed her in a fat body; she was a victim trapped by her weight:

> But she doesn't think it through and realize she can change, that there still is hope. She just thinks it's too late for her. Mothers . . . when they're fat, they think there's nothing they can do, but they look at their kids and think, "I can do something about her." It's like that with Kelley. Her mom is fat but doesn't diet, but she keeps telling Kelley to diet even though she doesn't even need to. It's like her mom's afraid that the same thing that happened to her will happen to her daughter.

Amy's description of her friend Kelley raises the issue of how daughters feel about their overweight mothers telling them to lose weight. Would this anger the daughter, making her feel that her mother held two sets of standards about weight—one appropriate for herself, and another for her daughter? Reading carefully through girls' narratives revealed that most did not feel this way, particularly those who were close with their mothers. When an overweight mother provided suggestions to her daughter on how to lose weight and had a positive relationship with her, the daughter seemed able to accept her mother's comments regardless of her size.

The following story exemplifies this issue. Fifteen-year-old Debbie, who was 5′2″ and weighed 145 pounds, frequently dressed in tee shirts adorned with peace symbols, oversized jeans, and a suede fringed jacket. She wanted to lose about thirty pounds and had been told that she needed to by her mother. Her mother weighed well over two hundred pounds and had been working at losing weight for about a year. When asked how she felt about her mother's telling her to diet, Debbie replied:

> I don't mind, 'cause I know I need to and coming from her it doesn't bother me. 'Cause she doesn't say it in a mean way. And my dad, it bothers me, because he comes around real sarcastically and he's like a jerk. But my mom, you know, she just states the facts and says, "You know, you'd look better if you lost this much weight and stuff." My mom's been heavy all her life . . . it kinda runs in her family. Actually it runs in both my parents' families, so it's kinda hard.

Debbie had joined her mother in her diet about a week before our interview and had already begun to lose weight. She was very proud of her mother's successful weight loss, and now that they were trying to lose weight together, they were encouraging each other to stick to their diets. Debbie felt that this shared activity and encouragement was drawing them closer together.

By telling their daughters not to eat too much ice cream or junk food, by offering to enroll them in formal weight-loss programs, and through gentle encouragement, the mothers described thus far facilitated their daughters' weight loss. From the daughters' perspective, the messages were helpful because they themselves wanted to be thinner. Mothers' messages were rooted in an understanding of the importance of thinness and a desire to see their daughters develop and maintain a culturally appropriate body shape. From another perspective, however, these mothers could be criticized for encouraging their daughters to conform to stereotypical notions of beauty rather than teaching them self-acceptance. I return to this theme shortly.

Although I did not interview the mothers of girls in the study because I had promised the daughters confidentiality, I did conduct interviews on dieting and body image with other mothers of teen-aged girls. One woman I spoke with, a forty-five-year-old health professional, was a single mother who had a fourteen-year-old daughter. During our interview she told me that when her daughter was ten, she had been extremely concerned about her because she was much heavier than her friends—so much so that even buying clothes for her posed a problem. She didn't want her daughter to suffer "the bad fate of being the fattest girl in the grade," as she once had. Worried that her daughter might enter into a "deep depression," she had taken her to their pediatrician, who had put her on an eight-hundred-calorie-per-day diet. She recalled that the doctor herself was rail thin because "she drank Diet Cokes and smoked cigarettes all day long." After a few frustrating weeks of failed dieting, the mother concluded that this was not the answer for her daughter. She called the doctor and said, "I'm not going to put a cigarette in her mouth and a Diet Coke in her hand so she can stay thin." As time went by, the mother adopted another strategy, which was to promise her daughter that once "her hormones kicked in and she started to grow, her body would thin out." "I was banking on that," she told me, "and thank God it worked! I knew she would never be really thin because her father's side of the family, whom she resembles, all have the bodies of stocky Russian peasants." "But," she said proudly, "I taught her how to eat healthy and how to manage her weight and now she looks good."

Given genetic parameters, this mother had tried to work with her daughter to avoid the possibility of a weight problem, which she herself had experienced and still vividly remembered. This example is instructive because it reveals the dilemma of a mother who wants her daughter's body to conform to cultural dictates of beauty but does not want to subject her to harmful weight-loss strategies. As the responsible agent for her daughter's appearance, she initially adopts one of the few options she sees open to her.

A mother's anxiety about having a heavy daughter can dramatically affect the daughter's socialization, even at an early age. The following is an excerpt from an interview conducted by my husband, anthropologist Mark Nichter, with a mother visiting her four-year-old daughter in the hospital. The girl had been admitted for malnutrition and a respiratory tract infection.[12] During the interview, the mother explained why she had placed her daughter on a "special diet":

> I don't give her fats in her diet and no sweets! I'm trying to keep down her number of fat cells so she'll have an easier time of it when she grows up. I'm always dieting and it never works for long. Maybe it's in my blood, 'cause my mother's fat and so is one of my sisters. My other sister is blessed; she's always been thin. She's one of those finicky eaters so she probably has less fat cells. I read an article about that. I want that for my daughter, so I put her on this special diet. The doctor scolded me. Now it may appear to him that I don't love my girl, but he couldn't be more wrong. Someday she is going to hug me and say, "Mom, I just don't know how to thank you." And she is going to have her pick of the men who come calling. Not like me.

This mother aims to teach her daughter that her body is a valuable commodity, a tool to get what she wants. Although this strategy has been ineffective for her, she has seen it work for other women in her family and so decides that it's worth trying on her daughter.

Before condemning her for the obvious shortcomings of her logic and the harm she is causing her young daughter, consider the following excerpt by feminist therapist Judith Rabinor. Although written with reference to eating-disordered patients and their families, it speaks to the topic at hand: "To blame the mother [for the daughter's eating disorder] fails to account for the social context in which a woman's appearance is often the most obvious or the only socially condoned form of power openly afforded her . . . It is a mark of female resilience that in the face of access to no real power, mothers do train their daughters to have access to the only power that exists: body power."[13] By reframing the mother's emphasis on dieting and weight loss from competition to loyalty and connection, Rabinor attempts to reaffirm the strength of the mother-daughter bond.

The point to recognize here is that some mothers' attempts to "help" their daughters are desperate moves in situations where they feel there are few viable alternatives. In such contexts, having a good body is a form of control and a source of empowerment because it opens up more choices in life. This rationale became clear in a follow-up interview with the mother of the sick young girl, who noted that "being fat was like trying to move through life with an anchor strapped to your dreams, it just doesn't let you get very far."

◆   ◆   ◆

Mothers and Daughters in Conflict

In mother-daughter relationships that were stressful, messages to lose weight were often rejected or met with ambivalence by the daughter. To some extent, girls who fought with their parents were able to dismiss these messages as just one more thing their parents were telling them that they didn't want to hear.

Sixteen-year-old Karen lived with her father because she and her mother could not get along. Growing up, Karen had always considered herself overweight, but in the past year, she had dropped about twenty-five pounds. According to her, this had just happened—she had not actively been trying to lose weight. Recalling her mother's attitude toward her weight, Karen noted:

> All my life my mother's been telling me to lose weight. She never helped me do anything about it, she just told me I should. She always used to tell me that she knew what it was like to go through life as a fat kid. She didn't want me to have to go through that too. But I hated her telling me. And I still look in the mirror now and I see somebody who's like this wide [gestures], you know, when they turn sideways. And my boyfriend always yells at me that

I don't see what I really am . . . and you know I can't help that. All my life I was told that I was huge. You know, one year really isn't enough to change that.

Karen's response to her mother's message is markedly different from that of the girls discussed earlier in this chapter. Rather than accepting her mother's message to lose weight, Karen resented her for telling her she needed to slim down. As she explains, her mother had not provided her with any help in losing weight—she had just told her that she needed to do it. In addition, Karen may not have wanted to accept such a message from her mother, whom she claimed to dislike.

Two best friends who were both in continuous battle with their parents used their large body size as a symbol of their defiance of their parents' will. Jennifer, who was 5′6″ and weighed approximately 240 pounds, was discussed in Chapter 1 as the girl who continually asked whether I was capable of understanding her experience of growing up fat. When asked if her parents had told her to lose weight, she replied that both her mother and her father had:

> Well, you know, they're just like [changes to high, whiney voice], "Well, we want you to be healthy and we want you to do this and we want you to do that," you know. But, I don't know. It's like they don't really understand. You know because it's not like they've ever—like my mom always says that she's overweight, I mean when she says it, you know, it's like she was like 10 pounds overweight or something. Which is like nothing, you know. It's like, you know, she's like, "Well I just don't understand." And I'm just like, "Well you don't," because she couldn't . . . They say, "Well we want you to do this and we want you to do that" [reference to diet programs]. But it doesn't really matter. You know, because if *I* don't want it, it really doesn't matter if *they* want it or not.

Jennifer went on to describe how, following one big fight with her mother, she and her best friend, Carey, had gone to the local convenience store and bought a gallon of ice cream, which they had sat down and shared. She went on:

> Well basically I think I can eat anything I want at any time. Because you know it's like, I'm in charge. And it's like my mom will say, "You can't eat that." I'm just like, "Well, yeah I can." And I go, "This isn't your body, it's mine." You know, I can do whatever I want. You know and sometimes they'll say like, "Well, as long as you're living under our roof, you'll do what we tell you to do," you know, they'll say that a lot and it's just stupid. You know because Carey can come over and just take me anywhere I want to go. If I say Dairy Queen, she can take me to Dairy Queen.

Her friend Carey, who weighed close to 200 pounds, expressed a similarly defiant attitude toward her parents' requests for her to lose weight. Carey's mother, a dietician, and her father, an athletic trainer, were beside themselves with their adoptive daughter's refusal to lose weight. In fact, over the course of the study, they called project staff several times to discuss their frustration with Carey's weight problem. Her mother stated that she was confident that her daughter knew more about good eating habits than other girls her age, yet she refused to lose weight. Her parents were aware that conflicts between their daughter and them were being expressed at the site of the body. Given their professions, their daughter was touching a nerve privately and calling attention to her parents as "failures" publicly. A control battle was afoot.

During one interview, Carey remarked that though she was aware that she needed to lose weight, she would do it "in her own time." "The thing is, it's up to me. If my mom says something about what I'm eating, I get really mad at her. It's like, 'Mom, I can eat what I want to eat' . . . and I get furious with her. And at my dad too." In her battle with her parents, Carey retained control by *not* watching her weight. In fact, earlier that year Carey had lost some weight to look good for her boyfriend. "He liked me the way I was, but I thought I'd look better if I were thinner." After he had moved away, however, she regained the weight she had lost and continued to gain more. Her weight gain was, in part, a protest against family domination. She viewed her parents' dictates to lose weight not as supportive but rather as critical of her as a person.

I observed similarly defiant attitudes while studying smoking behavior among these girls. Like eating—or not eating—smoking is a behavior that is good ammunition in a control battle. In a non-supportive environment, where control is exercised and an adolescent's sense of self is threatened, cigarettes become a symbol of resistance to parental domination. Just as girls told their parents that they could eat what they pleased, they told them that if they wanted to, they could smoke. As children become older, parents must contend with their teens' increasing autonomy as well as with their own loss of control. Power struggles ensue between parents and their adolescent daughters about these and other issues, like breaking curfew or failing to obey other household rules. Under such circumstances, parents need to consider their adolescent's need to feel empowered rather than deprived of personal power. The key is for youth to feel independent through exercising responsibility and making personal choices, rather than engaging in symbolic protest against parents they view as controlling.

◆　◆　◆

Competition between Mothers and Daughters

Another weight-related conflict that existed between mothers and daughters was evident in households in which the mother was very attractive or thinner than her daughter. In such cases, if the mother told her daughter to lose weight, the daughter felt threatened. In the mother-daughter pairs discussed below, the daughters resented their mothers, who used their own appearance as the standard of beauty that they felt their daughters needed to achieve.

Fifteen-year-old Traci continually battled with her mother. One of their bones of contention was that Traci was always being told to lose weight. Peering out from long, stringy bangs that dangled over heavily made-up eyes, Traci explained, "Like when we go out and I want to order a piece of cake for dessert, my mom tells me I shouldn't eat it. She says, 'You're going to look like me . . . you're going to get fat . . . you're going to get ugly like me' . . . she's like, 'Somebody has got to tell you.'" I asked Traci how she responded to such comments. "I laugh at her and tell her she's wrong," she explained. "I'll never look like her! I order the cake, and of course, she resists ordering some . . . and she won't even take a bite of mine! Then she tries to make me feel guilty, as if I should be working on my body like she does!"

In an unsolicited gesture, Traci reached into her backpack and took out her wallet. Flipping quickly through photos of friends, she stopped at a picture of her mother and handed it to me to examine. Far from being ugly (as her description had suggested), her mother was extremely attractive and young looking. Anticipating my next question, Traci told me that her mother had given birth to her at age fifteen and was now thirty years old. Fearful that her daughter might also become pregnant at a young age, her mother was protective of her and restricted her from going out on dates. Traci was frustrated by her mother's youth and attractiveness, especially since she "just acted so old." When her friends commented on how young and pretty her mother was, Traci would reply, "Yeah, but you don't really know her." During our interview, she recalled with annoyance an incident in which her mother had arrived at a party to pick her up and some of the guys had flirted with her, not realizing that she was Traci's mother.

Traci's relationship with her mother raises the issue of whether some girls felt jealous of their mother's looks, particularly her body size. Traci did not view her mother's suggestions to refrain from eating sweets as positive or helpful. Her anger with her in other areas of life prevented her from perceiving her comments as supportive. Although the message may not have been so different from that of the mothers described earlier, what differed was how it was delivered and how Traci interpreted her mother's reasons for saying what she did. Traci felt threatened by having an attractive mother who was considered "hot" by boys her age. Compared with her mother, Traci felt that she was nothing special. But looks can be deceiving, Traci noted, and her mother wasn't all she appeared to be.

Although the theme of mother-daughter competition did not emerge in many interviews, there were a few girls who alluded to it. Maria, who at 5′6″ and 140 pounds was an athletic ninth-grader involved in a team sport, told me that her mother was skinny and weighed 10 pounds less than she did. She also looked far younger than her age. "I don't think that's fair," Maria demurred. "I'm jealous 'cause she's skinnier than me. Everyone says she looks my age when they see us from far away. And the thing is, she's like that normally. That's the way her whole family is. They're all skinny. Unfortunately, I take after my dad's side of the family." When asked if her mother had ever told her to lose weight, Maria talked about the scrutiny she experienced in her household:

> She says my stomach sticks out a little bit when I'm like wearing shorts. "Wow, you need to lose weight, Maria. Your stomach's sticking out a little more than it usually does." But then other days she'll say that my stomach sticks out less than it usually does. She's always like really inspecting me. And all my brothers and sisters say that I need to lose weight. 'Cause they're all skinnier than me.

When asked how she responded to their comments, Maria looked away, her voice barely audible, her hands clutched together: "It's just really hard for me . . . I don't know . . . I just feel really bad. I need to lose about five, well maybe ten pounds, and then I'll be perfect." Maria did not think of herself as capable of losing weight, and she jokingly told me that "the word 'diet' always makes me hungry." "I just don't have will power," she complained. "If I'm hungry and there's food in the house and I shouldn't eat because I've been eating all day, I still eat. I just like eat and eat and eat. I'm compulsive. It's disgusting."

Maria's self-disgust at her voracious appetite was hardly warranted. As a member of the swim team, she was in the pool practicing for about three hours each day. No wonder she was so hungry! Maria was not fat, yet she was growing up in an environment where she was critically evaluated by family members. Having a mother and siblings who were thinner than she was, coupled with her belief that she could not diet successfully, Maria felt in competition with members of her household who had "more perfect" bodies than she did. The statement, "If only I could lose 5 or 10 pounds, life would be so perfect" was one I heard repeated in numerous interviews.

◆   ◆   ◆

Fathers' Comments

Although fewer girls had received messages from their fathers to lose weight than from their mothers, there was a difference in how mothers and fathers delivered these messages. Fathers were more likely to be very direct and blunt. Fathers who had been fairly tolerant of their daughter's weight and body shape as she was growing up suddenly began to notice the budding young woman in their midst. Critiques came in the form of appraising looks, kidding quips, put-downs, and snide comments like, "When did *you* start getting boobs?"

In interviews, the girls provided examples of how their fathers made uncomfortably direct comments about their weight and general appearance. At the time of our interview Darlene, who was 5'5" and weighed 140 pounds, was living with her mother after her parents' recent divorce. Each time she visited her father, she was offended by his critiques of how she looked. She recalled that during her last visit her dad had pointedly asked her, "How much do you weigh?" This had upset Darlene immensely and she had tried to end the conversation by telling him sharply that she didn't know her weight. Her voice was raised and angry as she continued. "The next time he says anything about my weight I'm going to say, 'If you're going to worry about how much I weigh then I'm not going to come see you anymore.'" Her father's comments were particularly offensive to her because he was overweight yet seemed unconcerned about his *own* body shape. Darlene believed that he had no right to criticize her body when he was not caring for his own. Her father was also concerned about her skin, which was slightly broken out. Recalling his comments, she noted, "He'll always be complaining, 'Your face is breaking out. When do you wash it? Are you washing it?'"

It was the seemingly blatant disregard for his daughter's feelings that rendered her father's remarks so offensive. Typically, girls in the study reported that their fathers understood much less about the intricacies of their lives than their mothers did. Fathers were described as more judgmental and less overtly caring than mothers.[14] Mothers were more willing to engage in conversation about the vagaries of everyday life, and discussed details of their own lives with their daughters. In one study of parents and their adolescent daughters, it was found that more than 50 percent of girls agreed with the statements, "My father does not express his true feelings to me," and "My father does not talk openly to me," compared with only 10 percent of girls who said this about their mothers.[15]

Lori, a tenth-grader whose father weighed more than 250 pounds, had been told by him that she was fat and that she needed to lose weight. She was 5′5″, weighed 135 pounds, and was angry at him for telling her that: "He's always telling me, 'Don't eat everything in the refrigerator.' It makes me feel really bad. I tell him, 'At least I'm not like you.' I try to get back at him, but I still don't think it's right what he says. He needs to take a good hard look at himself in the mirror!" Lori's mother, with whom she was very close, sided with her, telling her father that his comments to Lori and her sister (whom he also "accused" of being fat) were inappropriate. Because of her mother's comments, her father had reduced the frequency of his acrimonious remarks, although he still continued to make them occasionally.

Some daughters seemed afraid to let their fathers know how much their comments hurt or angered them. A few girls told me what they wished they could say in response to their fathers. Sixteen-year-old Shelley told me that although her father had teased her all her life, as she got older, the content of his teasing had changed:

> My dad, he's always said something to me about my appearance because I've always had chubby cheeks since I was born, so he always used to comment about them and pinch them. But now he'll say things like, "Oh, you've gained a little weight, haven't you?" or something like that . . . When he says that I feel like turning around and screaming, "You're one to talk . . . you can't even see your toes on a good day!" but I know I'd get in trouble if I said that, so I just laugh it off.

Shelley's relationship with her parents was strained. At 5′7″ and 135 pounds, she clearly did not need to be concerned about her weight. Weight was a way for her father to get at her, striking where she was vulnerable. But she would not give him the satisfaction of showing the hurt that she felt. Like several girls I spoke with, Shelley downplayed the impact that her father's teasing had on her. Laughing it off was a coping response. Other girls reacted similarly after describing negatives remarks by their fathers, adding, "It wasn't a big deal," or "I didn't really care," or "Oh, it just goes in one ear and out the other!" Yet further into these interviews, their anger would surface.

Whether the topic was fatness or thinness ("you need to lose weight"; "you're too thin"), girls' bodies served as a convenient object for their fathers' off-handed commentaries. The gaze of fathers reproduces the social values and power relations of Western patriarchy wherein males—from fathers at home to boys at school—have a cultural license to dominate females through behavior and speech. Some girls accepted this lesson without resistance. In other households, however, mothers defended their daughters against teasing or overly harsh statements about weight. Ironically, in many of the same households, mothers would later offer their daughters dieting tips.

The girls generally considered their fathers less attentive than their mothers to the "progress" they made when they attempted to lose weight and unappreciative of how difficult it was—especially at puberty or just beyond. Trisha, who at 5′5″ and 158 pounds had been told to lose weight by both parents, was surrounded by talk about body weight:

> Like my parents just said things like, "You'd look so much nicer if you lost five or ten pounds." That kind of stuff, you know, not really harsh things, because I'm not that much overweight . . . I know I need to work on it. My mom told me that I need to do a little bit more, to work at losing it. My dad suggested it a couple of times but my dad doesn't really seem to see the progress that I really have made . . . But you know for a while he didn't really think that I was doing anything to help. I was really trying and he didn't think I was, and he told me that, and I got really mad at him. And I told him it wasn't fair for him to say that to me. And you know, he even went and talked to my mom about it . . . this whole thing about my not trying . . . and my mom yelled at him. She said, "You shouldn't be thinking that and you shouldn't be telling her that. She's done a lot better than you think she has." So now he doesn't say anything.

Although Trisha described herself as close to both her parents, her father displayed less sensitivity toward her dieting efforts and was more focused on measurable results. Because her mother spent more time with her, she was aware that Trisha was trying to lose weight and was supportive of her intention. From their own experiences, mothers knew the

difficulties encountered while trying to sustain a diet, especially when the results are not what television ads have promised. Mothers understood that even when you managed to
lose weight, it didn't always come off in the right places! This
rendered them less likely than fathers to criticize their daughters for their lack of progress and more likely to applaud their
efforts in trying to lose weight "where it counts."

What is the lesson these girls are learning from their relationships with their fathers? Disquietingly, they listen and internalize a message that they are somehow unacceptable as
they are, that their bodies need to be more perfect, closer to
the feminine ideal. Gendered standards for acceptable body
weight are played out in the kitchen. While the daughter is
held accountable for her food consumption, her father is not.
The situation is complex, borne out of issues of both gender
and generation. The daughter may find herself in a double
bind—because she is female and because of her social status
as daughter, it is inappropriate for her to talk back in defense
of her body shape. Silently, she must listen to her father's
message, turning to her mother for solace.

As an outsider looking into the home lives of these girls, I
found that solace from their mothers was insufficient compen-
sation for the hurt inflicted on them by their fathers. Most
troubling to me as a researcher was my awareness that learning to accept male critiques of their bodies was an inevitable
part of growing up for these girls.

❖   ❖   ❖

Dieting in Families

Even if parents were talking about the importance of controlling weight, how common was it for mothers and fathers to be
dieting—thus sending an overt message that this is normal behavior? On our survey we examined the frequency with which
mothers and fathers were dieting to lose weight, by asking
girls to complete the following statement, "My mother (step-

mother) tries to lose weight . . ." with response choices ranging from *always* to *never.* The same question was asked with regard to fathers (stepfathers). Responses were *always* (mothers, 14 percent; fathers, 2 percent); *often* (mothers, 22 percent; fathers, 9 percent); *sometimes* (mothers, 43 percent; fathers, 39 percent); *never* (mothers, 21 percent; fathers, 50 percent).

Just as in Chapter 4, where we saw that mothers were found to be worrying about their weight more than fathers, mothers were also found to diet with far greater frequency than fathers. What was the body shape of parents who were dieting? Were parents who were perceived to be heavy more likely to attempt to lose weight? What were the differences in perceived body shape and dieting between mothers and fathers? To answer these questions, I examined the body size of the parent as perceived by the daughter (discussed in Chapter 4) in relation to the parent's dieting attempts.

Among mothers described by their daughters as "just about right," 33 percent dieted always/often compared with only 3 percent of fathers in this category. Indeed, 60 percent of fathers who were described as "just about right" never dieted, as compared with only 37 percent of mothers who fell into this category. A similar pattern emerges for mothers classified as "the right weight but out of shape": 35 percent dieted always/often compared with just 4 percent of fathers. More than one-half of fathers who were "the right weight but out of shape" never dieted, as compared with 18 percent of mothers. In addition, almost 40 percent of mothers who were "kind of fat" dieted "always/often" as compared with 12 percent of fathers. Of those mothers who were "very fat," 66 percent dieted "always/often" compared with only 33 percent of fathers whose dieting attempts fell into this category (see Appendix B, Tables 5 and 6).

What emerges from these gender-based comparisons is just how common it is for mothers to diet, even when their daughters consider them to be "just right." Regardless of weight, mothers are *trying* to diet with far greater frequency than fathers, at least as reported by their daughters. This is consistent with research that has found that women are about twice as likely as men to be currently trying to lose weight or to have a history of weight-loss efforts.[16]

The majority of girls we spoke with lived in homes where their mothers expressed discontent with their body shape and displayed an active interest in losing weight. In contrast, fathers only occasionally acknowledged that they were out of shape and needed to lose a few pounds. It is hardly surprising that daughters mirror their mothers concerns through self-surveillance and self-monitoring. As one girl poignantly noted, "When I reached the seventh grade, I cared how I looked. Then I knew from that day on, until the day I die, I'm going to worry about what I eat. Just like my mom, I know I'm always destined to diet in one way or another."

Does sharing similar concerns translate into similar rates of dieting? Our survey data suggest that it does not: daughters do not diet with the same frequency as their mothers. Whereas more than one-third of the mothers dieted "always/often," only 14 percent of daughters did so. This finding suggests that dieting among women may increase with age. As discussed in Chapter 2, much of the dissatisfaction with body shape among teen-aged girls emerges in discourse about weight and does not result in actual dieting and weight loss. Thus, girls may be developing body concerns similar to their mothers', although these may not be observable in measurable reports of dieting. No doubt, many daughters of dieters are actively internalizing their mothers' world view about the virtue of thinness. Unlike their daughters, mothers have more freedom to maintain their diets. Not only do they have more choices and resources available to them, but they may also face less temptation than their daughters, who are surrounded by peers and environments laden with junk food.

Although in our survey questions we did not investigate "watching what you eat" in relation to mothers, it is plausible that research among middle-aged women might reveal a pattern of watching similar to that which we found among teens. A recent survey among adults lends support to this idea: whereas 27 percent of those surveyed claimed to be on a diet, another 40 percent reported that although they were making a serious attempt to control their weight, they did not consider themselves to be on a diet. Instead, they were controlling and monitoring their food intake, what the girls we spoke with referred to as watching what they ate.[17]

In a large readership study conducted by *Glamour* magazine, daughters of dieters reported that their mothers' approval or disapproval of their body was most keenly felt during adolescence.[18] More than two-thirds of the four thousand women (average age, twenty-seven) who responded to the survey considered themselves "daughters of dieters," and 64 percent reported that their mothers were critical of their teenage weights. Those women who had observed their mothers dieting reported doing so themselves, in repetitive cycles that many found difficult to break as adults. Seventy percent of the daughters of dieters reported that they were still dieting, and 33 percent of these women reported "always worrying" about their weight. On a sobering note, the *Glamour* survey revealed that the younger the daughter was when she started to diet, the higher her current weight was at the time of the survey.

What might be the effect of a mother's criticism of her daughter's body? Psychologists Kathleen Pike and Judith Rodin studied mother-daughter pairs and found that girls who exhibited disordered eating were much more likely to have mothers who were critical of them. Mothers of eating-disordered daughters rated their daughters as significantly less attractive than their daughters rated themselves, as compared with mothers and daughters in the comparison group, in which daughters did not have weight or food problems.[19]

Psychologist Michael Levine and his colleagues surveyed white girls in middle school to investigate the extent to which mothers influenced their daughters' dieting. Girls were asked how often their mother dieted, how important it was for her to be thin, and how important physical appearance was to her. The mother's investment in her own slenderness (a composite variable formed by summing the girl's response to these three items) was the most significant predictor of the daughter's dieting, surpassing other key predictors, including changes in menstrual status, dating status, and desired shape. Thus, girls who dieted were likely to have mothers who dieted. Among girls who had eating disorders, mothers were found to have given overt verbal messages to them about the importance of being thin.[20] In another study of high school girls, those who were compulsive dieters reported that their restrictive dieting was positively related to "feelings of success in living up to what were perceived to be their mother's standards."[21]

Given a common interest in weight loss, I wondered how often mothers and daughters dieted together and, when they did, what the dynamic was between them. On our survey, girls were asked: When your mother (stepmother) diets, how often do you diet with her?" Responses were *always* (2 girls; 1 percent); *sometimes* (57 girls; 32 percent); and *never* (121 girls; 67 percent). Twenty girls reported that their mother did not diet.

In interviews, I asked the girls who had dieted with their mothers to describe their experience. Helen, a shy ninth-grader who was 5'6" and weighed 135 pounds, lived with her mother, whom she described as "more like a friend than family," and her eleven-year-old brother. Her narrative speaks to their dieting history:

> Every once in a while my mom will say, "Let's go on a diet," and I'm like, "OK" ... We do it about once a month for about a week and that usually doesn't last the whole week, but we try ... and well sometimes I'm like, "Mom, I have to have a piece of cake! I'm dying ... we've been so good," and she'll be like, "OK, go ahead," or sometimes you know we'll just quit eating things and we'll start eating regular food again 'cause usually we'll eat nutritional dinners you know and you can microwave those and we'll eat those 'cause they have less calories ... And then every once in a while my mom's like, "Let's go get some dessert, we've earned it," and I'm like, "Mom, I'm not hungry, we just had dinner," and she's like, "Oh, just a piece of cake," and I'm like, "OK." So we'll just do that every once in a while when we

have to have something, it's like a craving, and then it's, "OK, time to diet again!"

Later in the interview, Helen told me that dieting with her mother "makes it more fun." An important issue can be highlighted in the narrative of this mother-daughter pair: love is expressed by displays of affection that take the form of both control and release. On the one hand, mother and daughter show mutual support for each other by participating in continual, short-term diets. On the other hand, they engage in release as they indulge in the satisfaction of one of their desires. Both expressions of control and release are valued in white American culture.[22] Indulging after a period of dieting is part of a cycle wherein control is celebrated by its opposite, which triggers a need to control again.

Dieting as control also emerges in the following mother-daughter pair. In describing her dieting history, Melissa recalled how when she had visited her biological mother in Los Angeles one summer she had gained five pounds. Upon her return, her stepmother had noticed her weight gain and had told her that if she wanted to go on Jenny Craig, or join any other type of diet program, she would join with her. After thinking about the offer, Melissa, who at 5'3" weighed 127 pounds, decided to enroll in Jenny Craig. She realized that her stepmother really didn't need to lose weight but went on diets regularly as a means of "gaining control over her life." Having been overweight as a child, her stepmother still saw herself as fat. "It's just her way of, when she feels like she's going to gain weight, she goes on a diet to like put her life on some kind of schedule. Like, sometimes she starts to gain weight, like when she gets stressed and she starts eating, so she goes on Jenny Craig to keep her off of eating like that."

Although Melissa did not say so directly, it appeared that she was being encouraged to adopt a similar plan of preventive "weight and life control." Control expressed through dieting was a coping mechanism for dealing with the problems of everyday life. Not insignificantly, like other girls who joined organized programs, Melissa felt empowered by the experience of learning "how to eat right, like how to measure fats and all that stuff." In addition, going to the weight-loss center for weekly meetings was fun because other girls from her high school also attended.

In some cases, dieting in families was initiated not for the sake of the mother or daughter but for a younger sister who was gaining weight during puberty. Dieting then became a family activity in which all the females in the household participated as a sign of support. As one girl described:

> We eat a lot of healthier foods 'cause my sister, she's ten, she's going through the stage I was going through. Like she's chubby, but I don't know, we eat more healthy food and are watching what we eat. My mom does Weight Watchers, they have it for kids too, well my sister doesn't go to the meetings but she follows it at home. And I do it to support her. I don't like to go to the meetings either. My mom goes for both of us and we use her stuff.

Two points about this family are worth noting. First, rather than explaining to the daughter that her weight gain was a normal part of puberty (which the mother may not have known), the mother motivated her older daughter to help her sister through this stage. Second, the father was also overweight, though he did not participate in the females' dieting activities and, in fact, ate as he pleased.

Another girl who explained that her whole family was "always on diets" noted that she found herself dieting more as she got older and also found herself watching out for her younger sister. She explained:

> With my little sister, it's like, "Michelle, stop eating that," and she's like, "No, I can maintain my weight," and so she's like eating all day long and I'm like, "Michelle, I said the same thing when I was your age. No, don't do it, stop eating so much!" and I'd like take the food away from her and she says, "You're so mean!" and I'm like, "When you get

older, you'll understand," so I guess you just become more aware of what's going on.

The multigenerational nature of surveillance is evident in this
family, where the older sister, who is only fifteen herself, is
already carefully watching over her younger sister, who is
eleven. She understands that a girl must be educated at an
early age about a woman's need to rein in her appetite.

Group dieting in households where there are two or more
daughters is also evident in Erica's family. A ninth-grader who
felt she needed to lose about ten pounds, Erica, who was 5'4"
and weighed 150 pounds, watched what she ate and dieted occasionally with her mother and sister. She believed that she
had inherited her mother's metabolism, which, "you know,
isn't the best in the world." However, she made it a point to tell
me that although she listened to her mother's weight-related
advice with interest, she retained control over her own eating.
It was important for her sense of self to exercise the freedom to
choose. She explained, "My mom and my sister and I, we all
watch what we're eating and we watch out for each other a lot.
And, um, I have pretty much control, you know, if my mom
tells me not to eat something, and I feel like eating it, I'll do it
anyway, you know, I have control over how much and what I
actually eat." When discussing family meals at a later point in
the interview, however, Erica explained, "Sometimes my mom
fixes real little bits just to make sure nobody eats too much.
She's got basic control over that one." She also explained that
her mother got mad at her, would nag her, and would "almost
kill her" if she ate foods—like chocolate—that her mother
thought she should avoid. Although Erica described their relationship as close, it was clear that her mother's attempted control over her food intake was an issue that had meaning beyond food and dieting. Erica felt a need to assert her own will.

Although Erica valued the support of her mother and sister in her weight-loss attempts, she also exercised her freedom
to indulge and cheat with her sister:

> Yeah, like me and my sister watch out for each
> other. Like yesterday we went to the store and we

both got this craving to have something chocolate so we went and bought a Twix bar and split it [laughs]. Don't tell my mom . . . It was just a little sneak on that one, but that's you know, just sometimes. But, usually me and my sister will sit there and tell each other, you know, "Don't eat that," and we help each other out a lot. That's nice having someone there 'cause you're not the only one just going through the problems and staying in one place and never losing weight.

She went on to explain that when her mother was in high school, she had dieted by herself, which had been difficult for her: "She didn't like being alone with it, so I guess she doesn't want me or my sister to go through it alone, which is nice."

Beyond mother-daughter pairs, dieting sometimes occurred as a multigenerational affair, extending from grandmothers to granddaughters. One girl told me that she and her mother were following a diet suggested by her grandmother. When I asked her if her mother needed to lose weight, she replied with a smile, "No! She's not fat at all, she just thinks she is, so she wants to lose some weight." Aware of her own daughter's dissatisfaction with her weight and her granddaughter's "need" to diet, the grandmother had sent detailed instructions on a diet plan that she had once followed with great success. Although physically absent from the household, the grandmother continued to contribute to the family dieting enterprise by sharing strategies from afar.

Even when the daughter was not actively dieting with her mother, she was often observing her mother's weight-reducing strategies. Diane, a tall, lanky ninth-grader with a mouthful of braces, described how reading through her mother's books about dieting had helped her develop ideas about how she could look and what she could do to change her body. She recalled a day when she was alone in the kitchen, eating her way through a bowl of potato chips after school. Flipping through one of her mother's books on dieting, she had come across a

story about Bill Cosby's experience at "Camp Happy Thighs."
As she remembered it:

> He said they had to stand in front of the mirror every day and say, "Mirror, mirror on the wall, who has the flabbiest ass of all." And you would have to stand there until you got a thorough hatred for your body. Then they would have to go for a 24 km. run or something. For dinner they had room service and they didn't even have to open the door to get the plate . . . it was just a leaf of lettuce and two celery sticks. The story kinda made me laugh, but then I went in front of the mirror and I looked at myself . . . I just looked at myself and I thought, "You know, I could turn a lot of this fat into muscle. And if I really wanted to, I could, you know, I could start getting a lot of nutrition that I need. And I could lose weight and look better.

Although Diane had not yet actively dieted, after reading her mother's dieting book she began to consider it. Thus, the seed of dieting and the accumulated knowledge about weight loss resident in their kitchen is planted in her mind long before she actually begins to diet and attempts to change her body shape. Even when a daughter does not join her mother on a diet, the daughter is exposed to weight-loss strategies as well as notions of appropriate body shape for women. As the daughter grows older and her body changes, she may put this knowledge to work.

◆　　◆　　◆

Watching and Dieting in Families: Reducing Health Risks

Achieving a thin body was not the only reason family members dieted or watched what they ate. In some families, dieting and watching were initiated to reduce health risks. Allison, a tenth-grader, explained that she and her mother watched what they ate because her grandmother had died of a heart attack at age fifty-three. She told me that her grandmother had lost a lot of weight before she died, "like a hundred pounds or something. She was looking real good right before she died, but then, you know, her heart just kind of gave out on her." That prompted the family to examine carefully the behavior that contributed to her early death. "She always sat right in front of the television with food in her hand," Allison explained. After her mother was diagnosed with high blood pressure, the teen's family had increased their awareness of their food intake.

A similar story was recalled by Sandy, an eleventh-grader, who explained that her heightened awareness of her food intake was due to the fact that her grandmother was about fifty pounds overweight. Her grandmother had suffered heart problems and high cholesterol, "probably from just lugging that extra fat around." Sandy watched what she ate and exercised because she recognized that prevention needed to start early. She told me that she always "considered the nutritional value of foods" and that she routinely asked herself whether the food she craved was a "psychological or a physical hunger." "What makes me want this? What makes me want the fat, what makes me want something sweet? That is what I ask myself." An important part of her decision-making process when it came to what to eat was the concept of food addiction, which her mother had introduced to her. As she explained, "Food addiction to me is using food or alcohol to make yourself forget your problems or stress and stuff." Her mother had told her that her grandmother had a problem with food addiction, and had warned Sandy about it in great detail.

In some families, heightened health concerns were connected with a parent's level of physical activity. Stephanie, introduced in Chapter 1 as the girl who aspired to be a model, was an articulate eleventh-grader whose father was a marathon runner. She expressed a heightened awareness about foods because of what she described as her father's obsessive concern about how the family ate: "It's gotten pretty bad the last year. The more the magazines are printing, and the more he reads about it, the more he becomes a little doctor on the subject of nutrition." In describing how her father hassled her about her food intake, she recounted the following story:

> Like this morning I had a Pillsbury toaster strudel with nine grams of fat and thirteen milligrams of cholesterol. For crying out loud, my dad told me he wouldn't even have a bite of it 'cause it had too much fat in it. That's just how he is, you know . . . But the food I like is healthy except for my Pillsbury toaster strudels . . . I mean I always get the lowest fat. I'm very conscious about it too but sometimes you've got to eat something with fat, I mean you only live once and . . . it's not going to kill you to have fat once in a while. I mean I never eat things like Twinkies or candy bars. I just don't eat that.

Her father was also very concerned that she get regular physical exercise, and he would ask her each day whether she had exercised at a level sufficient to elevate her heart rate. While preaching to her about the value of exercise, he criticized her behavior: "When you're older you're going to regret that you didn't exercise every day." Stephanie was concerned that if she became involved in regular exercise such as running, "then I'm gonna wake up one day and think, 'Oh, God, I *have* to get up and go running today.' I don't want to make myself think *I have to do* something. Just like, if you like running, go run. If you don't, just don't sit in front of the television."

Embedded in Stephanie's narrative are questions about the meaning of a healthful lifestyle. While she realizes that her father is reducing the family's health risks by monitoring their food consumption and exercise, she questions whether his extreme behavior is, in fact, healthy. "Is too much control healthy?" she wonders. Stephanie expresses concern about the stress that is imposed on her while eating her Pillsbury strudel, and she defies the thought of having to run each and every day. She seems to recognize that her father's behavior is obsessive or addictive in nature. Though she has adopted many of his concerns, she wants a more balanced lifestyle in which she can eat fat every once in a while, because after all, as she says, it's not going to kill her. At a young age, Stephanie acknowledges and has internalized the value of moderation in her life.

Considering the negative appraisals that girls receive from others, the paucity of positive messages from parents, and the proliferation of media messages replete with directives to be thin, it is not surprising that so many girls were dissatisfied with their bodies. Girls are not alone with this dissatisfaction; many of them also contend with their mother's unhappiness with her own weight.

Some mothers taught their daughters to interpret continual surveillance of their bodies as a form of empowerment connected to self-love. In direct conversations with their mothers, in observations of what was consumed by whom at family mealtime, girls have ample opportunity to learn about gender roles and notions of appropriate femininity. Dieting as a socialized practice enabled some girls to feel better about themselves. In learning to control their bodies through dieting, they felt that they were also learning to take control of their lives.

Funds of shared information in the household support the hegemony of the thin beauty ideal and all it entails. Listening to accounts of fat talk and prescribed antidotes proffered in the kitchen, I wonder whether mothers are contributing significantly to their daughters' unrealistic body-shape ideals. This certainly seems to be the case in households in which competition exists between mother and daughter. Some of the mothers I interviewed, by contrast, struggled with how to deal effectively with daughters who were dissatisfied with their weight or body shape. Telling her daughter that she was "beautiful as she was" or that dominant beauty ideals were unrealistic would certainly be a positive step on the part of the parent, but such messages may not be accepted by the daughter, given the reality of peer competition and messages in the media telling her otherwise. Positive messages about body acceptance need to be heard from diverse and credible sources, including parents, so that girls can begin to acknowledge the importance of this message.

The comment of a mother I interviewed who had a four-teen-year-old daughter aptly characterizes the tension of knowing that something needs to be said, but being uncertain of what it should be. Privy to her daughter's self-effacing comments and painful dissatisfaction with her body, this mother expressed frustration that was as much about herself as it was about her daughter:

> I know that I shouldn't be so concerned about my weight. I realize that I should have more self-acceptance and appreciate myself for who I am rather than measure myself against others. But I find it very difficult to do this. I'm always worried about my weight. When it comes to my daughter . . . it's even harder for me to figure out how I should cope with her insecurities about her body. I'm really not sure of what I should be doing to help her.

Like other mothers described in this chapter, she adopts both a worried and a watchful stance over her daughter. To some extent, present cultural dictates prescribe that she behave that way. Susie Orbach explains that a "good mother" should be mindful of her daughter, reprimanding her excesses in order to avoid her own personal and social condemnation. In other words, her daughter's physical appearance is a reflection of her own capacity for self-governance.[23] However, a mother walks a fine line—if she monitors her daughter's actions too closely, she may risk putting too much stress on their relationship at a time when the daughter is already trying to establish herself as an autonomous person.

Both mothers and fathers need to foster healthy eating and exercise habits as an alternative to dieting and to teach their children to be more self-accepting. But is that enough? Daughters need to be encouraged to have pride in themselves and to learn, in the words of one African-American girl, "to make what they've got work for them" rather than buying into a cultural ideal. Such a reframing can empower girls to be active agents in establishing their own identity. As will be discussed in the next chapter, this approach was common among African-American girls and their families but was rarely encountered in my interviews with white and Latino girls. Both in the family and with peers, it is important to consider how a critical consciousness about the body and beauty work can be established and maintained in the face of pressures to conform.

6

Looking Good among African-American Girls

> INTERVIEWER: What would you do if a friend
> complained about being fat?
> CHARISE (AGE 16): I'd tell her, "Don't think nega-
> tive. People who think negative
> aren't gonna get nowhere."

THE QUOTE ABOVE from Charise, a
sixteen-year-old African-American girl,
is strikingly different from the fat talk I heard from white girls.
I wondered whether she was typical of her African-American
peers. My readings on the subject, mostly reports of surveys,
showed that African-American girls were more satisfied with
their body weight and were less likely to diet than white or
Latino girls.[1] But there were few explanations given for why
these ethnic differences existed, although the reports all made
vague references to "cultural factors." As anthropologists interested in the culture of teen-aged girls, we wanted to explore what led African-American girls to accept their body
shape when so many of their white peers were dissatisfied
with theirs.[2]

Differences in cultural standards for acceptable weights
have been reported among both adult women and teen-aged
girls. Janet Allan, in a study of weight-management activities
among African-American women, found that although most of
the women she spoke with had been overweight for years by

biomedical standards, they did not perceive themselves to be overweight. Awareness of being overweight came from outside the immediate family, usually from a social or health encounter. As Allan explains, these women had evaluated their body size not "in relation to the White ideal in the media but in comparison to other African American women who on the average are heavier than white women."[3] Moreover, most women she spoke with did not define being overweight as unhealthy.

Shiriki Kumanyika and her colleagues, drawing on a sample of five hundred African-American women between the ages of twenty-five and sixty-four, found that about 40 percent of the women in the overweight categories (based on body mass index) considered their figures attractive or very attractive.[4] Almost all these women recognized that they were overweight by biomedical standards. Further, only one-half of the women who were moderately or severely overweight reported that their husbands or boyfriends were supportive of their dieting efforts. Almost unanimously, overweight women reported that their body size had not been a source of difficulty in their personal or family relationships.

Nationwide survey results indicate that, in contrast to African-American girls, white and Latino girls perceive themselves to be overweight even when their weight falls within "normal" parameters for their height as established by the National Center for Health Statistics.[5] As they get older, white girls express increasing dissatisfaction with themselves, whereas African-American girls report a relatively stable and positive sense of self-worth.[6]

This discrepancy in self-esteem is reflected in the rates of eating disorders among these different groups. Anorexia nervosa and bulimia nervosa are estimated to affect 1–3 percent of the white population, and studies indicate that the frequency of eating disorders is similar among Latino girls and women.[7] To date, few cases of anorexia nervosa and bulimia nervosa have been reported among African-American females. A comparative study of bulimia among African-American and white college women found that fewer African-American women experienced a sense of fear and discouragement surrounding food and weight control than did their white counterparts.[8] Some researchers have speculated, however, that increased affluence and acculturation of African Americans into white culture may result in a higher incidence of eating disorders as blacks seek to emulate white middle-class ideals.[9] Indeed, one study of African-American female college students found that higher levels of assimilation to white racial identity were associated with greater food restriction, fear of fat, and drive for thinness.[10] Researchers who have studied eating-disorder symptoms among obese populations have found significant rates of disordered eating in overweight African-American women.[11] It may be that professionals misdiagnose eating disorders among African Americans owing to stereotypical ideas that such problems are restricted to white women.[12]

Psychologists Ruth Striegel-Moore and Linda Smolak found that when African-American girls or women experienced weight-related social pressures, they were likely to want to be thinner, to attempt to lose weight, or both. These authors raise concerns that the present understanding of eating disorders is based almost exclusively on data obtained from clinic-based samples among white women.[13]

Drawing on in-depth interviews with African-American and Latino women, sociologist Becky Thompson highlights the risk of generalizing about class and thinness among women of color. The diversity of experiences among the women she interviewed makes it clear that African-American and Latino women may be equally vulnerable to the emphasis on thinness. "Media permeation of even the most remote areas of the country," writes Thompson, "makes it unlikely that any ethnic or racial group is unaware of the premium placed on dieting and thinness."[14]

Beyond considerations of weight, several researchers have noted that women of color are compelled, at various points in their lives, to compare their appearance to the dominant white ideal. Such comparisons extend beyond body shape to hair and skin color.[15] Some have argued that the African-American woman is twice victimized because she must respond to the desires and expectations of African-American men as well as to white cultural values and norms.[16]

Research conducted up until the last decade tended to highlight the self-contempt some African Americans experienced about their appearance as a result of the dominant white beauty ideal.[17] More recently, researchers have pointed to the manner in which African-American women are supportive and appreciative of one another's efforts to fashion a positive identity.[18] To date, however, little research has focused on the actual experience of African-American teenaged girls and the extent to which conflict about appearance affects their lives in various social settings. This led us to wonder what type of self-presentation is culturally valued by African-American girls, in what context, and for what reasons.

Richard Majors and Janet Billson, writing on African-American males, suggest that one coping strategy adopted to deal with oppression and marginality has been "cool pose"—a "ritualized form of masculinity that entails behaviors, scripts, [and] physical posturing that deliver a single, critical message: pride, strength, and control."[19] By striking a cool pose through dress and animated movement, black males feel in control of their psychological and social space. "Styling" provides an individual voice for males who might otherwise go silent and unnoticed. On the street, young men who are "looking good" (that is, who are very well dressed) are given greater personal space and respect than those whose dress is more ordinary.[20]

While Majors and Billson do not specifically discuss African-American women, other researchers have noted the importance to women of styling and the construction of self in an environment where style is both valued and commented upon.[21] Flexibility and personal style, rather than conformity to a mainstream style, are admired. What is missing from the literature is an understanding of how African-American adolescent girls negotiate their gender identities and how they relate to their bodies in a variety of settings.

In the third year of our study, we were fortunate to receive additional funding from the National Institutes of Health to investigate body image and dieting issues among African-American girls. This study was conducted over one year. Fifty high school girls were invited to participate in interviews and focus groups. Like the white and Latino girls we interviewed, the African-American girls were from lower-middle and middle-class families. Interviews and focus groups took place primarily in the schools and in community settings and were facilitated by Sheila Parker and Colette Sims, two of our African-American colleagues. These girls also completed the survey that we had developed based on our research with white and Latino girls.

◆　　◆　　◆

Survey Findings

In order to assess differences between white and African-American girls with regard to weight-related issues, we compared responses to the survey question, "How satisfied are you with your weight?" Responses show distinct differences between the two groups. Seventy percent of the African-American girls responded that they were satisfied or very satisfied with their current weight. While 82 percent of these girls were at or below the normal weight-for-height range for African-American girls their age, 18 percent were significantly overweight (defined as above the eighty-fifth percentile).[22] Only 15 percent of the girls who were of normal weight expressed dissatisfaction with their present weight (see Appendix B, Table 7). By contrast, a similar survey question about body shape directed at white girls revealed that almost 90 percent were dissatisfied with their bodies.

Despite the differences in body satisfaction expressed by African-American and white girls, responses to other survey questions on weight-control behaviors reveal few significant differences between the two groups. This was initially puzzling to us. In response to the question, "How often have you tried to lose weight during the past year?" 48 percent of the African-American girls stated that they had not tried to lose weight, as compared with 39 percent of the white girls. Approximately 30 percent of girls in both ethnic groups had tried to lose weight one or two times in the past year. Eleven percent of girls in both groups said they were always trying. (See Appendix B, Table 8.)

In response to the question, "Are you trying to change your weight now?" 54 percent of African-American girls answered in the affirmative as compared with 44 percent of white girls. We found no significant differences between ethnic group responses on this question (see Appendix B, Table 9).

Data derived from this survey seemed contradictory. While African-American girls appeared similar to white girls with respect to dieting practices, they expressed much greater satisfaction with their weight than white girls did. Why did these African-American girls report trying to lose weight if they were satisfied with how much they weighed? During discussions among project staff and a panel of African-American youth, several issues emerged: Did answering questions on a survey primarily designed for a white population mask differences in attitudes and behaviors of African-American girls? To what extent were their answers shaped by the questions asked and the context in which they were asked? Was it plausible that the language of the survey reflected dominant cultural values? Would language that engaged African-American girls yield different responses? We wondered if there were characteristics of this African-American sample that might lead them to adopt forms of behavior similar to their peers. African Americans are a minority group in a largely white and Latino population in the area where the study was conducted. Were their peers mainly white and Latino girls, and did this influence their practices and attitudes?

Members of the research team expressed concern that the survey results from the African-American girls did not reflect differences in body image and perceptions of self expressed during focus groups and individual interviews. We therefore developed a second survey designed specifically for African-

American girls that employed language and addressed themes that emerged during interviews and discussions.

◆　　◆　　◆

The Ideal Girl: An African-American Perspective

African-American perceptions of beauty are markedly different from white perceptions despite frequent media images of black models and dancers who depict white beauty ideals. In focus-group discussions, African-American girls were asked to describe their sense of the ideal girl. Commonly, girls responded with a request for clarification: Were we asking about an African-American ideal girl or a white one? This response signaled to us that the girls were keenly aware of differences in ideals of beauty between the African-American and the dominant white culture.

This notion was confirmed in the new survey we administered to African-American girls in which they were asked whether there was a difference between their ideal of beauty and that of white girls. More than 60 percent of the girls agreed that there was, while the remaining girls reported that there was little difference. In response to the open-ended question, "If yes, what is the difference?" girls wrote comments such as: "White girls have to look like Barbie dolls and Cindy Crawford to be beautiful," and "White girls want to be perfect." African-American girls noted that "their attitudes and the way they wear their clothes is different," and that white girls "want to be tall, be thin and have long hair."

When we asked the African-American girls for their description of an ideal black girl, their response often began with a list of personality traits rather than physical attributes. The ideal African-American girl was smart, friendly, not conceited, easy to talk to, fun to be with, and had a good sense of humor. Many girls noted that their ideal girl did not have to be "pretty," just "well-kept" (that is, well-groomed). When asked about physical attributes, girls tended to respond that ideal girls had it "going on." This referred to making what they had work for them: be it long nails, pretty eyes, big lips, nice thighs, a big butt—whatever. Notably, the skin color of the "ideal girl" was described as dark, medium, or light depending on the skin color of the respondent.

What was particularly striking in African-American girls' descriptions, when compared with those of white adolescents, was the deemphasis on external beauty as a prerequisite for popularity. As sixteen-year-old Yolanda explained:

> There's a difference between being just fine or being just pretty . . . because I know a lot of girls who aren't just drop-dead fine but they are pretty, and they're funny, all those things come in and that makes the person beautiful. There are a lot of bad-looking [physically beautiful] girls out there, but you can't stand being around them.

Girls were aware that African-American boys had more specific physical criteria for an "ideal girl" than the girls themselves had. They commented that boys liked girls who were shapely, "thick," and who had "nice thighs." One girl noted that "guys would be talkin' about the butt . . . it be big." Sixteen-year-old Valerie explained:

> I think pretty matters more to guys than to me. I don't care. Just real easy to talk to, that would be the ideal girl for me, but the ideal girl from the guys' perspective would be entirely different. They want them to be fine, you know what guys like, shapely. Black guys like black girls who are thick—full-figured [laughs].

When we asked how they would feel if they were with a friend who was slimmer than they were, fifteen-year-old Anitra responded, "It's okay with me. Guys like thicker girls, healthier girls, someone who's got some meat on their body."

African-American girls were notably less concerned than their white counterparts with the standards for an "ideal girl" depicted in the media. What emerged from interviews was a sense of self-esteem that led several girls to describe the ideal girl in terms of themselves—not somebody "out there" to be emulated. Fifteen-year-old Leila noted: "The ideal girl? That's me. I don't know. I'm happy with the way I am. My friends like me the way that I am and they don't think that I should change and neither do I."

African-American girls did not describe beauty in relation to a particular size or set of body statistics. They noted that beauty was not merely a question of shape; it was important to be beautiful on the inside as well as on the outside, and to be beautiful a girl had to "know her culture." One girl explained that "African-American girls have inner beauty in themselves that they carry with them—their sense of pride." This sense of pride was commonly described as a legacy they received from their mothers.

We asked the girls to describe the qualities they admired in a black woman. Girls noted that they admired a woman who "keeps herself up and acts like herself" and "is strong on the inside, knows what she wants, and looks good on the outside and inside." One girl explained that a beautiful black woman is "a woman who accepts who she is but yet can stand up for herself, and a woman who truly believes in herself, works hard and doesn't accept negative things in her life that will bring her down." Having a positive attitude and "not worrying about your looks too much" were important components of a beautiful woman. Attitude eclipsed body parts as a measure of value.

In focus-group interviews, we asked the African-American girls if they heard or engaged in much fat talk with their friends. Sixteen-year-old Christina explained:

> I don't hear that a lot. I hang out with black people and they don't care. We don't worry if we're fat because we'd all be drawn away from that. We want to talk about what's going on, you know, about where we're going for lunch. We're not concerned with that.

Standards for body image and beauty among these African-American adolescents can be summed up in what the girls term "looking good." "Looking good" or "got it goin' on" entails making what you've got work for you, by creating and presenting a sense of style. In an article on body-size values among white and African-American women, Janet Allan and her colleagues similarly report that "looking good" among African-American women is related to public image and overall attractiveness rather than to weight.[23] Adolescent informants explained that regardless of a girl's body size or shape, height, weight, skin color, hairstyle, and so on, if she can clothe and groom herself and have the personality to carry off her individual style, she is "looking good." "Looking good" had to do with projecting one's self-image and confidence—having "tude" (attitude) and "flavor." "Throwing your attitude" means establishing your presence, creating a "certain air about yourself," being in control of your image and "things around you," being able to improvise effectively, and maintaining poise under pressure. "Flavor" refers to one's sensuality beyond physical appearance.

African-American perceptions of beauty are flexible: they include and exceed physical characteristics. In the survey we developed specifically for African-American girls, we asked them to select one of several possible answers to complete the statement, "In my opinion, beauty is . . ." Almost two-thirds (63 percent) of these girls responded that beauty is "having the right kind of attitude and personality when you deal with others." Thirty-five percent responded that beauty is "making what you got work for you in your own way." Only 2 percent of the sample noted that beauty is "making yourself look as close as possible to an ideal body shape and face."

Another theme that emerged in discussions with African-American girls was that beauty is fluid rather than static. Beauty is judged on the basis of "how one moves" rather than on what one weighs. We observed that when African-American girls and women tried on clothes and looked in the mirror, they had a greater tendency to move around than to strike a series of static poses, behavior more typical of white women. Similarly, the importance of movement and body language has been noted with reference to Black English. Linguists Barbara Speicher and Sean McMahon noted that the people they interviewed described style in conversation as a means of projecting self.[24] As one woman noted, "When you're trying to get your point across, there's style, there's movement, there's a lot of moving." Another informant described Black English as a "very interactive form of language," noting that "it has to do with eliciting an audience's response, not just an audience's listening and understanding, but very much a visceral response, a physical response."[25] The emphasis was as much on how a person moved and the sense of style she projected as on what she actually said.

Style was very important to peer-group members. "Putting it together," according to the black girls, entails creating style that not only fits one's person, but projects an attitude. The black girls we interviewed were far less likely than the white girls to purchase ready-made "looks" off a rack or to derive identity from wearing brand-name labels. By contrast, wearing brand-name clothes and recognizable styles was a major identity issue among white girls, especially in middle school (indeed, white girls in middle school were more label-conscious than their counterparts in high school).[26] Economics, as well as the cut of clothing (most ready-made clothes are fit for a Caucasian body), affected African-American girls' efforts to create a style. Although brand names continued to be recognized as a sign of status, they did not dominate the girls' fashion statements. Brands did not create distinction in and of themselves.

Creation of a style that "works" involves making a personal statement and projecting a unique presence. This presence reflects not only on one's person, but also on the African-American community at large. As Susan Taylor notes, style is strongly linked to ethnic pride:

> Black style is our culture. It's our collective response to the world. Our style is rooted in our history and in knowledge of our inner power—our power as a people. Black style is the opposite of conformity. It's what others conform to. In fact, quiet as it's kept, our style is envied and emulated throughout the world.[27]

Beginning in early adolescence, an African-American girl is encouraged by her community of friends and family to develop a look that "works," given her physical endowments and her social and economic environment. In a context in which the beauty standards of the larger society are often the antithesis of African-American physical attributes (facial features, body shape, body size, and hair), positive feedback from other members of the community is important, especially given the constant barrage of ideal standards from the dominant white culture and negative stereotypes generated about African Americans:

> For who among us has not at some point in time succumbed to the propaganda, looked in a mirror and felt ourselves to be wanting? Wanting because our skin is too dark, or our noses too wide or our hips too large, or because our hair wouldn't grow and never blew in the wind, or just because we never seemed to measure up.[28]

How an African-American female is valued within her family and community will determine whether or not she succumbs to this constant assault on her person.

◆   ◆   ◆

African-American Girls and Their Mothers

African-American girls have needed to move beyond the internalization of racial denigration to develop pride in who they are. This involves confronting and rejecting oppressive negative evaluations of being black and female, "adopting instead a sense of self that is self-affirming and self-valuing."[29] An African-American girl needs to evaluate negative distortions, "understand their origins and whose interests they serve, and must ultimately look beyond these demeaning portrayals by embracing the admirable qualities of black womanhood that these images obscure, particularly the unique wisdom, strength and perseverance of African American women."[30] Thus, black girls often turn to older women in their community as role models and for support. In our interviews, several African-American girls described their mothers as their role model. Because women's knowledge increases as they get older, mothers are respected as the people who can teach girls "how to make it"—how to survive in a potentially hostile environment.[31]

Ana Marie Cauce and her colleagues have described how African-American mothers establish themselves as the adults in charge. Given the reality of a hostile environment, mothers need to enforce strict rules in order to protect their daughters—this in contrast to white mothers, who often do not make their rules for behavior adequately known. Nonetheless, the most consistent message African-American girls receive from their mothers is to be self-reliant and resourceful. As Janie Ward writes:

> African Americans have particularly high expectations for their daughters. Historically, black daughters have been socialized toward both traditional care (nurturing wife and mother) and nontraditional roles (worker or employee). Parents recognize that their daughters will be at least partially, if not totally, responsible for the financial survival of their families. This orientation to the dual roles of mother and worker and the values placed on black women's strength and perseverance are important elements of their healthy self-esteem.[32]

In her recent work, Ward describes the home as an important and primary site where black children learn from their parents how to deal with racism and prejudice and how to construct a positive image. She writes, "The process of self-creation depends upon the Black's ability to invoke an 'oppositional gaze,' to observe the social world critically and to oppose ideas and ways of being that are disempowering to the self."[33]

Learning respect for elders and obedience to parents is an important goal of child socialization in African-American families. Interestingly, the girls we interviewed were well aware of the differences between white and African-American parent-child interactions. As one African-American girl described, "I have a [white] friend who ran away last week and she still hasn't gone home. Why would I *ever* run away? It's like she ran away 'cause her mother wanted her to clean her room! Black girls don't run away 'cause their room ain't clean [laughs] or because they can't go out tomorrow night. I have white friends who say stuff to their parents that I wouldn't ever dream of saying to my mom."

Among African-American girls, closeness to family—particularly to one's mother—has been found to be central to overall self-esteem. Community reinforcement is an important component that sustains this self-esteem at high levels.[34]

◆   ◆   ◆

Positive Feedback

The African-American girls in the study reported routinely receiving compliments from other African Americans of both sexes for "having it going on." Comments were received from people of close as well as casual acquaintance, in public as well as in private, as a matter of course without any offense taken. Interview data strongly suggest that African-American girls receive far more positive than negative feedback about how they look from their families and friends. At the same time, however, they are taught to maintain their composure in verbal battles (that is, "playing the dozens") in which their opponents attempt to exploit areas of potential sensitivity and vulnerability.[35]

In focus groups, girls also talked about receiving positive feedback from family members, friends, and community members for "looking good."[36] This is consistent with the findings of Patricia Collins, who notes that in traditional African-American communities, black women "share knowledge of what it takes to be self-defined Black women with their younger, less experi-

enced sisters."[37] Collins further contends that there is a sister-
hood among black women in their extended families, in the
church, and in the community-at-large.

In our survey African-American girls reported receiving
positive feedback for creating their own style around their
given attributes. In contrast, white girls received support for
altering their looks to fit established beauty ideals. Support for
dieting was commonly articulated by white girls but rarely
mentioned by African-American girls. Other researchers confirm these findings, noting that African-American women were
influenced by friends and family to maintain a larger body
size.[38]

In contrast to the envy and competitiveness that mark
white girls' comments of others whom they perceive to be attractive, African-American girls described themselves as being
supportive of each other. On the survey we designed specifically for African Americans, we asked girls what their response was when they saw a girl "who's got it going on"—a girl
who has put her personal resources and attributes together.
Almost 60 percent noted that they would "tell her she's looking good," while another 20 percent noted that they "would
admire her but wouldn't say anything." Only 11 percent of
girls noted that they "would be jealous of her." These findings
stand in stark contrast to the discussion in Chapter 2 about
competition among white girls.

In the African-American community, a girl's peer group
serves an important function in her socialization. Being the
same age as other group members is not as important for
group membership as it is for white girls. Broader-based group
membership and support contribute to flexibility in the way
beauty and style are perceived and accepted. Groups do engage in surveillance, however, and hold members accountable
for how they look, how they carry themselves, and whether or
not they are "taking care of business." As sixteen-year-old
Adrian noted:

> Other people, our peers, like when they don't like
> what you have on they will tell you and if they like it

they will say so ("that's fresh") . . . the white girls, oh whatever, they say, "that's nice," even if it's not, they will say it anyway.

Similar perceptions about white girls' behavior with regard to hairstyles, as distinct from that of African-American girls, is described by psychologist Midge Wilson. She explains:

> Among White girls, seemingly every major hair deci-sion—whether to perm, dye or cut—requires constant feedback and reassurance from her closest friends. An unwritten social rule in the White community seems to be that whatever a White girlfriend does to her hair, however it may look, it is essential to tell her, "it looks great!" Privately one may think the friend is vain, insecure, or silly for experimenting the way she does, but one must never question her decisions or motives. Among Black teenage girls, however, hair decisions are subject to more critical feedback from friends, because hair styles are laden with political overtones.[39]

Another difference between white and African-American perceptions of beauty involves the manner in which age is represented. Age is perceived as physical deterioration in the dominant white culture. Age is an enemy to be fought with vigilance through the use of wrinkle creams, dieting and exer-cise programs, and, when all else fails, cosmetic surgery. Na-omi Wolf, citing interviews with editors of women's maga-zines, notes that the airbrushing of age from women's faces is routine in their work. Wolf contends that to airbrush age off a woman's face is to erase her identity, individuality, power, and history.[40] For adolescents, the failure to portray adult white women as beautiful adds an increasing pressure for them to achieve the beauty ideal during the teen-age years.

Among African Americans, less emphasis is placed on be-ing young as a criterion for being beautiful. This theme emerged during focus groups and was something we speci-fically asked about on the African-American survey. In response to the question, "As women get older, what will happen to them in terms of how they look?" 65 percent of girls said that they would get more beautiful, and 22 percent said they would stay the same. Only 13 percent of girls thought women would lose their looks as they became older.

For African-American girls, beauty is not associated with a short window of opportunity as it is for most white girls. Beauty may be achieved, maintained, and enhanced as a female grows older and more sure of herself. The number of African-American girls who spoke of their mothers as "beautiful" far exceeded that of white girls, who tended to speak of their mothers either in terms of their youth ("when she was young") or as "alright for a mother," implying that as a woman became older, the chances of her being beautiful were reduced.

◆   ◆   ◆

Attitudes toward Dieting

Beauty work is closely tied to dieting in dominant white culture. Among African Americans, by contrast, dieting carries less significance. On the African-American survey, we asked girls to complete the statement, "For your health, is it better to be . . ." Responses included "a little overweight" or "a little underweight." Sixty-four percent of the girls thought it was better to be "a little overweight," while the remaining 36 percent chose "a little underweight" as their response. In the same survey, girls were asked to respond to the question, "For people who are normal weight or underweight, I think dieting is . . ." Responses indicate that 40 percent of girls thought it was "okay if you want to do it," whereas 42 percent thought dieting was "harmful to your body." Only 12 percent of girls thought it was "good because it puts you in control of your life."

Most African-American girls agreed that dieting was appropriate for someone who was "very overweight." A girl who was "very overweight" was defined in focus-group interviews as "someone who takes up two seats on the bus." Sixteen-year-old Cheree explained, "Being fat is when you have three stomachs . . . when you sit down your stomachs fold up like just-washed clothes." Some girls noted that harming the body through dieting was a sin inasmuch as one's body was God-given. Notably, girls who reported on surveys that they dieted articulated a different set of cultural values related to dieting and body image in focus groups and individual interviews.[41]

◆　◆　◆

Self-Esteem

During group discussions, African-American girls expressed a greater acceptance of their bodies than did white girls. Rather than reaching for an abstract ideal, these girls talked about achieving their own personal ideal. As one girl noted:

> I think that black people, black kids, we're all brought up and taught to be realistic about life, and we don't look at things the way you want them to be, or how you wish them to be. You look at them the way they are.

The African-American family and community are sources of positive feedback that serve to enhance self-esteem and supplant negative comments from outside directed against individuals.[42] African-American children, especially those in lower socioeconomic groups, are taught by their parents to function in an oppressive and hostile society in which they are expected to survive and excel.[43] Children are raised with the knowledge of "how it is." Parents teach their children that though resources may not be available to them, they can succeed if they learn to "make what they got work for them." The church reinforces this message by preaching acceptance of self from an early age.

African-American parents must prepare their children to

understand and live in two cultures. W. E. B. Du Bois, writing in the early 1900s, described the idea of a double consciousness. "Blacks have to guard their sense of blackness," noted Du Bois, "while accepting the rules of the game and cultural consciousness of the dominant White culture."[44] To achieve the former, children are raised to be part of an African-American community as well as a member of an African-American family. For many black women, this entails developing a spiritual self, which becomes "the greenhouse in which a woman can nurse her self-image and build her self-esteem."[45] In Christian belief, the body is seen as the temple of the Holy Spirit, and in the black community, the church is one of the places where a sense of style is displayed and appreciated.

In this chapter, I have contrasted two distinct ideologies that are articulated at the site of the body. While these ideologies coexist, they affect white and African-American women in different ways.

Gender ideology is reproduced at the site of the body through working toward bodily perfection, a task that engages the imagination, if not the lives, of a majority of young white women in America. This ideology has promoted critical assessment of girls' physical attributes (leading young women to be dissatisfied with their bodies), fostered competition and envy among women, and encouraged the pursuit of goals that are impossible to maintain or obtain. In a multicultural nation, the idealized beauty of white culture has been valorized and a multitude of products have been made available to women of color promising "melting pot" success to help them pass in mainstream America.

A second ideology, propagated within African-American culture, is built around egalitarian ideals, the principle of reciprocity, and the recognition of strength and balance in diversity.[46] In this approach to life, improvisation is valued and identity is constructed through creativity and style. Writing about the ways in which knowledge is transmitted between mothers and daughters in an African-American community, Suzanne Carothers notes:

> Daughters learn competency through a sense of aesthetics, an appreciation for work done beautifully ... This aesthetic quality becomes one of the measures of competently done work as judged by the women themselves and by other members of their community.[47]

African-American girls learn from their mothers and through interactions with their peer groups and community that they can project an image and attitude of power through the way they dress and carry themselves. Competency is required in knowing how to present oneself in bicultural contexts ranging from the school and the street to the church and the job market.[48] In focus groups, girls continually noted the importance of style, not only to project an image of themselves as individuals, but in their role as representatives of the African-American family and community.

In African-American culture, one way in which lessons about freedom, competency, and community are learned is through aesthetic appreciation. In contrast to the more static image of beauty as bodily perfection found in white culture, a more fluid, flexible image of beauty prevails in black culture. Instead of competition that fosters envy and alienation, an egalitarian ethos is promoted, marked by mutual appreciation, cooperation, and approval of someone "who's got it going on."

Several researchers have noted that in African-American communities there is an emphasis on collective social strategies that contrast with the focus on individuals dominant in white culture.[49] Although among African Americans creating one's own style as an individual statement is important, a positive presentation of one's community is equally imperative. An egalitarian ethos does not imply the absence of hierarchy nor the absence of historical tensions and interpersonal power struggles that form part of daily existence.[50] What it does imply is that while individuality in the form of personal style and attitude is respected, it is overshadowed by a strong sense of community.[51]

Some psychologists have contended that African-American women are becoming increasingly assertive in establishing their own identities:

> Rising above externally sanctioned characterizations of womanhood, some Black women are fashioning their identities based upon an analysis and understanding of their own struggles and successes. Further, Black women have united to support one another's efforts in the creation of newly defined roles and identities. Within this dynamic of self-determination, the Black woman is proactive rather than reactive, aggressive rather than passive, and assertive rather than receptive.[52]

Many of the African-American girls we interviewed expressed positive feelings about their bodies and their sense of style. Their responses may reflect egalitarian ideals and downplay internal conflicts that may emerge in contexts where positive feedback is not forthcoming. It remains to be seen whether they will be able to maintain these self-perceptions as they become older and obtain jobs in mainstream American society. Increased opportunities are available to women of color, particularly those who can operate in ways that conform to the norms of the dominant white culture.[53] Thus middle-class African-American women may be more likely to deemphasize their black identities in order to get ahead, and may be particularly vulnerable to the message of dominant white society that "thin is everything."[54] For example, feminist philosopher Susan Bordo claims that African-American women are as likely as other groups of women to have disturbed relationships with food. For evidence of this, she points to African-American magazines that have an increased number of articles on weight, dieting, and exercise issues.[55] The extent to which dominant cultural values discussed in popular magazines are ignored and/or resisted by individuals or groups of women bears consideration. Entering the mainstream job market may increase pressure for women of color to be "perfect" in order to counteract negative racial stereotypes. Of relevance here is whether this will translate into body discipline in the form of dieting by those girls who aspire to make it, or whether preexisting sensibilities will alter the way in which beauty and success are perceived in the black community.[56]

Teens expend considerable time and energy negotiating a sense of style when they are on display to their peers. While the African-American girls we interviewed clearly recognized the dominant white ideal of beauty, it did not play an influential role in negotiating their identities and their sense of self.

7

What We Can Do

The other day my girlfriend asked me, "Can you imagine what life would be like if we both lost fifteen pounds?" and I said, "Oh, wow!" Right now, I'm a little bit chubby and I like clothes but I just can't find the kind of clothes that I'd really like to wear. I just know that if I lost fifteen pounds, I'd be more self-confident. I'd be able to walk past the soccer team and not feel all embarrassed. I could just walk right up to those guys and say, "Hi, how are you doing?" I'd feel so much better about my-self if I were thinner.

VANESSA, *AGE 16*

IT WAS A WARM spring day and Vanessa and I were seated in a quiet corner of the school under the shade of a large tree. This was one of the last interviews that I would conduct, and I was feeling a little sad that the project was coming to an end—at least the face-to-face interviewing component of it. My formal interview with Vanessa ended a bit early, so I took the opportunity to ask her a few additional questions. I asked nonchalantly, "If you could do anything that you wanted to this summer, what would it be?" half expecting a response about a trip to some beautiful beach or a visit to friends or family in a faraway place. Despite having talked with so many girls who were obsessed with their bodies, I was a bit taken aback by Vanessa's response, which detailed her frustration with her weight. What she really hoped for was to lose fifteen pounds that summer! Just as she finished her sentence, the bell rang and Vanessa jumped up, rushing off to her next class.

As I was driving home from the high school, Vanessa's final comments were turning over in my mind. At age sixteen, she dreamed only of losing weight. Of course, I had heard this before from other girls her age, but it was all the more disconcerting to hear such talk that day, during my final interview. I could not help wondering whether my interview questions had inadvertently made things worse by bringing to Vanessa's consciousness how she felt about her body, the pressures she experienced in school, and her relationship with her mother, who also wanted her to lose weight. I knew that my concerns were shared among other Teen Lifestyle Project members, some of whom had come to feel increasingly self-conscious about themselves while conducting our interviews. During one of our weekly meetings, a twenty-four-year-old interviewer and graduate student remarked:

> Listening to girls' fat talk has really jogged my own memory of what I was like when I was their age. I guess I had really put all that out of my mind, but when I hear girls buzzing around the locker room about how fat they feel, I remember that I used to talk that way too! Sometimes when I go to the high school to do interviews, I feel so self-conscious . . . so conspicuous . . . as if everyone is looking at me . . . it's as if I'm fifteen all over again! I even feel like I should be wearing makeup or something to make myself more attractive!

Another interviewer complained about her own paradoxical behavior. "Since I've been working on this project, I'm a lot more conscious of what I see in magazines," she told me. "Sometimes, when I'm reading *Vogue* or *Elle*, I have this scathing critique running through my mind of how women are represented. I get really angry when I see how skinny the models are, and I remember how girls have said that they want to look just like them! But later that same day, I'll catch myself picking at my food because I'm concerned with my weight! I get so annoyed at myself for thinking one way and acting another!"

I myself was not immune to this kind of thinking, and I appreciated my colleagues' honesty in disclosing their frustrations. The problem was not just that we as women judged ourselves by our weight. It was far more insidious than that. Being an ideal weight was a marker of a woman's identity, achievement, and self-control, and by extension, a statement of her moral virtue and overall self-worth. The conversation and actions of the girls in the study showed that they themselves and not simply some outside other were reinforcing the importance of meeting the dominant ideal of beauty. Although fathers, brothers, and boys at school were enforcers of the preferred body shape, other girls and women were at least as, if not more, responsible for defining and enforcing female beauty standards.

In our study, girls turned their critical gaze inward toward themselves and outward toward other females. Participation in fat talk was a critical component of peer-group membership and made girls appear no better than their friends. By affirming that their friends were not fat, girls helped one another keep their self-effacing thoughts about their bodies in check. Girlfriends served as buffers for one another, mediating the potentially harmful effects of others' gazes, envious looks, and negative comments. Nonetheless, while girls appear to be closely connected with their peers, beauty politics are often divisive, causing rifts in their social world.

It is clear from the girls' narratives about their lives at home and at school that they have deeply internalized these beauty ideals. These ideals are reinforced by media messages that blatantly link thinness with an enhanced sense of well-being and, ultimately, a "more perfect" life. This theme is aptly captured in an advertisement for a new miracle weight-loss product: "Lose weight and find yourself!" As a result of being preoccupied with their physical selves, particularly during early adolescence, girls often fail to understand that they are far more than how they look. The comparisons that they draw between themselves and imagined and real others direct their energy away from more meaningful pursuits.

In direct contradiction to previous research findings, the majority of girls in this study did not diet with any great frequency or intensity. In fact, most girls who dieted did so for less than one week and more than two-thirds of girls who dieted had lost ten pounds or less on their diet. On food records, only 14 percent of the girls reported that they were dieting, although 40 percent had reported dieting on our survey. Many girls demonstrated not pathology, as has been reported in numerous studies, but a desire to be healthy, and as a result they were actively involved in watching what they ate as opposed to dieting. Although girls who watched often still worried about their weight, the majority of them were more concerned with maintaining their present weight than with losing weight. Nonetheless, dieting, watching, and fat talk are all manifestations of personal surveillance, albeit to varying degrees.

African-American girls, by contrast, downplayed weight and body statistics as a measure of self-worth, emphasizing instead that how one moved and projected 'tude (attitude) are important qualities contributing to a female's beauty. While these findings were anticipated by our African-American colleagues, they were surprising to some of our white team members. In project staff discussions, several white interviewers explained that thinking about their presentation of self in terms of style and movement instead of weight and body shape was helping them re-evaluate their "beauty." Their consciousness of what constituted beauty was expanding.

◆   ◆   ◆

What Should We Do Next?

In group meetings after all the data were gathered, our multi-disciplinary team (which included cultural and medical anthropologists, a nutritionist, and a health educator) debated our next steps. We had concerns about simply writing up and disseminating our research findings without engaging in problem solving. If we did that, would we ourselves be adding to the hype about weight? Did we have an obligation to at least pilot a meaningful research-based intervention that would attempt to foster healthier lifestyles and raise girls' critical consciousness about the media? Given our inability to change girls' home lives, what could we realistically hope to achieve with an intervention?

Having spent several years carrying out ethnography in middle and high schools, I was struck by two observations. First, despite the national concern with adolescent girls as a group at risk for low self-esteem, unhealthful eating and excessive dieting, eating disorders, and obesity, we were not paying as much attention to, or allocating as many resources for, prevention. Girls received little practical information on the developmental process, eating healthfully, and physical activity. Second, little school time was spent on developing critical thinking skills in relation to media images and advertising.

In the high schools in which I worked, health education was required as a one-semester course. During the four years of high school, a student was exposed to a maximum of five class periods on nutrition. There was considerable latitude as to what was included in these classes, and some health education teachers chose to include only one or two lessons on nutrition. In the absence of ethnography on teens' everyday eating behavior, the content of these nutrition classes tended to be general, with a focus on food groups or the food pyramid. What was not addressed were the multitudes of questions that young people had about foods that they typically consumed. These questions involved not just health but beauty work and practices that girls engaged in for the sake of weight management. Considering the lack of information on how to make healthful food choices, coupled with the over-accessibility of high-fat foods and soda in the lunchroom and in vending machines, was it realistic to expect teens to eat healthfully?

Although I recognized that much of a teen's socialization

into food consumption and taste preferences occurred at home, it was also apparent that patterns of eating were influenced by peers and the mass media. Food advertisements and nutritional "advice" given in fashion magazines clearly influenced girls' ideas about eating and dieting. Discussions with girls in the Teen Lifestyle Project revealed that there was a lot of confusion about terms such as lite, low fat, fat free, cholesterol, and so on, as well as a great deal of interest about what constituted appropriate food choices if one wanted to eat healthfully, lose weight, or maintain one's weight. During interviews, girls voiced interest in the relative effectiveness of various dieting strategies that they had heard about or seen advertised in magazines. Did they work? Were they appropriate for teen bodies? What was best if they wanted to lose a little or a lot of weight? The problem was not too little information but rather too much information. How could we teach girls to make sense of the multitude of food and weight-related information that permeated their environment?

Findings of our nutritional intake and survey data raised concerns about the lack of particular nutrients in girls' diets. One concern was insufficient calcium consumption. On our survey we asked, "How much milk do you drink?" Responses included *three or more glasses per day* (twenty-eight girls; 14 percent); *two glasses per day* (forty-four girls; 22 percent); *one glass per day* (forty-three girls; 21 percent); *two glasses a week* (thirty-two girls; 15 percent); or *a glass or less a week* (fifty-seven girls; 28 percent). Combining these responses, we find that more than 40 percent of the girls in our study were drinking two glasses of milk a week or less! Low calcium consumption was confirmed on the girls' diet records. In sharp contrast to their low milk consumption, one-third of girls were drinking soda two to three times a day or more, while another 20 percent reported drinking soda once a day!

The trend among youth toward soda consumption over milk has been documented nationwide. Conservative estimates have children and teens guzzling more than sixty-four gallons of soda per year (much of which is caffeinated), an amount that has tripled for teens since 1978.[1] The average thirteen-to-eighteen-year-old female soda drinker consumes more than two cans a day, and 10 percent of females consume five or more cans a day. Soda is the main beverage of youth and provides many young people with 20 to 40 percent of their daily calories.[2] This is occurring not only in schools, but also at home. Nutritionists warn that caffeine may threaten developing bone mass, and when substituted for more wholesome foods, may impede the overall nutrition of youth. Of particular concern to women, the replacement of milk with soda may herald increasing rates of osteoporosis in future years.[3]

It is not just soda machines that have worked their way into schools through corporate promises of revenue and other much-needed resources to financially strapped administrators. Between 1991 and 1996, the percentage of public schools participating in the sale of brand-name fast foods increased dramatically, from about 2 percent to 13 percent. Burgers, fries, and pizza from popular chains have become increasingly available in the school cafeteria.[4] Across the nation, homerooms in almost 40 percent of high schools start the day with news and commercials, some of which are direct endorsements for food products. Commercial logos for Pepsi, Coke, and popular teen breakfast cereals can be found on free software provided to schools by Fortune 500 corporations for "educational purposes" as well as on school signs. In the city in which I live, schools advertise their connection to major food and beverage corporations (Coca Cola, Taco Bell) on their marquees. Other companies, like Hershey's, have developed and disseminated free curricula to middle schools, teaching about the place of chocolate in a balanced diet! At some schools, free book covers are distributed to students advertising popular brand-name clothing (for example, Calvin Klein) adorned on the bodies of thin young models.[5] Increasingly, youth are being targeted as consumers, even on school grounds.

Given this reality, what type of useful intervention could we mount in the high school? During some of our final focus-group discussions, we learned from girls that they valued talking about issues relating to body image, eating, and dieting in a non-judgmental environment. When asked what they would want in the form of education, girls told us that they would like information and practical tips on eating better and exercising. Some girls who were not on athletic teams voiced frustration that they had little opportunity to exercise. This was particularly the case with overweight girls who had experienced teasing in their required physical education classes and as a result were embarrassed to join other exercise classes.

We also asked girls what grade would be the best to target for an educational program. There was no consensus, but some girls expressed the opinion that it would be beneficial to bring students across the four years of high school into a single group. Their rationale was that a mixed group would allow older girls (juniors and seniors) to talk with ninth-graders about the difficulties of being a first-year student and how to deal with the pressures of "fitting in." On the basis of our discussions, we concluded that an intervention that targeted girls' lived experience would be popular.

Drawing on our ethnographic research, we recognized that girls already had existing funds of knowledge about what they believed was good for their health. We wanted to build upon what they already knew and practiced, reinforcing positive attitudes and behaviors such as watching what they ate—avoiding junk foods and eating more fruits and vegetables. We also wanted to provide a corrective for negative attitudes and potentially harmful behaviors identified among this population. Issues that needed to be addressed included limited calcium intake, high consumption of caffeinated sodas, and harmful dieting practices. We saw a need to adopt both a primary prevention and a harm-reduction strategy to working with teens. The first informs a population about the risks and benefits of different types of behavior, whereas the second dwells on what to do when faced with sub-optimal choices, specifically after engaging in a risky or unhealthful behavior ("pigging out").

In order to ground our advice in the world of teens, we had to review patterns of existing behavior and consider options as they saw them (that is, self-efficacy). What healthful choices could they make when they went to fast-food restaurants without feeling embarrassed? We also needed to consider how they processed information when making decisions. How did they understand nutritional labels and what terms did they pay attention to? What distinctions did they make, if any, among foods that were labeled "low fat," "low cholesterol," and "low calorie"? For girls who wanted or needed to lose weight, was there a way they could "do it right," or at least avoid "doing it wrong"?

We did not see the goal of our intervention as preventing eating disorders or obesity. However, we felt it was important for girls to recognize that while anorexia nervosa and bulimia nervosa affect 1–3 percent of girls, obesity is far more prevalent (21 percent for whites; 30 percent for African Americans).[6] Furthermore, obesity in adolescent girls has increased in the last thirty years, particularly among African Americans.[7] We wanted to discuss with girls why they thought this might be the case. Our hope was that through a historical consideration of obesity, we might get them to think beyond eating and nutrition to activity patterns and exercise.

It was clear that a class on nutrition and exercise was unlikely to be popular unless these topics were discussed in relation to girls' real concerns. Our data showed that for many teen-aged girls, health work—including the "work" of eating—was closely aligned with beauty work. Our challenge was to broaden girls' concepts of beauty beyond rigid, narrow definitions and provide them with the knowledge and skills to work on themselves in a more holistic and healthful manner. The key was to introduce a more flexible alternative to "Barbie beauty," a sense of beauty based more on style and movement than on a number on a scale. A first step was to raise girls' awareness of unrealistic body images promoted through the media and to help them recognize and honor the diversity of body shapes that exists in the real world. Having heard so much of the anguish that girls (particularly white and Latino girls) experienced from being teased for their body shape, we recognized the importance of teaching tolerance of others along with acceptance of self.

One way we hoped to do this was to bring girls of different ethnic backgrounds together to talk about cultural differences in how girls and women feel about their bodies. Shifting the focus of the discussion from the individual to the cultural level might provide girls with a much-needed perspective on their own attitudes and behaviors.

We felt that white and Latino girls could benefit from learning about African-American perceptions of beauty, which appeared more flexible and were based on attitude and self-presentation. But what would African-American girls gain? We believed that these cross-ethnic group discussions would provide positive reinforcement of cultural values for African-American girls, as well as an opportunity to learn from other girls whose experiences might be quite different from their own. Although the beauty ideals of African-American girls appeared more flexible than those of white and Latino girls, we were aware of studies documenting that one way African-American women move up the socioeconomic ladder is by dieting as a way to obtain the "right look" of the dominant culture.[8] We reasoned that African-American girls might benefit from hearing about the frustrations that other girls experienced as a result of continual self-monitoring and dieting. Given the growing public health concern over obesity, we reasoned that all girls could benefit from practical training in nutrition and exercise.

Our guiding philosophy was that there was much girls could learn by exploring their own experiences. We had found while conducting our research that discussion can serve as an intervention that empowers girls and allows them to take ownership of the knowledge that they gain. Therefore, our educational program incorporated few didactic elements and relied heavily on group discussion and experiential activities.

◆　　◆　　◆

Implementing the Program

Our intervention took place at three sites over the course of one year (a public high school and two community sites) and involved seventy girls.[9] My focus in this chapter is on the high school site, which involved twenty-two girls who were in the ninth to twelfth grades. The group was approximately one-third white, one-third Latina, and one-third African American. The project was conducted outside of regular school hours during two six-hour Saturday workshops and three ninety-minute after-school sessions (see Appendix B, Table 10). We chose to conduct our intervention outside the classroom so that we could target only girls in order to facilitate dialogue and engender rapport, particularly around sensitive topics such as body image. In public schools, where coeducation is mandated, there is little opportunity for a single-gender class-room experience.[10]

On the first day of the program, the girls viewed a slide show that used images from magazine advertisements of white, African-American, and Latino women to illustrate the pervasiveness of the dominant culture's influence on beauty ideals. The girls saw how women of color are often depicted in the media (that is, in magazines like *Seventeen* and *Glamour*) as looking extremely similar to white women in terms of body shape. The diversity of shape and color that exists in real life was not pictured.

The script for the show included phrases taken verbatim from Teen Lifestyle Project interviews, and was performed by girls from a drama class at a local high school. The lines they spoke portrayed how white girls felt about themselves when they saw either ads of women in the media or real girls who were beautiful: "I'd kill for her body"; "Oh, she's so perfect, I hate her"; "When I go to the mall and I see all these beautiful girls I just wonder why I was born." The purpose of the presentation was to provide girls with an opportunity to critically evaluate media messages and to begin to reflect on how these messages make them feel about themselves and other girls. One of the themes highlighted in the narrative was how notions of beauty negatively influence social relations between girls by creating jealousy. Images and dialogue in the show also focused on themes such as "having it all" (by eating diet foods and cheating just a little) and media representations of women as body parts rather than as whole people. The dialogue and the discussion that followed guided girls to view the images and cultural ideals behind them as unrealistic and problematic, rather than something to which they should aspire.

After viewing the slide presentation, the girls were encouraged to discuss concepts of beauty, body image, and weight control. Referring to pictures of African-American, white, and Latino women incorporated in the slide show, we discussed cross-cultural perceptions of beauty. Girls discussed cultural differences in ideal body type, and they listened intently when girls of different cultural backgrounds talked about male expectations of women and the media's influence and portrayal of beauty. The discussion made it obvious to all participants that media images were marketing discontent, and even girls who appeared to match the dominant cultural ideal (that is, girls who were white, blond, and thin) were driven to be dissatisfied with their appearance.

The African-American, Latino, and white girls learned much through their honest communication and interactions. African-American girls talked about body acceptance and the importance of "makin' what you got work for you" rather than striving for an ideal image portrayed in magazines. White and Latino girls became more aware of the cultural dimensions of beauty and body image and discovered that what was desirable in white culture was not generally the ideal among African Americans. All of the girls learned that how they felt about themselves was culturally as well as individually mediated, providing them with insights into their own behaviors and attitudes. The intervention also provided opportunities to expand their notions of what was beautiful. African-American girls talked about moving with style and looking good no matter what a person weighed. For African-American girls, these discussions and the reactions of the white and Latino girls reinforced the positive nature of their cultural models of beauty. When African-American girls heard white girls talk about being "perfect," they also gained a greater understanding of the problems caused by rigid and unrealistic beauty ideals.

In keeping with the theme of "makin' what you got work

for you," we created a practical session entitled "Putting Your Best Foot Forward," in which girls explored their own style through color and clothing style. One of our team members who had a background in fashion design led this session, which was intended to introduce girls to factors other than body shape and size that influence body image and how we present ourselves to others. As some girls draped themselves in cloth of different colors, other girls commented on how the colors complemented or detracted from their appearance. Discussion during this segment focused on the importance of feeling good about ourselves, and how we need to recognize our assets and limitations and learn how to work with them.

◆ ◆ ◆

Eating Healthfully

Topics covered during the nutrition sessions included dietary assessment, information on healthful eating, and a cooking demonstration. On the first day, girls completed food records of what they had eaten the previous day. We analyzed these food recalls for use during the nutrition session to allow girls to see what was contained in the foods they ate (nutrients and hidden fats). Exploring their actual food consumption helped initiate a discussion of how they currently made food choices both in school and at home. Girls also learned hands-on skills in healthful preparation of foods that were easy to make and commonly eaten (french fries and taco salad).

During the nutrition sessions, the girls raised a number of questions, including: "Why can some people eat and eat and eat and never gain weight and other people just look at food and get fat?" "Why do we need fat anyway?" "Is there a way that we can turn fat into muscle?" "What does the word 'metabolism' really mean? Is it fixed over your life or can you change it?" "What can I do if I've really pigged out?" Responses to these questions by an expert made nutrition come alive for the girls.

Becoming Physically Active

The physical activity components of the intervention were designed to introduce girls to exercise options. We had learned in our research that some girls were hesitant to participate in physical activity because they thought if they breathed hard or sweated it was an indication that they were out of shape. Because of this awareness, we directly addressed this issue in our intervention. After learning that sweating and breathing hard were normal outcomes of exercising, girls were more willing to be physically active.

In the first of the physical activity components, a creative movement specialist and artist in African dance engaged the girls in discussion about body movement and self-esteem and led the group in dance routines. Her presentation, which emphasized moving gracefully with confidence, embodied African-American notions of presence and sense of style. She followed the dance activity with a discussion of how movement and grace come from within and how we as individuals are much more than how we look on the outside.

In interviews, some girls had told us that they often danced in their rooms at night. Even though this could be a rigorous aerobic exercise, few girls recognized that this "qualified" as a physical activity. Their perception was that only organized sports or activities done at a gym constituted "exercise." Following the African-American dance segment, a funk aerobics class was held, which used popular music and current dance steps to make the exercise fun as well as vigorous. The funk aerobics class was extremely popular because it demonstrated that a favorite activity (dancing) could be a fun and effective way of exercising.

Two other sessions were developed to demonstrate strength-training exercises and teach girls proper alignment. The emphasis was on weight training that could be done at home using conventional five- and eight-pound barbells or milk jugs filled with water or sand. Girls had the opportunity to practice a variety of low-tech exercises that they could replicate in their homes. A follow-up session on strength training gave the girls another opportunity to work one-on-one with a fitness trainer who answered their questions, corrected their form, and gave them handouts to use for future reference. Girls were able to purchase barbells used during the sessions, which we had bought at a used sporting goods store for $5 a set. All sets were sold, suggesting that many girls had decided to begin, or at least experiment with, a home exercise program. Providing inexpensive options for exercise equipment (hand weights and milk jugs) also helped to dispel notions that exercise could only be done in a gym on expensive equipment.

◆   ◆   ◆

Girls' Response to the Intervention

Did the girls benefit from this intervention? An assessment of the project, conducted by an independent evaluator, found that girls valued the participatory nature of the curriculum because it provided an opportunity for open discussion. Because girls felt they were in a non-judgmental learning environment, they felt free to discuss sensitive issues like their appearance and feelings about their bodies. Although we knew girls frequently talked about such things with friends, discussing the same topics with a more diverse group (in terms of age, social group, and ethnicity) was insightful. Several girls acknowledged that through these group discussions they realized that other girls shared similar concerns. By recognizing that issues about the body were not simply individual problems, girls became less critical of themselves and more critical of media representations of beauty. As one ninth-grader commented, "It was the first time I realized that I didn't *have to* be this way. There are other ways to think about myself besides how much I weigh!" Many girls commented on how different the experience seemed "without boys being there," and how they felt more free to talk about issues that were important to them without worrying about being judged or teased by their male peers.

I wondered whether boys could also benefit from training in critical thinking about the media in a coed group environment. Shortly after our high school intervention was completed, I was invited to address a coed eighth-grade class on body image and the media. I approached this as a good opportunity to experiment. To my dismay, as boys viewed the slide show of representations of women in the media, they responded with catcalls. The ensuing discussion between girls and boys was hostile, with girls stating that boys had no right to comment on girls' bodies in the ways they typically did. Whereas the all-girl group in our intervention had moved to a discussion of strategies to deal with the comments of males toward girls' bodies, the coed group discussion did not. Rather than teaching girls to evaluate the media critically, the coed middle school experience brought up issues of boys' critically evaluating girls.

Although some of the topics discussed in the intervention were also covered in the regular school curriculum (for example, cooking and nutrition), girls noted that because they were not under pressure to take an exam, they enjoyed them more in the intervention. In addition, they felt more at ease asking what they felt might otherwise have been perceived as "stupid" questions.

Girls expressed a keen interest in developing an ongoing project similar to the one they had just completed. Although we recognized that our pilot project needed much refinement, we took these comments as an indication of girls' need and desire to have opportunities to discuss these topics in a non-threatening environment.

We asked the girls how a project like this could be structured in the school setting. After some discussion, they suggested that an after-school club would be a better format for a continued program than a project conducted in class. Rather than have the program run by high school teachers, girls said they would like to bring in outsiders to talk about specific topics of concern. They liked that our program had numerous presenters including fitness experts, nutritionists, a fashion person, and a media specialist, and they wanted to continue with that rather than have a single instructor who would function as an expert in all areas.

Their enthusiasm about the funk aerobics class led them to request an after-school aerobics class at their school, for which they were willing to pay a small fee. This idea was equally endorsed by girls from all ethnic groups represented in the intervention. This signaled to us both that girls wanted to be more physically active than they currently were but did not have available outlets to do so, and that they valued exercising in a supportive environment with other girls.

Girls also requested more information on the following topics: cooking for themselves; making healthful food choices in their everyday environment; understanding food labels; and working out with weights. Although these topics were already included in the curriculum, girls thought that additional sessions would help them further expand their knowledge and establish routines in these areas.

An important issue for those involved in the prevention of eating disorders and obesity has been the age at which programs should be introduced for maximum benefit. Some researchers have suggested that programs geared toward middle and high school students come too late in girls' development and that programs are best introduced in elementary school, followed by booster sessions in middle and high school.[11] Having worked with both middle- and high school–aged girls in our three intervention sites, we felt that our program was particularly relevant for high school girls because of their level of physical and social maturity. As one girl commented, "A couple of years ago before my body changed, I really wouldn't have learned much." High school girls told us that at their age, they were capable of implementing the food choices and other behavioral changes that were discussed in the sessions. In addition, they were able to identify with the images and themes introduced in the media-awareness slide show and were thus able to engage in a more insightful discussion of how such images affected them. Future interventions need to pay close attention to the changing developmental concerns of girls across adolescence.

◆   ◆   ◆

Involving the Household

We recognized that working with girls was not enough; we also needed to consider what could be done in the home. What messages needed to be introduced in the home and what modes of communication needed to be cultivated? Answering these questions requires a consideration of how parents respond to developmental changes in their daughters.

Physical changes that accompany puberty often serve as triggers for parental concerns about a daughter's physical appearance. Very few of the parents of girls in the study had told their daughters that the weight gain they were experiencing was a necessary component of physical maturation. Because they were troubled by their daughter's growth, some parents attempted to restrict her food intake at a time of increased caloric needs. A disturbing ramification of this finding is that parents who did not understand the normal process of puberty themselves were unable to explain it to their adolescent daughters. An understanding that weight gain and an accumulation of fat are "normal" at this time, and indeed an integral part of becoming a woman, might help girls and their parents respond to physical changes in a healthier, less judgmental manner.

Parents, particularly mothers, need to talk with their daughters about the physical changes the daughter is experiencing, as well as the sense of vulnerability that often accompanies these changes. In my prevention work in the fields of dieting and smoking, I have found that parents often avoid directly discussing sensitive or potentially volatile issues with their children, particularly if they feel the information has already been discussed at school. Some mothers have the impression that girls receive adequate information about developmental changes in school, which they do not. Although daughters could benefit from frank discussions about the biological realities of the female body, mothers feel they lack the facts to engage their daughters.

Many of these same mothers offer advice to their daughters about dieting. I have been careful not to lay blame on those mothers who feel they are "helping" their daughters at a time of vulnerability by teaching them how to diet. But I am concerned about the impact of both their dieting advice and practices that serve to normalize the daughter's dissatisfaction with her body, regardless of whether she actually begins to diet. Without education, this cycle of dissatisfaction with body shape and weight will more than likely be repeated once again as these daughters become mothers. Mothers need to instill pride in their daughters for who they are, not for who they may become. At this critical juncture in girls' lives, mothers may be in a unique position to mitigate or prevent negative outcomes for their daughters. At home, they can create a place where it is safe to speak, to listen, and to share in each other's experiences.

In addition to developmental changes occurring on the physical level, adolescence is also marked by changes in cognitive processes that influence how a girl feels about herself and others. As girls move from childhood to early adolescence, they become increasingly focused on physical appearance, bodily changes, and personal behavior. A girl may feel she is always on stage, with others monitoring and evaluating her appearance and activities. This adolescent egocentrism leads many girls to assume falsely that others are as preoccupied with their appearance as they themselves are. Their heightened self-absorption may contribute to the prevalence of their requests for parental input on how they look ("Do I look fat?"; "Does my butt look big today?"). Paradoxically, it may also account for the hypersensitivity that many girls expressed about the comments they did receive from family members and the lingering salience of the social commentary on their bodies. Adolescent egocentrism may also lead to a discounting of comments from parents—whether good or bad ("only what I think counts!"). For the adolescent, these newly acquired cognitive structures may be liabilities, inasmuch as they may be difficult to control or apply effectively.[12]

A better understanding of how their daughters' cognitive abilities are changing across adolescence may help parents tolerate what might appear at times to be irrational behavior or an overreaction to small comments. While it is often easy to criticize teens for being overly sensitive to others' comments, it is important for parents to remain open and non-judgmental when listening to their daughters' responses to experiences at home and at school. As children mature, they begin to pull away, spending more time with peers, increasingly asserting their own will at home. Parents may mistake this striving for independence as a sign that their daughter no longer wants to be close with them. Parents need to see their adolescent's growing independence in a more positive light, recognizing that adolescents learn healthy independence best in the context of a close parent-child relationship.[13]

◆   ◆   ◆

Eating with the Family

What is going on around the table? Traditionally, family meals were a time when parents and their children would come together to partake of food and review what had happened that day—a time for parents to "check in" with their children and learn what was going on at school. During the course of our research, we learned that this culturally valued ideal rarely matched the reality of girls' lives. As part of our survey we asked, "How many times do you eat dinner together with your family each week?" Responses were as follows: *every night* (sixty-three girls; 26 percent); *4–6 times per week* (forty-four girls; 19 percent); *2–3 times per week* (sixty-nine girls; 29 percent); and *less than once a week or never* (sixty-two girls; 26 percent). Moreover, we found a significant reduction in family meals by grade level. Whereas 35 percent of ninth-graders reported eating dinner with their families every night, only 16 percent of tenth-graders reported the same. By tenth grade, 41 percent of the girls in our sample were eating with their family just 2–3 times per week. From interviews, I knew that this had as much to do with a daughter's or other siblings' schedule as it did with the parents' schedule.

If girls were not eating with their families, what were they doing? Did someone prepare a meal for them that they were consuming later? Were they preparing their own meals and, if so, was this monitored? We asked girls, "How many times a week do you decide what you will eat for your own dinner?" Responses were as follows: *usually every night* (thirty-four girls; 17 percent); *4–6 times a weeks* (twenty-four girls; 12 percent); *2–3 times per week* (sixty girls; 30 percent); and *less than once a week or never* (eighty-seven girls; 41 percent). Collapsing these figures, we find that almost one-third of girls were deciding what they would eat for themselves most nights. The most common foods prepared by girls when they were on their own were sandwiches, macaroni and cheese, and spaghetti. Salads or vegetables were consumed by less than 5 percent of girls when they prepared their own dinner. One girl explained that her parents worked very late and were tired when they came home. "The last thing my mom wants to do is make dinner," she explained. "It's not like we go without dinner, it's like we really don't eat dinner together. We eat when we want, wherever we want."

One outcome of families' eating together less often is that it has become increasingly difficult for parents to monitor their daughters' food choices and consumption levels. One advantage of eating at a table is that parents at least have a sense of who's eating what. Without knowing what constitutes a meal, teens find it difficult to value or be able to create nutritious meals as they go off on their own. As one girl jokingly told me, "When I have a family, I'll just have to order out!"

These findings reaffirm the importance of teaching teens, many of whom are left in charge of themselves and their younger siblings at mealtime, how to make healthful food choices at home and in the supermarkets where they shop. Training youth to be educated and skillful consumers and teaching them how to read food labels and recognize deceptive advertising are important priorities for healthy survival.

Both parents and teens are inundated with information about what to eat, how to diet, and what products to purchase in order to enhance their appearance. At every turn, they are confronted with headlines and sound bites heralding the latest medical breakthrough on health and the latest weight-loss product. What is considered to be healthy one week is believed to place a person "at risk" the following week. Rather than feeling empowered by this multitude of ever-changing information, young girls especially can feel disempowered and vulnerable. In order to help teens negotiate their way through conflicting messages about diet and weight loss, educators and parents must work toward creating a critical social consciousness among youth, a consciousness that will allow them to move with grace and competency into the next millennium.

Appendix A: Research Strategies

T HIS BOOK is based on a three-year
longitudinal study of white and Latino
girls and a one-year cross-sectional study of African-American
girls. Both studies were funded by the National Institute of
Child Health and Human Development. The intervention described in Chapter 7 was funded by Canyon Ranch.

A Brief History of the Project

The Teen Lifestyle Project was conducted over a three-year period by a team of cultural and nutritional anthropologists con-
sisting of Mark Nichter, Cheryl Ritenbaugh, Nancy Vuckovic,
and myself. The genesis of the study was a year of discussion
and exploratory research on the relationship among girls' body
image, dieting, smoking, and advertising. Initially we conducted interviews and focus groups on these topics with college students at the University of Arizona and then applied for
funding to follow a cohort of girls from middle school to high
school. After obtaining funding, we spent the first year of the
study doing pilot ethnographic research with seventy-five
eighth-, tenth-, and twelfth-grade girls. The purpose of the pilot
year was to identify topics that would engage girls and determine how best to frame questions we wished to include in the
longitudinal study in a youth-friendly and developmentally
sensitive manner.

Participants

The longitudinal study began with a cohort of 240 girls (130 eighth-graders and 110 ninth-graders) recruited from two middle and two high schools in Tucson, Arizona. After we made presentations about the project in the classrooms, we distributed consent forms and a letter of endorsement from the school administration to all girls who expressed interest in participating. The consent form, which required the signature of the girl and one parent, explained the project in detail and stressed the confidentiality of all responses. There were no criteria for inclusion in the study.

The mean ages of the eighth- and ninth-graders who agreed to participate in the study were 13.6 (sd = .5) and 14.7 (sd = .5), respectively. The sample included Anglo (70 percent), Latino (10 percent), Asian-American (2 percent), Native-American (2 percent), and African-American (1 percent) girls. Fifteen percent of the girls did not provide information on ethnicity. There were no significant differences between the ethnic backgrounds of the girls who joined the study in year 1 and that of those who remained in the study at year 3. In the spring of year 3, 211 girls remained in the study, resulting in an overall attrition rate of 12 percent. This was extremely robust, given that one of the high schools we worked in had a very high transient population.

In terms of educational status of the parents, 8 percent of mothers had not graduated from high school; 23 percent were high school graduates; 16 percent had some college or vocational training; 23 percent had a four-year college degree; and 10 percent had education beyond college. Twenty percent of the daughters reported that they were unsure of their mother's education. As far as the fathers were concerned, 5 percent had not graduated from high school; 19 percent were high school graduates; 13 percent had some college or vocational training; 19 percent had a degree from a four-year college; and 17 percent had education beyond college. Twenty-seven percent of the daughters reported that they were unsure of their father's education. There were no significant differences between parental education for the girls who joined the study at year 1 and parental education of those who remained in the study at year 3.

With regard to family composition, 57 percent of the girls lived in intact two-parent families. Twenty-seven percent lived in households headed by a single parent; of these, 89 percent were headed by mothers. Sixteen percent of the girls lived with one biological parent and a stepparent. Recognizing the shifts in family structure that characterize many American families, we were careful during each interview to ask the girl who she was living with, and whether there had been a change in family composition in the past few months.

Data Collection

Annual data collected from each girl for three years included one in-depth interview, two telephone interviews, one survey, six days of food records, and measured height and weight. The in-depth interview, which lasted fifty minutes, took place at the school in a location that allowed for privacy. Each interview was tape-recorded. I conducted approximately 30 percent of the interviews each year, and six advanced female graduate students in anthropology whom I had trained in ethnographic interviewing techniques conducted the rest. Typically, new interviewers accompanied me on at least two occasions to observe how an interview was conducted before they began working alone. To maintain quality control, I periodically listened to interview tapes and provided feedback to interviewers about interviewing techniques and points to follow up and clarify with the girls.

School officials and teachers appreciated the importance of the study and were extremely cooperative in helping us schedule interviews with students. Our research team spent full days at the school, arriving for the first period and staying until the end of the school day. This allowed us to conduct multiple interviews and to spend time with girls during lunch periods, making observations of what they were eating, who they were hanging out with, and what was being discussed. It also allowed us to observe carefully what foods were available in the lunchroom and at what cost.

School-based ethnography is challenging because students are subject to a constant barrage of tests and pop quizzes, as well as to mood shifts predicated on an ever-changing and intense social scene. Our interview plans were often compromised by girls' absences, unannounced tests, and their emotional ups and downs. Above all else, we tried to be flexible and accommodate girls' schedules as much as possible.

When the weather permitted, we conducted the interviews outside school buildings on the periphery of the campus. Often, other students would come by and inquire as to what was going on. Girls would proudly point to the tape recorder and say, "I'm being interviewed for a study that I'm in at the University of Arizona. I've been in it since middle school!" Participation in the study was a point of pride for many girls.

Interviews were semi-structured and focused primarily on issues of body image, dieting, and smoking as they related to the individual girl, as well as her perceptions of teen-aged behavior in general. Although interviewers followed a question guide, we encouraged flexibility in the interviews. As researchers, we followed the girl's lead, listening to what she said as well as posing questions for which we wanted responses. When a girl was troubled or experiencing difficulties in school or at home, the interview topics of body image, dieting, and smoking appeared relatively unimportant in relation to her more pressing life issues. In such cases, we deviated from our interview topics and listened to her story. We then attempted to reschedule the planned interview for a later date.

Although many questions on the interview remained the same from year to year, we also included new questions to reflect the developmental age of the girls, and new directions of research that emerged during ongoing data analysis. In the second year of the study, I developed a series of questions on household communication and conflict and girls' perceptions of their parents' dieting and smoking behaviors. These questions were asked of all the girls and formed the basis for my doctoral dissertation on parents' influences on their daughters' body image, dieting, and smoking, discussed in Chapters 4 and 5.[1]

Each year, we also conducted approximately ten focus groups composed of five to six girls who were friends. Focus groups were facilitated by Nancy Vuckovic and myself and typically explored specific themes that had emerged in individual interviews. For example, to explore the topic of "watching what one ate" as a strategy for controlling or maintaining weight, we called together groups of friends who had identified in interviews that they practiced this behavior. Focus groups tended to be excellent forums for eliciting natural speech, as girls would challenge one another's responses and tease one another about what they said.

All semi-structured interviews were tape-recorded and later transcribed and entered into the Notebook software program to permit retrieval of quotations and enable thematic analysis across informants on particular topics. Ethnograph, another computer program for analyzing qualitative data, was utilized to identify particular themes across girls' narratives (such as descriptions of the perfect girl, eating in front of boys, fat talk, and so on). Although qualitative data-analysis programs were useful, I based my analysis more on my own reading and rereading of all the girls' transcripts, identifying patterns among girls and selecting those who were particularly insightful on specific topics. My continued reading of the transcripts allowed me to gain familiarity with individual girls' stories as well as to obtain a sense of important themes for this age cohort. Emergent themes were discussed at weekly meetings attended by our transdisciplinary team of anthropologists and nutritionists (both faculty and graduate students). By familiarizing myself with the transcripts, I was able to select the quotes that seemed to be most representative of the cohort. I also analyzed survey data to identify girls who fit particular criteria, such as those who had dieted with their mothers or had been told to lose weight by one of their parents. Once I identified these girls, I went back to their transcripts to consider differences and similarities in mother-daughter dieting pairs.

In Chapters 4 and 5, I sometimes refer to the quality of a girl's relationship with her mother or father as positive or stressful; these classifications were derived from a careful reading of the transcripts. A positive relationship was marked by open and free-flowing communication, shared activities, and a sense of mutual respect between the daughter and her parent(s) ("I can tell my mom everything I do"; "My mom's like my best friend"). Stressful relationships, by contrast, were marked by routine confrontations or avoidances between the daughter and her parent ("Me and my mom, we just argue, argue, argue"; "Whenever I talk with my mom, it just always ends up in a fight"). After selecting categories and representative quotes on the quality of relationships, I presented them to a co-researcher on the Teen Lifestyle Project. In order to determine inter-rater reliability, I asked her to classify a list of twenty quotes into the positive or stressful category. Inter-rater reliability was found to be 95 percent.

Body Image and Dieting Questions

The questions listed below are a sampling of those asked of each participant in the study that relate to the findings presented in this book. The actual questionnaire was much longer and included questions on smoking attitudes and behavior and a range of other issues.

Year One:

Where do you get ideas about how you want to look?
If you could change the way you looked, would you? How?
Would you like to lose or gain weight?
Would you say that you diet or just watch what you eat? How do you do that? How long have you been doing it?
Do you think it's easier to watch what you eat than to diet? What does it mean to you to be on a diet?
Does anyone in your family diet? Who? Do you think they need to? How do they diet?

Do you exercise with any of your family members? Who? What do you do together?

Do your parents encourage you to exercise?

Do you think a lot of girls in your class are concerned with their weight?

Do you hear a lot of girls saying "Oh, I'm so fat?" Do you say that too?

When do girls say it—is it more at school or at home?

Would girls say it in front of a guy?

What do you say when a friend says "I'm so fat?" Do you ever say "yeah, you are?"

Years Two and Three:

How has your body changed since last year? Have other people commented on it? Has it changed how you act or your style of dress?

Has your mother/father or other family member said anything about it? [If body has not changed, probe similar questions about how others have responded.].

Could you describe your parents? Do you take after either of them?

Do you think the way your mother looks affects your ideas about your body? How about the way your dad looks?

When you look at family members, do you get ideas about how you might look when you're older? Who? How?

Has anyone in your family told you to lose (or gain) weight? When? What did they say?

Last year, we heard girls say "I'm so fat" even when they weren't fat. Do you think that's more common among girls in middle school than among high school girls? Why?

Does your mother ever say "I'm so fat"? What do you say to her when she says that?

Have you ever dieted with anyone in your family? Who suggested it? How did that go?

Do you look at the nutritional labels on foods? What do you look for? Are there things you are trying to avoid?

Does that affect the choice of what you actually eat?

If you're going to a party, does that affect what you eat during the
    day?

Are there certain foods that you eat when you're alone that you
    wouldn't eat with friends?

Telephone Interviews and Surveys

Girls were also contacted at home by telephone in the fall and
spring of each year. These interviews lasted approximately
twenty to thirty minutes and included a range of questions
about their households, including who they currently lived
with; their parents' current employment status; how many
times they had prepared their own dinner in the past week;
how many times they had eaten fast food in the past week;
and so on. Questions also focused on parents' and siblings'
dieting behavior in the past two weeks, the methods utilized
during their diets, and the number of times various family
members had exercised in that time frame. Extensive questions were asked about the girl's own dieting behavior during
her most recent attempt to lose weight, including what
method(s) she had utilized, how long her diet had lasted, and
how successful she felt her diet had been. Girls were asked to
report on behaviors during the past two weeks in an attempt
to reduce recall bias, which may occur when informants are
asked questions about behaviors carried out over a longer period of time. In addition, telephone interviews allowed us to
document the extent to which girls' behaviors were changing
over time.

Each spring, a survey questionnaire of approximately 110
items was administered to all study participants in the schools.
Questions focused on attitudes and behaviors regarding body
image, dieting, and smoking and were derived from the literature and from information gained in ethnographic interviews.
While core survey questions remained consistent from year to
year, new questions were added as necessary. After the girls
completed the survey, height and weight measurements were
taken in the privacy of a separate room.

Dietary Data Collection and Coding

Food records were requested from each girl for a total of six days per year. Recording days were randomly assigned, blocked as two weekdays and one weekend day each semester.[2] During the first year of the study, project nutrition staff conducted food-record training sessions with all informants. Girls were taught how to estimate portion sizes and how to record in adequate detail all the foods they consumed. Twenty-four-hour food-intake record forms and return self-addressed envelopes were sent to each participant before each assigned date. Food-intake record forms included the date on which they should be kept, instruction reminders for noting what was eaten and when, and additional questions, including whether this was a day on which the girl had dieted to lose weight. Project staff called girls on the night of the assigned record to remind them to complete the form.

Every returned food record was reviewed by a nutrition staff member, and girls were called promptly to follow up on inadequate information. By the third year of the study, the food records were of consistently high quality. Participant observation within school lunchrooms and at local eating establishments confirmed reported food choices and portion sizes. In the third year of our study, each girl completed at least one food record, with an average of 3.23 per girl. This response is similar to response levels of adult women in national surveys. Because we wanted to keep the girls involved in all aspects of the study (particularly the interviews), we only attempted one make-up call for each missed day. Since completing the food records was the most burdensome part of the project for many girls, we decided not to bother them if they had not completed them.

Food records were coded and entered into the project database by trained staff using Nutritionist III v.6, utilizing all standard quality-control/quality-assurance protocols of the Nutrition Core of the Arizona Cancer Center. We developed an extensive database of foods eaten by these teens, including standard portion sizes and nutrients for all local fast foods and all foods prepared or served at the schools. Twenty-five percent of the records were entered twice for quality control.

Conducting Research with African-American Girls

In the third year of the longitudinal study, Sheila Parker received a minority supplement to the Teen Lifestyle Project to conduct a similar study of body image, dieting, and smoking among African-American girls. Weekly meetings of key project personnel ensured that a study protocol similar to the original one was followed with the fifty girls who consented to participate. African-American graduate students were hired to conduct the interviews and received training in ethnographic interviewing techniques. Interviews were conducted in schools and in community settings and were coordinated by Colette Sims. Although many of the questions asked of the African-American girls were the same as those used in our longitudinal study, we spent considerable time identifying questions that more clearly reflected African-American notions of beauty and style.

We administered two surveys to this population. The initial survey, which was the one we had developed for the longitudinal study, did not reveal pronounced differences in perceptions of beauty, body image, or weight management between white and African-American girls. These differences emerged only when a culturally sensitive survey was constructed following ethnographic research and administered by African-American researchers. We learned two lessons. First, survey instruments on body image and weight control designed largely for white populations mask important differences that exist between African-American and white girls. Second, performance on such surveys by African-American youth attending predominately white schools may reveal more about their bicultural competency than about the way they think about beauty and body image. Because questions in the initial survey did not address issues relevant to African-American girls, responses tended to conform to those expected of the dominant white population.

appendix a

Final Considerations

I have tried throughout this book to protect the confidentiality of the girls who were interviewed by changing their names, the intimate details of their lives, and other identifying characteristics that were revealed in their narratives. At the same time, I have sought to maintain the integrity of their stories. For the most part, the quotations are unaltered, except when I deemed it necessary to change a word or two to enhance readability.

One concluding point about conducting ethnographic interviews with teens should be noted. Some of the girls we interviewed did not yet have the cognitive capabilities or insight to reflect on their experiences either in their households or with their peers. Thus, these girls were limited in the explanations they could provide for their own behaviors as well as for those of their parents. By contrast, other girls were extremely articulate and demonstrated a cognitive maturity beyond their years. This speaks to the range of levels of articulation and maturity that exists among teens participating in an ethnographic study. Although this may be an issue in a sample of informants of any age, it is more marked during adolescence.

Appendix B: Tables

Table 1 Characteristics of girls using different weight-control strategies

Variable	Dieters	Watcher/Dieters	Watchers	Neither
Number (%)	19 (8%)	98 (42%)	84 (36%)	30 (13%)
Weight (lbs.) $x \pm$ SD	144.6 ± 21.4^{ab}	141.6 ± 25.9^{cd}	123.6 ± 18.5^{ac}	115.6 ± 18.8^{bd}
Body Mass Index $x \pm$ SD (kg/m^2)	24.4 ± 3.6^{ab}	23.2 ± 3.6^{cd}	20.8 ± 2.8^{ac}	19.6 ± 3.5^{bd}
Exercise $x \pm$ SE (times/week)	3.7 ± 0.5^{abc}	3.4 ± 0.3^{ad}	2.9 ± 0.3^{b}	1.9 ± 0.4^{cd}

abcd. Values in same row with same superscript are significantly different from each other at $p < 0.05$.

tables

Table 2 **Behaviors on dieting days versus non-dieting days**

	Dieters	Watcher/Dieters	Watchers	Neither
Total number of food records[a]	53	293	300	110
Dieting days (%)	29 (55%)	32 (12%)	4 (1%)	0
Energy intakes on dieting and non-dieting days (mean ± S.E.):				
Dieting days (Kcals)	1464 ± 152	1379 ± 193[b]	2272 ± 248	–
(*n*)	13	15	4	–
Non-dieting days (Kcals)	1664 ± 138	1842 ± 65[b]	1829 ± 60	1988 ± 102
(*n*)	9	86	82	30

a. Not all records had answers to the "dieting day" question. Only those records with an answer are included in this table. Twenty-one records had missing dieting day information, distributed as follows: 6 dieters, 6 watcher/dieters, 9 watchers, 0 neither.
b. Non-dieting days for watcher/dieters are significantly different from dieting days only at $p < 0.05$, by paired students' t-tests.

Table 3 Average nutrient intakes by behavioral category (mean ± S.E.)

Nutrients	Dieters	Watcher/Dieters	Watchers	Neither
	$n = 19$	$n = 98$	$n = 84$	$n = 30$
Energy (Kcals)	1533 ± 109.3[abc]	1806 ± 58.1[a]	1840 ± 54.3[b]	1993 ± 104.3[c]
Vitamin A (RE)	485.8 ± 113.9[abc]	677.8 ± 38.1[ad]	842.1 ± 50.4[bd]	717.2 ± 78.3[c]
% RDA	60.7 ± 14.2	84.7 ± 4.7	105.2 ± 6.3	89.7 ± 9.8
Vitamin E (TE)	5.52 ± 0.73[abc]	6.76 ± 0.34[a]	6.77 ± 0.31[b]	7.74 ± 0.46[c]
% RDA	69.0 ± 9.1	84.5 ± 4.3	84.6 ± 3.9	96.8 ± 5.8
Calcium (mg.)	629.3 ± 78.2[abc]	844.5 ± 40.5[a]	941.8 ± 41.7[b]	842.6 ± 70.2[c]
% RDA	52.4 ± 6.5	70.3 ± 3.4	78.5 ± 3.5	70.2 ± 5.9
Iron (mg.)	8.6 ± 0.8[abc]	11.0 ± 0.4[a]	11.5 ± 0.4[b]	12.8 ± 1.2[c]
% RDA	57.3 ± 5.3	73.3 ± 2.7	76.7 ± 2.7	85.3 ± 8.0

abcd. Values in same row with same superscript are significantly different from each other at $p < 0.05$, by student's t-test.

Table 4 **Cross-tabulation of body mass index (BMI) and whether the daughter had received a message to lose weight**

| | Received message to lose weight | | | |
| | Yes | | No | |
BMI	n	(%)	n	(%)
Low BMI[a]	—	—	57	100
Mid BMI[b]	33	27.3	88	72.7
High BMI[c]	31	51.7	29	48.3

Note: $n = 238$; $p < .001$
a. Low BMI (≤ 19.18); mean = 17.84
b. Mid BMI ($\geq 19.8 \leq 22.76$); mean = 20.83
c. High BMI (≥ 22.76); mean = 26.03

Table 5 Cross-tabulation of perceived frequency of dieting among mothers by perceived body shape

| Perception of mothers' body shape: | Perceived frequency of mothers' dieting | | | | | | Total |
| | Always/Often | | Sometimes | | Never | | |
	n	(%)	n	(%)	n	(%)	n
Too thin	–	–	3	50.0	3	50.0	6
Just about right	20	32.2	19	30.6	23	37.0	62
About the right weight, but out of shape	19	34.5	26	47.2	10	18.1	55
Kind of fat	33	37.9	43	49.4	11	12.6	87
Very fat	8	66.0	4	33.3	–	–	12

Note: Always/Often ($n = 80$); sometimes ($n = 95$); never ($n = 48$); Chi-square $= 24.81$; d.f. $= 8$; $p < .001$

Table 6 **Cross-tabulation of perceived frequency of dieting among fathers by perceived body shape**

| Perception of fathers' body shape: | Perceived frequency of fathers' dieting | | | | | | Total |
| | Always/Often | | Sometimes | | Never | | |
	n	(%)	n	(%)	n	(%)	n
Too thin	–	–	3	42.8	4	57.1	7
Just about right	5	3.0	27	34.1	47	59.4	79
About the right weight, but out of shape	4	4.0	16	39.0	21	51.2	41
Kind of fat	7	12.0	28	50.0	21	37.5	56
Very fat	5	33	4	26.6	6	40.0	15

Note: Always/Often ($n = 22$); sometimes ($n = 78$); never ($n = 100$); Chi-square = 15.96; d.f. = 8; $p < .04$

Table 7 Responses of African-American girls aged 14–18 ($n = 44$) to question, "How satisfied are you with your present weight?"

BMI	Very dissatisfied	Dissatisfied	Satisfied	Very satisfied	Total
Low[a]	25%	25%	25%	25%	10% ($n = 4$)
Mid[b]	4	11	71	14	72 ($n = 32$)
High[c]	14	57	29	–	18 ($n = 8$)

Note: BMI was calculated according to A. Must, C. Dallal, and W. Dietz, "Reference Data for Obesity," *American Journal of Clinical Nutrition,* 53 (1991): 839–846.

a. Low BMI indicates girls below the 15th percentile of BMI.
b. Mid BMI indicates girls above the 15th and below the 85th percentile.
c. High BMI indicates girls above the 85th percentile.

Table 8 Responses to survey question, "How often have you tried to lose weight during the past year?"

Sample	Haven't tried	1–2 times	4–6 times	Once a month or more	Always trying
White (*n* = 211)	39%	28%	14%	8%	11%
Black (*n* = 46)	48	30	7	4	11

Table 9 Responses to survey question, "Are you trying to change your weight now?"

	No	Yes, I'm trying to gain	Yes, I'm trying to lose
White (*n* = 211)	51%	5%	44%
Black (*n* = 46)	39	7	54

Table 10 Components of the high school–based intervention

Session 1 (Saturday)	Pre-test
	Food recalls
	African dance/creative movement
	Funk aerobics
	Media awareness
Session 2 (after school)	Review of food recalls
	Healthy food choices
	Food labels
Session 3 (after school)	Cooking demonstration
	Question and answer session
Session 4 (after school)	Weight training I
Session 5 (Saturday)	Goal setting for healthy lifestyles
	Weight training II
	Putting your best foot forward
	Post-test

Notes

INTRODUCTION: BARBIE AND BEYOND

1. J. Rodin, L. Silberstein, and R. Striegel-Moore, "Women and Weight: A Normative Discontent," in T. Sondregger, ed., *Nebraska Symposium on Motivation, vol. 32: Psychology and Gender* (Lincoln: University of Nebraska Press, 1985), pp. 267–308; J. C. Rosen and J. Gross, "Prevalence of Weight Reducing and Weight Gaining in Adolescent Girls and Boys," *Health Psychology*, 6 (1987): 131–147; American School Health Association, Association for the Advancement of Health Education and Society for Public Health Education, Inc., *The National Adolescent Student Health Survey: A Report on the Health of America's Youth* (Oakland, Calif.: Third Party Publishing, 1989); T. Walden, G. Brown, G. Foster, and J. Linowitz, "Salience of Weight-Related Worries in Adolescent Males and Females," *International Journal of Eating Disorders*, 10 (1991): 407–414; F. M. Berg, "Harmful Weight Loss Practices Are Widespread among Adolescents," *Obesity and Health* (July/August 1992): 69–72.

2. M. A. Males, *The Scapegoat Generation: America's War on Adolescents* (Monroe, Me.: Common Courage Press, 1996).

3. R. F. Hill and J. D. Fortenberry, "Adolescence as a Culture-Bound Syndrome," *Social Science and Medicine*, 35 (1992): 73–80.

4. N. Wolf, *The Beauty Myth: How Images of Beauty Are Used against Women* (New York: Anchor Books, 1991); S. Bordo, *Unbearable Weight: Feminism, Western Culture and the Body* (Berkeley, Calif.: University of California Press, 1993); S. Hesse-Biber, *Am I Thin Enough Yet: The Cult of Thinness and the Commercialization of Identity* (New York: Oxford University Press, 1996); B. Fredrickson and T. Roberts, "Objectification Theory: Toward Understanding Women's Lived Experiences and Mental Health Risks," *Psychology of Women Quarterly*, 21 (1997): 173–206.

5. S. Orbach, *Fat Is a Feminist Issue* (New York: Berkeley Books, 1982);

K. Chernin, *The Obsession: Reflections on the Tyranny of Slenderness* (New York: Harper and Row, 1981); K. Chernin, *The Hungry Self: Women, Eating and Identity* (New York: Harper and Row, 1985).

6. R. P. Troiano, K. M. Flegal, R. J. Kuczmarski, S. M. Campbell, and C. L. Johnson, "Overweight Prevalence and Trends for Children and Adolescents: The National Health and Nutrition Examination Surveys, 1963 to 1991," *Archives of Pediatric and Adolescent Medicine,* 149 (1995): 1085–1091; Centers for Disease Control and Prevention, "Update: Prevalence of Overweight among Children, Adolescents, and Adults–United States, 1988–1994," *Mortality and Morbidity Weekly Report,* 46 (1997): 199–202.

7. M. P. Levine and L. Smolak, "Media as a Context for the Development of Disordered Eating," in L. Smolak, M. P. Levine, and R. Striegel-Moore, eds., *The Developmental Psychopathology of Eating Disorders: Implications for Research, Prevention and Treatment* (Mahwah, N.J.: Lawrence Erlbaum Associates, 1996), pp. 235–257; K. Jasper, "Monitoring and Responding to Media Messages," *Eating Disorders,* 1 (1993): 109–114.

8. A. Gonzalez-Lavin and L. Smolak, "Relationships between Television and Eating Problems in Middle School Girls" (paper presented at the Meeting of the Society for Research in Child Development, Indianapolis, Ind., March 1995).

9. C. Downs and S. Harrison, "Embarrassing Age Spots or Just Plain Ugly? Physical Attractiveness Stereotyping as an Instrument of Sexism on American Television Commercials," *Sex Roles,* 13 (1985): 9–19.

10. Ibid.

11. E. D. Evans, J. Rutber, C. Sather, and C. Turner, "Content Analysis of Contemporary Teen Magazines for Adolescent Females," *Youth and Society,* 23:1 (1991): 99–120.

12. Levine and Smolak, "Media as a Context for the Development of Disordered Eating."

13. D. Stewart, "In the Cutthroat World of Toys, Child's Play Is Serious Business," *Smithsonian* (December 1989): 73–83.

14. Ibid. According to the marketing manager for Mattel, Barbie's manufacturer, Barbie's popularity is in part due to the fact that she is not locked into one role. Barbie doesn't have a personality; she takes on a different persona with each outfit she adorns. In this sense, Barbie is like a flawless model who is supposed to be polymorphous enough to take on any role.

15. Mark Nichter and Mimi Nichter, "Hype and Weight," *Medical Anthropology,* 13 (1991): 249–284.

16. R. Freedman, *Bodylove: Learning to Like Our Looks—and Ourselves* (New York: Harper and Row, 1989).

17. M. C. Martin and P. Kennedy, "Advertising and Social Comparison: Consequences for Female Preadolescents and Adolescents," *Psychology and Marketing,* 10:6 (1993): 513–530; P. N. Myers and F. A. Biocca, "The Elastic Body Image: The Effect of Television Advertising and Programming on Body Image Distortions in Young Women," *Journal of Communication,* 42 (1992): 108–133; M. L. Richins, "Social Comparison and the Idealized Images of Advertising," *Journal of Consumer Research,* 18 (1991): 71–83.

18. C. Lasch, *The Culture of Narcissism: American Life in an Age of Diminishing Expectations* (New York: Warner Books, 1979).

19. H. Stein, "Illness as Metaphor," *Journal of Psychological Anthropology,* 3 (1980): 33–38; H. Stein, "Neo-Darwinism and Survival through Fitness in Reagan's America," *Journal of Psychohistory,* 10 (1982): 163–187.

20. M. Douglas and A. Wildowski, *Risk and Culture* (Berkeley, Calif.: University of California Press, 1983).

21. D. Hebdige, *Subculture: The Meaning of Style* (London: Methuen, 1979); A. McRobbie, "Second-Hand Dresses and the Role of the Ragmarket," in A. McRobbie, ed., *Zoot Suits and Second-Hand Dresses* (London: Macmillan, 1989); P. Willis, *Learning to Labor: How Working Class Kids Get Working Class Jobs* (New York: Columbia University Press, 1981).

22. Mimi Nichter, Mark Nichter, N. Vuckovic, G. Quintero, and C. Ritenbaugh, "Smoking Experimentation and Initiation among Adolescent Girls: Qualitative and Quantitative Findings," *Tobacco Control,* 6 (1997): 285–295.

1. In the Presence of the Perfect Girl

1. C. Gilligan, "Women's Psychological Development: Implications for Psychotherapy," in C. Gilligan, A. G. Rogers, and D. L. Tolman, eds., *Women, Girls and Psychotherapy: Reframing Resistance* (Binghamton, N.Y.: Harrington Park Press, 1991), pp. 5–32; L. Brown, "Narratives of Relationship: The Development of a Care Voice in Girls Ages Seven to Sixteen" (Ph.D. diss., Harvard University, 1989).

2. L. Brown, *Raising Their Voices: The Politics of Girls' Anger* (Cambridge, Mass.: Harvard University Press, 1998), p. 195.

3. D. Eder, with C. C. Evans and S. Parker, *School Talk: Gender and Adolescent Culture* (New Brunswick, N.J.: Rutgers University Press, 1995), p. 114.

4. P. Eckert, "Cooperative Competition in Adolescent 'Girl Talk,'" *Discourse Processes,* 13 (1990): 91–122.

5. Eder, Evans, and Parker, *School Talk,* p. 118.

6. A. Fallon and P. Rozin, "Sex Differences in Perceptions of Desirable Body Shape," *Journal of Abnormal Psychology,* 1 (1985): 102–105; J. Eisele, D. Hertsgaard, and H. Light, "Factors Related to Eating Disorders in Young Adolescent Girls," *Adolescence,* 21 (1986): 82–87; H. Katchadourian, *The Biology of Adolescence* (San Francisco: Freeman Press, 1977).

7. W. Feldman, E. Feldman, and J. Goodman, "Culture versus Biology: Children's Attitudes toward Thinness and Fatness," *Pediatrics,* 2 (1988): 190–194.

8. W. Kinston, L. Miller, P. Loader, and O. Wolff, "Revealing Sex Differences in Childhood Obesity by Using a Family Systems Approach," *Family Systems Medicine,* 8 (1990): 371–386; B. Mendelson and D. White, "Development of Self-Body-Esteem in Overweight Youngsters," *Developmental Psychology,* 21 (1985): 90–96.

9. American Association of University Women, *Shortchanging Girls, Shortchanging America: Executive Summary* (Washington, D.C.: American Association of University Women, 1991).

10. J. Brooks-Gunn, "Pubertal Processes and Girls' Psychological Adaptation," in R. Lerner and T. Foch, eds., *Biological-Psychosocial Interactions in Early Adolescence* (Hillsdale, N.J.: Erlbaum, 1987), pp. 123–153; E. Grief and K. Ulman, "The Psychological Impact of Menarche on Early Adolescent Females: A Review of the Literature," *Child Development,* 53 (1982): 1413–1430.

11. American Association of University Women, *Shortchanging Girls, Shortchanging America.*

12. P. Orenstein, *Schoolgirls: Young Women, Self-Esteem, and the Confidence Gap* (New York: Doubleday, 1994).

13. C. P. Herman and J. Polivy, "Restrained Eating," in J. Stunkard, ed., *Obesity* (Philadelphia: W. B. Saunders, 1980), pp. 208–275.

14. J. Rodin, L. R. Silberstein, and R. H. Striegel-Moore, "Women and Weight: A Normative Discontent," in T. B. Sonderegger, ed., *Nebraska Symposium on Motivation, vol. 32: Psychology and Gender* (Lincoln, Nebr.: University of Nebraska Press, 1985), pp. 267–307.

15. R. M. Lerner, J. B. Orlos, and J. R. Knapp, "Physical Attractiveness, Physical Effectiveness and Self-Concept in Late Adolescents," *Adolescence,* 11 (1976): 313–326; B. Frederickson and T. A. Roberts, "Objectification Theory: Toward Understanding Women's Lived Experiences and Mental Health Risks," *Psychology of Women Quarterly,* 21 (1997): 173–206.

16. Rodin, Silberstein, and Striegel-Moore, "Women and Weight."

17. D. Holland and D. Skinner, "Prestige and Intimacy: The Cultural Models Behind American's Talk about Gender Types," in D. Holland and N. Quinn, eds., *Cultural Models in Language and Thought* (Cambridge: Cambridge University Press, 1987), pp. 78–111.

18. P. R. Costanzo, "External Socialization and the Development of Adaptive Individuation and Social Connection," in D. N. Ruble, P. R. Costanzo, and M. E. Oliveri, eds., *The Social Psychology of Mental Health* (New York: Guilford, 1992), pp. 55–80.

19. These rules are also mirrored in popular advertisements. A recent ad for Doritos features three teen-aged girls, happily munching on a large bag of chips. The copy reads: "Allowed to be Loud," which refers as much to the chips' "super loud, break-out-from-the-crowd taste" as it does to girls breaking out of the expected mold and making noise. The loudest taste on earth is good for girls because the chips are made with Olean, so they have one-third fewer calories and only one gram of fat!

20. Orenstein, *Schoolgirls*.

21. Eder, Evans, and Parker, *School Talk*.

22. Ibid., p. 108.

23. R. Freedman, "Reflections on Beauty as It Relates to Health in Adolescent Females," *Women and Health,* 9:2–3 (1984): 29–45.

24. Eder, Evans, and Parker, *School Talk*.

25. E. Kaschak, *Engendered Lives: A New Psychology of Women's Lives* (New York: Basic Books, 1992); S. L. Bartky, *Femininity and Domination: Studies in the Phenomenology of Oppression* (New York: Routledge, 1990); S. Bordo, *Unbearable Weight: Feminism, Western Culture and the Body* (Berkeley, Calif.: University of California Press, 1993); Frederickson and Roberts, "Objectification Theory."

26. R. Coward, *Female Desires: How They Are Sought, Bought, and Packaged* (New York: Grove Press, 1985), p. 229.

27. S. Basow, *Sex-Role Stereotypes: Traditions and Alternatives* (Monterey, Calif.: Brooks/Cole Publishers, 1980).

28. S. W. Kirkpatrick and D. M. Sanders, "Body Image Stereotypes: A Developmental Comparison," *Journal of Genetic Psychology,* 132 (1978): 87–95.

29. S. A. Richardson, A. H. Hastorf, N. Goodman, and S. M. Dornbusch, "Cultural Uniformity in Reaction to Physical Disabilities," *American Sociological Review,* 26 (1961): 241–247.

30. L. Steineger, "The Relationship between Body-Mass Index and Academic Achievement in Third Grade White Females" (M.S. thesis, University of Arizona, 1997).

31. Empirical research on adult women demonstrates that a woman's body size affects her life experiences. For example, obesity has been found to negatively affect women's but not men's social mobility, with obese women showing lower educational and economic attainments than their parents. Job discrimination and hostile work environments are more frequently reported by overweight women than by overweight men. See J. T. Snow and M. B. Harris, "Maintenance of Weight Loss: Demographic, Behavioral and Attitudinal Correlates," *Journal of Obesity and Weight Regulation*, 4 (1985): 234–255. For a broader discussion see Fredrickson and Roberts, "Objectification Theory."

32. D. Neumark-Sztainer, M. Story, and L. Faibisch, "Perceived Stigmatization among Overweight African-American and Caucasian Adolescent Girls," *Journal of Adolescent Health*, 23 (1998): 264–270.

33. E. Rothblum, "The Stigma of Women's Weight: Social and Economic Realities," *Feminism and Psychology*, 2:1 (1992): 61–73.

34. R. Crawford, "A Cultural Account of 'Health': Control, Release, and the 'Social Body,'" in J. McKinley, ed., *Issues in the Political Economy of Health Care* (London: Tavistock, 1984), pp. 60–101.

35. For a more in-depth discussion of how dissatisfaction fuels capitalism, see Mark Nichter and Mimi Nichter, "Hype and Weight," *Medical Anthropology*, 13 (1991): 249–284. See also H. Schwartz, *Never Satisfied: A Cultural History of Diets, Fantasies and Fat* (New York: The Free Press, 1986).

2. Fat Talk

1. H. Sullivan, *The Interpersonal Theory of Psychiatry* (New York: W. W. Norton, 1953).

2. C. Steiner-Adair, "The Body Politic: Normal Female Adolescent Development and the Development of Eating Disorders," in C. Gilligan, N. P. Lyons, and T. J. Hammer, eds., *Making Connections: The Relational Worlds of Adolescent Girls at Emma Willard School* (Cambridge, Mass.: Harvard University Press, 1990), pp. 162–188.

3. M. H. Richards and R. Larson, "The Life Space and Socialization of the Self: Sex Differences in the Young Adolescent," *Journal of Youth and Adolescence*, 18:6 (1989): 617–626; E. Duckett, M. Raffaeli, and M. Richards, "'Taking Care': Maintaining the Self and the Home in Early Adolescence," *Journal of Youth and Adolescence*, 18:6 (1989): 549–564; C. M. Leone and M. H. Richards, "Classwork and Homework in Early Adolescence: The Ecology of Achievement," *Journal of Youth and Adolescence*, 18:6 (1989): 531–548.

4. R. Larson and M. H. Richards, *Divergent Realities: The Emotional Lives of Mothers, Fathers, and Adolescents* (New York: Basic Books, 1994). See also D. Buhrmester and W. Furman, "The Development of Companionship and Intimacy," *Child Development*, 58 (1987): 1101–1113; R. C. Savin-Williams and T. Berndt, "Friendship and Peer Relations," in S. Feldman and G. Elliot, eds., *At the Threshold: The Developing Adolescent* (Cambridge, Mass.: Harvard University Press, 1990), pp. 277–309.

5. N. Chowdorow, *The Reproduction of Mothering* (Berkeley: University of California Press, 1978); C. Gilligan, *In a Different Voice: Psychological Theory and Women's Development* (Cambridge, Mass.: Harvard University Press, 1982).

6. Z. Rubin, *Children's Friendships* (Cambridge, Mass.: Harvard University Press, 1980); J. Youniss, *Parents and Peers in Social Development* (Chicago: University of Chicago Press, 1980).

7. D. Tannen, *You Just Don't Understand: Women and Men in Conversation* (New York: Ballentine Books, 1990).

8. D. Elkind, "Egocentrism in Adolescents," *Child Development*, 38 (1967): 1025–1034.

9. Ibid., p. 153.

10. R. Pesce and C. Harding, "Imaginary Audience Behavior and Its Relationship to Operational Thought and Social Experience," *Journal of Early Adolescence*, 6 (1986): 83–94.

11. B. B. Brown, S. A. Eicher, and S. Petrie, "The Importance of Peer Group ("Crowd") Affiliation in Adolescence," *Journal of Adolescence*, 9 (1986): 73–96; D. C. Dunphy, "Peer Group Socialization," in F. J. Hunt, ed., *Socialization in Australia* (Sydney: Angus and Robertson, 1972); D. Eder, with C. Evans and S. Parker, *School Talk: Gender and Adolescent Culture* (New Brunswick, N.J.: Rutgers University Press, 1995).

12. C. Hope, "American Beauty Rituals," in R. B. Browne, ed., *Rituals and Ceremonies in Popular Culture* (Bowling Green, Ohio: Bowling Green University Press, 1980), pp. 226–237.

13. R. Barthes, trans. A. Davis, *Mythologies* (London: Paladin, 1973).

14. S. Ogaitis, T. T. Chen, and G. P. Cernada, "Eating Attitudes, Dieting and Bulimia among Junior High School Students," *International Quarterly of Community Health Education*, 9:1 (1988). 51–61.

15. One could question whether commenting on another woman's weight loss is really a compliment, or whether it simply reinforces a self-definition that ultimately demeans and objectifies women.

16. Mimi Nichter, Mark Nichter, N. Vuckovic, G. Quintero, and C. Ritenbaugh, "Social Contexts of Smoking among Adolescent Fe-

males: Qualitative and Quantitative Findings," *Tobacco Control* (January 1997): 285–295.

17. M. H. Goodwin, *He-Said-She-Said: Talk as Social Organization among Black Children* (Bloomington, Ind.: Indiana University Press, 1990); M. H. Goodwin and C. Goodwin, "Children's Arguing," in S. U. Phillips, S. Steele, and C. Tanz, eds., *Language, Gender and Sex in Comparative Perspective* (Cambridge: Cambridge University Press, 1987), pp. 200–248.

18. D. Tannen, *Talking 9 to 5—Women and Men in the Workplace: Language, Sex and Power* (New York: Avon Books, 1995). See also Tannen, *You Just Don't Understand.*

19. W. W. Hartup, "Adolescents and Their Friends," in B. Laursen, ed., *New Directions for Child Development: Close Friendships in Adolescence* (San Francisco: Jossey-Bass, 1993), pp. 3–22; B. B. Brown, "Peer Groups and Peer Cultures," in S. Feldman and G. Elliot, eds., *At the Threshold,* pp. 171–196.

20. P. Mosbach and H. Leventhal, "Peer Group Identification and Smoking: Implications for Intervention," *Journal of Abnormal Psychology,* 97 (1988): 238–245; S. Sussman, C. W. Dent, A. W. Stacy, and C. Burciaga, "Peer Group Association and Adolescent Tobacco Use," *Journal of Abnormal Psychology,* 99 (1990): 349–352; K. A. Urberg, "Locus of Peer Influence: Social Crowd and Best Friend," *Journal of Youth and Adolescence,* 21 (1992): 439–450; M. M. Dolcini and N. E. Adler, "Perceived Competencies, Peer Group Affiliation, and Risk Behavior among Early Adolescents," *Health Psychology,* 13 (1994): 496–506; W. R. Downs and S. R. Rose, "The Relationship of Adolescent Peer Groups to the Incidence of Psychosocial Problems," *Adolescence,* 26 (1991): 473–491; B. B. Brown, S. D. Lamborn, N. S. Mounts, and L. Steinberg, "Parenting Practices and Peer Group Affiliation in Adolescence," *Child Development,* 64 (1993): 467–482; P. Eckert, *Jocks and Burnouts: Social Categories and Identity in the High School* (New York: Teachers College Press, 1989); B. B. Brown and M. J. Lohr, "Peer Group Affiliation and Adolescent Self-Esteem: An Integration of Ego-Identity and Symbolic Interaction Theories," *Journal of Personal and Social Psychology,* 52 (1987): 47–55; D. Eder, "The Cycle of Popularity: Interpersonal Relations among Female Adolescents," *Sociology of Education,* 58 (1985): 154–165.

21. Teens at the margin refashion their world and engage in the carnivalesque, a term employed by Bakhtin to connote a world outside of and in opposition to the disciplined social order. M. Bakhtin, *Rabelais and His World* (Cambridge, Mass.: Massachusetts Institute of Technology Press, 1968).

22. A study of gender and ideology among Latino gang girls, cholas, in California found that the body ideal of these girls was radically opposed to what is valued within Euro-American culture. The girls' status within their group was in part based on their physical power—their ability to beat up others. Cholas admired a large zaftig body—a body size that connoted power and strength. These girls were often athletes and were considered powerful, beautiful, and sexy. See N. Mendoza-Denton, "'Muy Macha': Gender and Ideology in Gang-Girls' Discourse about Makeup," *Ethos,* 61:1-2 (1996): 47-63.

23. J. Rodin, L. Silberstein, and R. Striegel-Moore, "Women and Weight: A Normative Discontent," in T. Donderegger, ed., *Nebraska Symposium on Motivation, vol. 32: Psychology and Gender* (Lincoln, Neb.: University of Nebraska Press, 1985).

3. Are Girls Really Dieting?

1. Centers for Disease Control and Prevention, "Youth Risk Behavior Surveillance—United States, 1995," *CDC Surveillance Summaries,* September 27, 1996, *Mortality and Morbidity Weekly* 45 (no. SS-4).

2. D. M. Kagan and R. L. Squires, "Dieting, Compulsive Eating, and Feelings of Failure among Adolescents," *International Journal of Eating Disorders,* 3 (1983): 15-26; J. C. Rosen and J. Gross, "Prevalence of Weight Reducing and Weight Gaining in Adolescent Girls and Boys," *Health Psychology,* 6 (1987): 131-147; E. Koff and J. Rierdan, "Perceptions of Weight and Attitudes toward Eating in Early Adolescent Girls," *Journal of Adolescent Health,* 12 (1991): 307-312; F. M. Berg, "Harmful Weight Loss Practices Are Widespread among Adolescents," *Obesity and Health* (July/August 1992): 69-72; S. A. French and R. W. Jeffrey, "The Consequences of Dieting to Lose Weight: Effects on Physical and Mental Health," *Health Psychology,* 13 (1994): 195-212; M. Story, S. A. French, M. D. Resnick, and R. W. Blum, "Ethnic/Racial and Socioeconomic Differences in Dieting Behaviors and Body Image Perceptions in Adolescents," *International Journal of Eating Disorders,* 18 (1995): 173-179.

3. D. M. Kagan and R. L. Squires, "Eating Disorders among Adolescents: Patterns and Prevalence," *Adolescence,* 14 (1984): 15-29; J. T. Kelly and S. E. Patten, "Adolescent Behaviors and Attitudes toward Weight and Eating," in J. E. Mitchell, ed., *Anorexia Nervosa and Bulimia: Diagnosis and Treatment* (Minneapolis: University of Minnesota Press, 1985), pp. 191-204; R. H. Streigel-Moore, L. R. Silberstein,

and J. Rodin, "Toward an Understanding of the Risk Factors of Bulimia," *American Psychologist,* 41 (1986): 246–263.

4. H. Schuman and G. Kalton, "Survey Methods," in G. Lindzey and E. Aronson, eds., *Handbook of Social Psychology,* vol. 1, 3rd ed. (New York: Random House, 1985), pp. 635–698; J. C. Rosen and D. Poplawski, "The Validity of Self-Reported Weight Loss and Weight-Gain Efforts in Adolescents," *International Journal of Eating Disorders,* 6 (1987): 99–111; S. A. French and R. W. Jeffrey, "Consequences of Dieting to Lose Weight: Effects on Physical and Mental Health," *Health Psychology,* 13:3 (1994): 195–212. French and Jeffrey note that estimates of dieting prevalence vary widely depending on the specificity of the questions asked. With regard to adults, 40 percent of women and 23 percent of men state that they are currently *trying* to lose weight. However, when asked if they are currently *dieting* to lose weight, only 26 percent of women and 14 percent of men report that they are doing so. Thus, within the dieting literature, subtle differences in the wording of questionnaires have revealed significantly different pictures of adult weight-related behaviors.

5. C. N. Meredith and J. T. Dwyer, "Nutrition and Exercise: Effects on Adolescent Health," *Annual Review of Public Health,* 12 (1991): 309–333; G. Frank, T. A. Nicklas, and L. S. Webber, "A Food Frequency Questionnaire for Adolescents: Defining Eating Patterns," *Journal of the American Dietetic Association,* 92 (1992): 313–318.

6. C. Ritenbaugh, M. Aickin, Mimi Nichter, and Mark Nichter, "Nutrient Intakes of Adolescent Females" (unpublished manuscript, 1998).

7. The survey confirms that a majority of Americans now recognize that dieting is a quick-fix, short-term solution to a weight problem and is largely ineffective. More people recognize that they need to be "controllers" of their weight (what I describe in this chapter as "watchers"), rather than dieters. *Calorie Control Commentary,* 20:1 (1998).

8. Youth Risk Behavior Survey, "Body Weight Perceptions and Selected Weight-Management Goals and Practices of High School Students—United States, 1990," *Morbidity and Mortality Weekly,* 40 (1991): 741–750.

9. L. Chassin, C. Presson, S. Sherman, E. Corty, and R. Olshavsky, "Predicting the Onset of Cigarette Smoking in Adolescents: A Longitudinal Study," *Journal of Applied Social Psychology,* 14 (1984): 224–243; L. Chassin, C. Presson, and S. Sherman, "Social Psychological Contributions to the Understanding and Prevention of Adolescent Cigarette

Smoking," *Personality and Social Psychology Bulletin* (March 1990): 133–151.

10. M. Nichter, A. Trowbridge, and D. Van Sickle, "Evaluation Report of the School-Based Tobacco Prevention Education Program in Pima County, Arizona" (unpublished manuscript, 1997).

11. This experimentation can also be found in dieting responses collected from surveys. Looking at data across three years of the Teen Lifestyle Project, I noted a fluctuation in reported ever-use of vomiting from year 1 (6.8 percent) to year 2 (2.3 percent) to year 3 (9 percent). Similarly, ever-use of diet pills fluctuated from year 1 (6.1 percent) to year 2 (5.3 percent) to year 3 (7.6 percent). This may represent experimentation on the part of these girls.

12. School lunches are often high in fat and sodium. One study of the nutritional content of school lunches found that the mean percent of total fat was 41.3 percent, and the mean percent of saturated fat was 16.1 percent. It is recommended that Americans receive no more than 30 percent of their daily calories from total fat and 10 percent of their calories from saturated fat. See B. G. Simmons-Morton, G. Parcel, B. Tom, R. Forthofer, and N. O'Hara, "Promoting Physical Activity and a Healthful Diet among Children: Results of a School Based Intervention Study," *American Journal of Public Health*, 81:8 (1991): 968–990. For recommended dietary intake, see *The Surgeon General's Report on Nutrition and Health* (Washington, D.C.: U.S. Department of Health and Human Services, 1989), publication 88-50201. For information on lunches brought from home, see L. R. Jones, J. F. Sallis, T. Conway, S. Marshall, and R. Pelletier, "Ethnic and Gender Differences in Request for and Use of Low/Non-Fat Foods in Bag Lunches," *Journal of School Health*, 69:8 (1999): 332–336.

13. R. C. Klesges, A. W. Meyers, L. M. Klesges, and M. E. LaVasque, "Smoking, Body Weight and their Effects on Smoking Behavior: A Comprehensive Review of the Literature," *Psychology Bulletin*, 106 (1989): 204–230; S. A. French, C. L. Perry, G. R. Leon, and J. A. Fulkerson, "Weight Concerns, Dieting Behavior and Smoking Initiation among Adolescents: A Prospective Study," *American Journal of Public Health*, 84 (1994): 1818–1820; S. A. French and R. W. Jeffrey, "Weight Concerns and Smoking: A Literature Review," *Annals of Behavioral Medicine*, 17 (1995): 234–244; S. A. French and C. L. Perry, "Smoking among Adolescent Girls: Prevalence and Etiology," *Journal of the American Medical Women's Association*, 51:1–2 (1996): 25–28.

14. Mimi Nichter, Mark Nichter, N. Vuckovic, G. Quintero, and C.

Ritenbaugh, "Smoking Experimentation and Initiation among Adolescent Girls: Qualitative and Quantitative Findings," *Tobacco Control*, 6:4 (1997): 285–296.

15. A. F. Subar, L. C. Harlan, and M. E. Mattson, "Food and Nutrient Intake Differences between Smokers and Non-smokers in the U.S.," *American Journal of Public Health*, 80:11 (1990): 1322–1329; N. E. Grunberg and D. E. Morse, "Cigarette Smoking and Food Consumption in the United States," *Journal of Applied Social Psychology*, 14:3 (1984): 310–317.

16. S. Adrian, "Rubbers and Romance: Heterosexual Condom Use in the U.S." (M.A. thesis, Department of Anthropology, University of Arizona, 1997).

17. One notable exception was reported in a recent article in the newsletter *Calorie Control*. On the basis of a teen survey, the newsletter reported that teens are less likely to be on a diet than are adults (23 percent vs. 27 percent), but that "teens are more likely to say that they are making a serious effort to control their weight (43 percent vs. 39 percent) even though they are not dieting. *Calorie Control Commentary*, 20:2 (1998).

18. The theme of striking a balance in one's life with relation to food was captured in a recent advertisement in a fitness magazine for Avia shoes. A highly toned woman pictured without a head (she is shown from just below her neck to above her knees) is clothed in a revealing running outfit which shows that she is a serious athlete. The caption reads, "I run because it's fun and for chocolate chip ice cream." The subtext is that her exercise regime is a tradeoff that permits her to eat what might otherwise be forbidden foods.

19. V. O'Connell, "Nabisco Portrays Cookies as Boost to Women's Sense of Self-Esteem," *Wall Street Journal*, July 10, 1998, p. B7.

20. J. T. Heimbach, "Cardiovascular Disease and Diet: The Public View," *Public Health Report*, 100 (1985): 5; J. T. Heimbach, "The Growing Impact of Sodium Labeling of Foods," *Food Technology*, 40:12 (1986): 102.

Dietary fat intake by Americans, which had been on a downward slide for twenty-five years, turned upward again from 1990 to 1995, according to a recent Department of Agriculture report. One reason for this change is that Americans are eating more of everything. The increase in calories comes largely from increased carbohydrate consumption. See Center for Nutrition Policy and Promotion, U.S. Department of Agriculture, "Is Total Fat Consumption Really Decreasing?" *Nutrition Insights* (April 1998).

21. S. Harris and S. Welsh, "How Well Are Our Food Choices Meeting Our Nutrition Needs?" *Nutrition Today,* 24 (1989): 20–28.

22. Four girls who "never" watched and "sometimes" dieted were excluded from further analysis because the group was too small to analyze separately and too conceptually distinct to be joined with the other category.

23. BMI is the current standard definition used by most researchers to define obesity. It was first established by the second National Health and Nutrition Examination Survey (NHANES II), a large population-based study sponsored by the U.S. Government during the years 1976–1980. BMI is derived by a formula of body weight and height (kg/m²). Recommended BMIs are generally within the 20–26 range for adult men and women. For a more complete description see G. A. Gaesser, *Big Fat Lies* (New York: Fawcett Columbine, 1996).

24. Gaesser, *Big Fat Lies,* p. 173. Whatever the case, yo-yo dieting has become a way of life for a great many women, a pattern triggered by personal markers of "goodness and badness," defined in relation to pounds, inches, or dress size, that take on surplus meaning. One marker is often an ideal that one dreams of obtaining or strives to obtain for short periods, a second lies in the realm of the acceptable, while the third is a marker that one is out of control. Depending on the person, the range between these markers may be narrow or broad.

25. E. Levine and J. F. Guthrie, "Nutrient Intakes and Eating Patterns of Teenagers," *Family Economics and Nutrition Review,* 10:3 (1997): 20–35; N. Bull, "Dietary Habits, Food Consumption, and Nutrient intake during Adolescence," *Journal of Adolescent Health,* 13 (1992): 384–388.

26. Mark Nichter and Mimi Nichter, "Hype and Weight," *Medical Anthropology,* 13 (1991): 249–284; Mimi Nichter and N. Vuckovic, "Fat Talk: Body Image among Adolescent Females," in N. Sault, ed., *Many Mirrors: Body Image and Social Relations* (New Brunswick, N.J.: Rutgers University Press, 1994), pp. 109–131.

27. A. Antonovsky, *Health, Stress and Coping* (San Francisco: Jossey-Bass Publishers, 1979); A. Antonovsky, "The Sense of Coherence as a Determinant of Health," in N. E. Miller, J. D. Matarazzo, S. M. Weiss, and A. J. Herd, eds., *Behavioral Health: A Handbook of Health Enhancement and Disease Prevention* (New York: J. W. Wiley and Sons, 1984), pp. 114–127.

28. Nichter and Nichter, "Hype and Weight"; C. Ritenbaugh, "Obesity

as a Culture Bound Syndrome," *Culture, Medicine and Psychiatry,* 6 (1982): 347-361.

4. WHO WILL I LOOK LIKE?

1. J. Brooks-Gunn and A. Petersen, *Girls at Puberty: Biological and Psychosocial Perspectives* (New York: Plenum Press, 1983).

2. R. Larson and M. H. Richards, *Divergent Realities: The Emotional Lives of Mothers, Fathers, and Adolescents* (New York: Basic Books, 1994).

3. J. Youniss and J. Smollar, *Adolescents' Relations with Mothers, Fathers, and Friends* (Chicago: University of Chicago Press, 1985).

4. One reason for the dearth of research on the topic is that it is difficult to gain permission from public schools to conduct research on puberty and youths' responses to their physical changes. See J. Brooks-Gunn and E. O. Reiter, "The Role of Pubertal Processes," in S. Feldman and G. R. Elliott, eds., *At the Threshold: The Developing Adolescent* (Cambridge, Mass.: Harvard University Press, 1990).

5. D. N. Ruble and Jeanne Brooks-Gunn, "The Experience of Menarche," *Child Development,* 53 (1982): 1557-1566. See also J. Brooks-Gunn and M. Zahaykevich, "Parent-Daughter Relationships in Early Adolescence: A Developmental Perspective," in K. Kreppner and R. Lerner, eds., *Family Systems and Life Span Development* (Hilldale, N.J.: Lawrence Erlbaum Associates, 1989), pp. 223-246.

6. Interestingly, boys may be even less prepared for puberty than girls are. In a small study of eighth- and ninth-grade boys, less than 15 percent had discussed ejaculation with anyone prior to its occurrence. A. Gaddis and J. Brooks-Gunn, "The Male Experience of Pubertal Change," *Journal of Youth and Adolescence,* 14:1 (1985): 61-69.

7. Judy Blume's novel *Are You There, God? It's Me, Margaret* (New York: Dell, 1970), a coming-of-age classic with menarche as its central focus, has enjoyed enormous popularity. By 1996, the book had sold more than six million copies.

8. R. Freedman, *Bodylove: Learning to Like Our Looks and Ourselves* (New York: HarperCollins, 1990), p. 56.

9. T. Apter, *Altered Loves* (New York: Fawcett-Columbine, 1990), p. 132.

10. L. Steinberg, "Autonomy, Conflict, and Harmony in the Family Relationship," in S. Feldman and G. Eliot, eds., *At the Threshold: The Developing Adolescent* (Cambridge, Mass.: Harvard University Press, 1990), pp. 255-277. N. Chodorow, *Feminism and Psychoanalytic Theory* (New Haven, Conn.: Yale University Press, 1989).

11. W. Wooley and S. Wooley, "Feeling Fat in a Thin Society: Women Tell How They Feel about Their Bodies," *Glamour* (February 1984): 198–252.

12. "Weighty Matters," *Ladies Home Journal* (September 1998): 159.

13. E. Rothblum, "The Stigma of Women's Weight: Social and Economic Realities," *Feminism and Psychology,* 2:1 (1992): 61–73; E. Rothblum, P. A. Brand, C. T. Miller, and H. J. A. Oetjen, "The Relationship between Obesity, Employment Discrimination, and Employment-Related Victimization," *Journal of Vocational Behavior,* 37 (1990): 251–266. See also J. T. Snow and M. B. Harris, "Maintenance of Weight-Loss: Demographic, Behavioral and Attitudinal Correlates," *Journal of Obesity and Weight Regulation,* 4 (1985): 234–255.

14. S. Gortmaker, A. Must, J. Perrin, A. Sobal, and W. Dietz, "Social and Economic Consequences of Overweight in Adolescence and Young Adulthood," *New England Journal of Medicine* (September 30, 1993): 1008–1010.

15. Steinberg, "Autonomy, Conflict, and Harmony in the Family Relationship"; Youniss and Smollar, *Adolescents' Relations with Mothers, Fathers, and Friends.*

16. H. Graham, *Hardship and Health in Women's Lives* (London: Harvester Wheatsheaf, 1993).

17. N. Grunberg and R. O. Straub, "The Role of Gender and Taste Preferences in the Effects of Stress on Eating," *Health Psychology,* 11:2 (1992): 97–100.

18. L. Lissner, J. Stevens, D. Levitsky, K. Rasmusson, and B. Strupp, "Variations in Energy Intake during the Menstrual Cycle: Implications for Food Intake Research," *American Journal of Clinical Nutrition,* 48 (1988): 956–962; G. Meijer, K. Westerterp, W. Saris, and F. Tenhoor, "Sleeping Metabolic Rate in Relation to Body Composition and the Menstrual Cycle," *American Journal of Clinical Nutrition,* 55 (1992): 637–640.

19. W. B. Cutler, G. Preti, A. Drieger, G. Huggins, C. Garcia, and H. Lawley, "Human Ancillary Secretions Influence Women's Menstrual Cycles: The Role of Donor Extracts," *Hormonal Behavior,* 20 (1986): 463–473.

5. Mothers, Daughters, and Dieting

1. I. Attie and J. Brooks-Gunn, "Development of Eating Problems in Adolescent Girls: A Longitudinal Study," *Developmental Psychology,* 25:1 (1987): 70–79. See also J. Graber, J. Brooks-Gunn, R. L. Paikoff,

and M. P. Warren, "Prediction of Eating Problems: An Eight-Year Study of Adolescent Girls," *Developmental Psychology,* 30 (1994): 823–834.

2. S. Orbach, "Anorexia and Adolescence," in M. Lawrence, ed., *Fed Up and Hungry* (New York: Peter Bedrick Books, 1987), pp. 74–85.

3. J. Youniss and J. Smollar, *Adolescents' Relations with Mothers, Fathers, and Friends* (Chicago: University of Chicago Press, 1985); L. Steinberg, "Reciprocal Relation between Parent-Child Distance and Pubertal Maturation," *Developmental Psychology,* 24 (1988): 122–128.

4. On the topic of mothers, daughters, and disordered eating, see Attie and Brooks-Gunn, "Development of Eating Problems in Adolescent Girls"; C. Costin, *Your Dieting Daughter: Is She Dying for Attention?* (New York: Brunner/Mazel, 1997); J. Graber and J. Brooks-Gunn, "Prevention of Eating Problems and Disorders: Including Parents," *Eating Disorders: The Journal of Treatment and Prevention,* 4:4 (1996): 348–363; A. Hill and J. A. Franklin, "Mothers, Daughters and Dieting: Investigating the Transmission of Weight Control," *British Journal of Clinical Psychology,* 37 (1998): 3–13; M. P. Levine, L. Smolak, A. Moodey, M. Shuman, and L. Hessen, "Normative Developmental Challenges and Dieting and Eating Disturbances in Middle School Girls," *International Journal of Eating Disorders,* 15 (1994): 11–20; M. Maine, *Father Hunger: Fathers, Daughters and Food* (Carlsbad, Calif.: Gürze Books, 1991); K. Pike and S. Rodin, "Mothers, Daughters, and Disordered Eating," *Journal of Abnormal Psychology,* 100:2 (1991): 198–204; M. Strober and L. L. Humphrey, "Familial Contributions to the Etiology and Course of Anorexia Nervosa and Bulimia," *Journal of Consulting and Clinical Psychology,* 55 (1987): 654–659; D. Waterhouse, *Like Mother, Like Daughter: How Women Are Influenced by Their Mothers' Relationship with Food—And How to Break the Pattern* (New York: Hyperion, 1997).

5. R. Striegel-Moore and A. Kearney-Cooke, "Exploring Parents' Attitudes and Behaviors about Their Children's Physical Appearance," *International Journal of Eating Disorders,* 15 (1994): 377–385. See also Graber and Brooks-Gunn, "Prevention of Eating Problems and Disorders."

6. Striegel-Moore and Kearney-Cooke, "Exploring Parents' Attitudes and Behaviors."

7. K. A. Matthews, "Myths and Realities of the Menopause," *Psychosomatic Medicine,* 54 (1992): 1–9.

8. R. Paikoff, J. Brooks-Gunn, and S. Carlton-Ford, "Effect of Reproductive Status Changes upon Family Functioning and Well-Being of

Mothers and Daughters," *Journal of Early Adolescence*, 11 (1991): 201–220.

9. E. Goffman, *Gender Advertisements* (New York: Harper and Row, 1976).

10. S. Bordo, *Unbearable Weight: Feminism, Western Culture, and the Body* (Berkeley, Calif.: University of California Press, 1993), p. 99.

11. Ibid.

12. Mark Nichter and Mimi Nichter, "Hype and Weight," *Medical Anthropology*, 13 (1991): 249–284.

13. J. Rabinor, "Mothers, Daughters, and Eating Disorders: Honoring the Mother-Daughter Relationship," In P. Fallon, M. A. Katzman, and S. T. Wooley, eds., *Feminist Perspectives on Eating Disorders* (New York: Guilford Press, 1994), pp. 272–286.

14. R. Larson and M. H. Richards, *Divergent Realities: The Emotional Lives of Mothers, Fathers, and Adolescents* (New York: Basic Books, 1994); Youniss and Smollar, *Adolescents' Relations with Mothers, Fathers, and Friends*.

15. Youniss and Smollar, *Adolescents' Relations with Mothers, Fathers, and Friends*.

16. M. R. Forman, F. L. Trowbridge, E. M. Gentry, J. S. Marks, and G. C. Hogelin, "Overweight Adults in the United States: The Behavioral Risk Factor Surveys," *American Journal of Clinical Nutrition*, 44 (1986): 410–416; S. French and R. Jeffery, "Consequences of Dieting to Lose Weight: Effects on Physical and Mental Health," *Health Psychology*, 13:3 (1994): 195–212; J. Horm and K. Anderson, "Who in America Is Trying to Lose Weight?" *Health Psychology*, 10 (1991): 274–281; R. Jeffery, S. Adlis, and J. Forster, "Prevalence of Dieting among Working Men and Women: The Healthy Worker Project," *Health Psychology*, 10 (1991): 274–281; M. G. Stephenson, A. S. Levy, N. L. Sass, and W. E. McGarvey, "1985 NHIS Findings: Nutrition Knowledge and Baseline Data for the Weight Loss Objectives," *Public Health Reports*, 102 (1987): 61–67.

17. "Controlling Weight No Longer Considered Dieting," *Calorie Counter Commentary*, 20:1 (1998): 1–4.

18. A. T. Fleming, "Daughters of Dieters," *Glamour* (November 1994): 222–252.

19. Pike and Rodin, "Mothers, Daughters, and Disordered Eating." See also A. Hill, C. Weaver, and J. Blundell, "Dieting Concerns of 10-Year-Old-Girls and Their Mothers," *British Journal of Clinical Psychology*, 29 (1990): 346–348.

20. M. P. Levine, L. Smolak, A. Moodey, M. Shuman, and L. Hessen, "Normative Developmental Challenges and Dieting and Eating Dis-

turbance in Middle School Girls," *International Journal of Eating Disorders*, 15 (1994): 11–20.

21. D. Kagan and R. Squires, "Dieting, Compulsive Eating, and Feelings of Failure among Adolescents," *International Journal of Eating Disorders*, 3 (1983): 15–26.

22. R. Crawford, "A Cultural Account of 'Health' Control, Release, and the 'Social Body,'" in J. McKinley, ed., *Issues in the Political Economy of Health Care* (London: Tavistock, 1984), pp. 60–101.

23. S. Orbach, Fat Is a Feminist Issue II: A Program to Conquer Compulsive Eating (New York: Berkley Books, 1982).

6. Looking Good among African-American Girls

1. J. Rosen and J. Gross, "Prevalence of Weight Reducing and Weight Gaining in Adolescent Girls and Boys," *Health Psychology*, 6 (1987): 131–147; S. Desmond, J. Price, C. Hallinan, and D. Smith, "Black and White Adolescents' Perceptions of Their Weight," *Journal of School Health*, 59 (1989): 353–358; R. Casper and D. Offer, "Weight and Dieting Concerns in Adolescents: Fashion or Symptom?" *Pediatrics*, 86 (1990): 384–390; Morbidity and Mortality Weekly Report, "Body Weight Perceptions and Selected Weight Management Goals and Practices of High School Students–United States, 1990," *Morbidity and Mortality Weekly Review*, 40 (1991): 741–750; K. K. Abrams, L. R. Allen, and J. J. Gray, "Disordered Eating Attitudes and Behaviors, Psychological Adjustment, and Ethnic Identity: A Comparison of Black and White Female College Students," *International Journal of Eating Disorders*, 14 (1993): 49–57; K. S. Kemper, R. G. Sargent, J. W. Drane, R. F. Valois, and J. R. Hussey, "Black and White Females' Perceptions of Ideal Body Size and Social Norms," *Obesity Research*, 2 (1994): 117–126; M. Story, S. French, M. Resnick, and R. Blum, "Ethnic/Racial and Socioeconomic Differences in Dieting Behaviors and Body Image Perceptions in Adolescents," *International Journal of Eating Disorders*, 18:2 (1995): 173–179.

2. Our interest in this topic was piqued by ongoing discussions with two African-American colleagues, Sheila Parker and Colette Sims, who confirmed our preliminary observations that beauty, body image, and fashion were markedly different among African-American women. They coordinated the research upon which this chapter is based. While the chapter describes "African-American" women in

relation to "white" women, I am well aware that these differences are cross-cut by class considerations and that cultural heterogeneity exists.

3. J. Allan, "Weight Management Activities among Black Women," paper presented at the Annual Meeting of the American Anthropology Association, Washington, D.C., November 15–19, 1989. Other national surveys have reported similar differences between African-American and white women.

4. An issue that has been raised is whether differences between African Americans and whites in bone size, body proportions, and frame size might affect measurement of African-American women. S. Kumanyika suggests that these errors are not significant and, in any case, would affect African-American women after adolescence. S. Kumanyika, J. Wilson, and M. Guilford-Davenport, "Weight Related Attitudes and Behaviors of Black Women," *Journal of the American Dietetic Association*, 93:4(1993): 416–422.

5. Morbidity and Mortality Weekly Report, "Body Weight Perceptions."

6. It is noteworthy that the American Association of University Women (AAUW) study from which this information is drawn found that African-American girls did show evidence of a significant decline in academic self-esteem over the course of their school careers. Thus, it seems that the African-American girls may not be relying on schools to provide them with a positive sense of self. American Association of University Women, *Shortchanging Girls, Shortchanging America: A Call to Action* (Washington, D.C.: American Association of University Women, 1991).

With respect to body image and self-image, it has been suggested that Latinas may be at elevated risk for mental health problems such as depression. Between the ages of nine and fifteen, Latinas show the most precipitous decline in the likelihood of endorsing the statement, "I am happy the way I am." Latinas may be an "at risk" population because they lack both the high self-esteem characteristic of African-American girls and the academic opportunities available to some (but certainly not all) white girls. For a more in-depth discussion of this issue, see P. Orenstein, *Schoolgirls: Young Women, Self-Esteem, and the Confidence Gap* (New York: Doubleday, 1994). Although we did not find the beauty ideals of the Latinas to differ from those of the white girls in our study, it is noteworthy that a few other researchers have done so. See, for example, T. Robinson, J. Killen, I. Litt, L. Hammer, D. Wilson, K. Haydel, C. Hayward, and C. B. Taylor, "Ethnicity and Body Dissatisfaction: Are Hispanic and Asian Girls at Increased Risk for Eating Disorders?" *Journal of Adolescent Health,* 19 (1996): 384–393.

7. C. G. Fairburn and S. J. Beglin, "Studies of the Epidemiology of Bulimia Nervosa," *American Journal of Psychiatry,* 147 (1990): 401–408; A. R. Lucas, M. Beard, W. M. O'Fallon, and L. T. Kurland, "50-Year Trends in the Incidence of Anorexia Nervosa in Rochester, Minn.: A Population Based Study," *American Journal of Psychiatry,* 148:7 (1991): 917–922. See also A. J. Pumariega, "Acculturation and Eating Attitudes in Adolescent Girls: A Comparative and Cultural Study," *Journal of the American Academy of Child and Adolescent Psychiatry,* 31 (1986): 802–809; J. E. Smith and J. Krejci, "Minorities Join the Majority: Eating Disturbances among Hispanic and Native American Youth," *International Journal of Eating Disorders,* 5 (1991): 179–186.

8. J. Gray, K. Ford, and L. Kelly, "The Prevalence of Bulimia in a Black College Population," *International Journal of Eating Disorders,* 6 (1987): 733–740.

9. G. Hsu, "Are Eating Disorders Becoming More Common among Blacks?" *International Journal of Eating Disorders,* 6 (1987): 113–124. A concern about affluence and anorexia deflects attention away from the fact that eating problems often relate to women's struggle against a "simultaneity of oppression." For a further discussion of this topic, see C. Clarke, *Narratives* (New Brunswick, N.J.: Sister Books, 1982); E. White, *The Black Woman's Health Book: Speaking for Ourselves* (Seattle, Wash.: Seal Press, 1990); G. Naylor, *Linden Hills* (New York: Ticknor and Fields, 1985). These researchers suggest that eating problems in the African-American community constitute responses to oppression and to being undervalued and overburdened at home as well as in the workplace. B. Thompson, "'A Way Outa No Way': Eating Problems among African American, Latina, and White Women," *Gender and Society,* 6 (1992): 546–561, notes that eating problems may begin as coping strategies against traumas ranging from sexual abuse to racism and poverty.

10. K. K. Abrams, L. R. Allen, and J. J. Gray, "Disordered Eating Attitudes and Behaviors, Psychological Adjustment and Ethnic Identity: A Comparison of Black and White Female College Students," *International Journal of Eating Disorders,* 14 (1993): 49–57.

11. S. Yanovski, "Binge Eating Disorder: Current Knowledge and Future Directions," *Obesity Research,* 1 (1993): 306–318.

12. T. Silber, "Anorexia Nervosa in Blacks and Hispanics," *International Journal of Eating Disorders,* 5 (1986): 121–128.

13. R. Striegel-Moore and L. Smolak, "The Role of Race in the Develop-

ment of Eating Disorders," in L. Smolak, M. Levine, and R. Striegel-Moore, eds., *The Developmental Psychopathology of Eating Disorders* (New Jersey: Erlbaum, 1996), pp. 259–285.

14. B. Thompson, "Food, Bodies and Growing Up Female: Childhood Lessons about Culture, Race and Class," in P. Fallon, M. A. Katzman, and S. C. Wooley, eds., *Feminist Perspectives on Eating Disorders* (New York: Guilford Press, 1994), pp. 335–378; see esp. p. 361.

15. M. Okazawa-Rey, T. Robinson, and J. Ward, "Black Women and the Politics of Skin Color and Hair," *Women and Therapy*, 6:1/2 (1987): 89–102; M. A. Gillespie, "Mirror Mirror," *Essence*, (January 1993): 73–79. See also R. T. Lakoff and R. L. Scherr, *Face Value* (London: Routledge and Kegan Paul, 1984).

16. Okazawa-Rey, Robinson, and Ward, "Black Women and the Politics of Skin Color and Hair."

17. For a critique of early studies of group identity preferences and self-esteem, which were largely based on studies of preschool children, see W. E. Cross, Jr., *Shades of Black: Diversity in African-American Identity* (Philadelphia: Temple University Press, 1991).

18. Ibid. See also Okazawa-Rey, Robinson, and Ward, "Black Women and the Politics of Skin Color and Hair."

19. R. Majors and J. M. Billson, *Cool Pose: The Dilemmas of Black Manhood in America* (New York: Lexington Books, 1992), p. 4.

20. Thomas Kochman explains that the respect and admiration that African-American males receive from their peers for the vitality of their dress contrasts markedly with the reception they get from whites in official settings such as schools. Whereas whites tend to adopt a utilitarian attitude toward dress, African Americans do not. African Americans consider hats and sunglasses to be "artistic adornments . . . calculated to create an attitude." When white officials insist that black students remove their hats and sunglasses, conflict arises because students do not want to alter the costume they have carefully crafted. T. Kochman, *Black and White Styles in Conflict* (Chicago: University of Chicago Press, 1981).

21. S. Fordham, "'Those Loud Black Girls': Black Women, Silence, and Gender 'Passing' in the Academy," *Anthropology and Education Quarterly*, 24:1 (1993): 3–32.

22. We classified the girls into these categories by computing BMI from height and weight measurements. BMI was then compared with normal values for African-American girls, based on NHANES I data. A. Must, G. Dallal, and W. Dietz, "Reference Data for Obesity," *American Journal of Clinical Nutrition*, 53 (1991): 839–846.

23. J. Allan, K. Mayo, and Y. Michel, "Body Size Values of White and Black Women," *Research in Nursing and Health,* 16 (1993): 323–333.

24. B. Speicher and S. McMahon, "Some African-American Perspectives on Black English Vernacular," *Language in Society,* 21 (1992): 383–407; see especially p. 391.

25. Ibid., p. 391.

26. It is important to note that white youth are also involved in the creation of style, which in some instances takes the form of recycling old or seemingly out-of-style clothing as a means of resisting dominant culture. On the creation of style, see A. McRobbie, "Secondhand Dresses and the Role of the Ragmarket," in A. McRobbie, ed., *Zoot Suits and Second-hand Dresses* (London: MacMillan, 1989). On the act of resistance, see two books by D. Hebdige, *Subculture: The Meaning of Style* (London: Methuen, 1979), and *Hiding in the Light* (London: Routledge, 1988).

    As discussed in Chapters 1 and 2, irrespective of differences in the ways in which white girls dress on the basis of the social group to which they belong, they maintain a thin body ideal. Hegemony carried out at the site of the body coexists with acts of resistance and attempts to express individual identity. The body is an area where social truths and social contradictions are played out and agency is expressed. It is a site of sensuality and creativity, as well as domination and struggle, a medium of expression affected by a confluence of meanings flowing from a variety of life spaces. See N. Scheper-Hughes and M. Lock, "The Mindful Body: A Prolegomenon to Future Work in Medical Anthropology," *Medical Anthropology Quarterly,* 1:1 (1987): 6–41.

27. S. L. Taylor, "In the Spirit: Cherishing Black Style," *Essence* (October 1982): 61.

28. Gillespie, "Mirror Mirror," p. 75.

29. T. Robinson and J. Ward, "A Belief in Self Far Greater Than Anyone's Disbelief: Cultivating Resistance among African American Female Adolescents," in C. Gilligan, A. Rogers, and D. Tolman, eds., *Women, Girls and Psychotherapy: Reframing Resistance* (New York: Harrington Park Press, 1991), pp. 87–103; see p. 91. On this topic, see also P. H. Collins, "The Social Construction of Black Feminist Thought," *Journal of Women in Culture and Society,* 14:4 (1989): 745–761; P. H. Collins, *Black Feminist Thought: Knowledge, Consciousness and the Politics of Empowerment* (Boston: Routledge, 1990); J. Ladner, *Tomorrow's Tomorrow* (New York: Doubleday, 1971).

30. Robinson and Ward, "A Belief in Self Far Greater," p. 92.

31. A. M. Cauce, Y. Hiraga, D. Graves, N. Gonzales, K. Ryan-Finn, and

K. Grove, "African American Mothers and their Adolescent Daughters: Closeness, Conflict and Control," in B. Ross Leadbeater and N. Way, eds., *Urban Girls: Resisting Stereotypes, Creating Identities* (New York: New York University Press, 1996), pp. 100–117.

32. J. Ward, "Raising Resisters: The Role of Truth Telling in the Psychological Development of African American Girls," in B. Ross Leadbeater and N. Way, eds., *Urban Girls: Resisting Stereotypes, Creating Identities* (New York: New York University Press, 1996), pp. 85–100; see p. 89.

33. Ibid., p. 87. On the subject of the "oppositional gaze," see bell hooks, *Black Looks: Race and Representation* (Boston: South End Press, 1992).

34. American Association of University Women, *Shortchanging Girls, Shortchanging America: A Call to Action* (Washington, D.C.: American Association of University Women, 1991). See also *AAUW Report: How Schools Shortchange Girls* (Washington, D.C.: American Association of University Women Educational Foundation and National Education Association, 1992).

35. For more discussion on communication differences between African Americans and whites, see Kochman, *Black and White Styles.*

36. It has been observed that African-American society involves a highly flexible and personalistic approach to interaction. See R. Abrahams, "Negotiating Respect: Patterns of Presentation among Black Women," *Journal of American Folklore,* 88 (1975): 58–80. The expressive or personalistic, rather than the instrumental or institutional, dimension of role validation is stressed in the black community. Respect must continually be earned and negotiated. In this context, smart talk and body language are important, and a competitive spirit is encouraged within the home as a survival skill. See also M. Ward, *Them Children: A Study in Language Learning* (New York: Holt, Reinhart and Winston, 1971). Given this pattern of interaction, positive feedback about one's looks is perceived by adolescent girls to far exceed negative feedback.

37. Collins, "The Social Construction of Black Feminist Thought," p. 762.

38. J. Allan, K. Mayo, and Y. Michel, "Body Size Values of White and Black Women," *Research in Nursing and Health,* 16 (1993): 323–333.

39. M. Wilson, *Divided Sisters: Bridging the Gap between Black Women and White Women* (New York: Anchor Books, 1996), p. 81.

40. N. Wolf, *The Beauty Myth: How Images of Beauty Are Used against Women* (New York: William Morrow and Company, 1991).

41. Considering the importance (at least traditionally) given among African-American women to knowing how to cook and serve a meal, it

may be culturally inappropriate to be on a diet. See G. Wade-Gayles, "'Laying on Hands' through Cooking: Black Women's Majesty and Mystery in Their Own Kitchens," in A. V. Avakian, ed., *Through the Kitchen Window: Women Explore the Intimate Meanings of Food and Cooking* (Boston: Beacon Press, 1997). See also N. Shange, *If I Can Cook, You Know God Can* (Boston: Beacon Press, 1998).

42. E. Barnes, "The Black Community as the Source of Positive Self Concept for Black Children: A Theoretical Perspective," in R. Jones, ed., *Black Psychology* (New York: Harper and Row, 1980), pp. 106–130.

43. Ladner, *Tomorrow's Tomorrow*.

44. W. E. B. Du Bois, *The Souls of Black Folk* (Greenwich, Conn.: Fawcett Publications, 1903/1961).

45. M. Lewis, *Herstory: Black Female Rites of Passage* (Chicago: African American Images, 1988), p. 64.

46. Fordham, "Those Loud Black Girls."

47. S. Carothers, "Catching Sense: Learning from Our Mothers to Be Black and Female," in F. Ginsberg and A. Lowenhaupt Tsing, eds., *Uncertain Terms: Negotiating Gender in American Culture* (Boston: Beacon Press, 1990), pp. 232–247; quote p. 239.

48. Collins ("The Social Construction of Black Feminist Thought") has explained that knowledge of how to behave is essential to the survival of the subordinate.

49. C. Stack, *All Our Kin* (New York: Harper and Row, 1974); B. Valentine, *Hustling and Other Hard Work* (New York: Macmillan, 1978). See also Collins, *Black Feminist Thought*.

50. See Fordham, "Those Loud Black Girls." The egalitarian ethos found in contemporary African-American "communities" is, in part, the result of an externally imposed lack of differentiation between "black peoples" associated with enslavement.

51. African American scholars writing on management styles and organizational environment have repeatedly drawn a distinction between Eurocentric and Africentric perspectives of social organization. For example, see N. Ak'bar, "Africentric Social Sciences for Human Liberation," *Journal of Black Studies*, 14:4 (1984): 395–414. M. Asanti, *Afrocentricity* (Trenton, NJ: Africa World Press, 1988). See also J. Baldwin, "African (Black) Psychology: Issues and Synthesis," *Journal of Black Studies*, 16:3 (1986): 235–249. W. Nobles, "African Philosophy: Foundations for Black Psychology," in R. Jones, ed., *Black Psychology* (New York: Harper & Row, 1980), pp. 23–37. J. Schiele, "Organizational Theory from an Afrocentric Perspective," *Journal of Black Studies*, 21:2 (1990): 145–161.

The Eurocentric model places emphasis on rationality, production, efficiency and individuality. The Africentric model, in contrast, places emphasis on group and system survival, viewing the individual as part of a collective in which horizontal communication and affective ties are high. The virtue of the Africentric approach is its flexibility, which is responsive to turbulent changes in the environment. See A. Daly, "African American and White Managers: A Comparison in One Agency," in A. Faulkner, M. Roberts-DeGennaro, and M. Weil, eds., *Diversity and Development in Community Practice* (New York: Haworth Press, 1994).

As distinct from a Eurocentric model of organization, in which emphasis is placed on "the correct way of doing the job," an Africentric approach places greater emphasis on raising group consciousness of problems and a consideration of alternatives that may work given a set of contingencies. This parallels the earlier discussion of the value of "making a look work for you" and "community feedback" about one's sense of style and aesthetic as a reflection on self, as well as community.

Researchers of African American child socialization have also laid emphasis on the way children are taught to bear individual burdens (self-suffering), as well as to adapt for the good of kin as a sign of strength and character . On this issue, see E. Higginbotham and L. Weber, "Moving Up With Kin and Community: Upward Social Mobility for Black and White Women," *Gender and Society*, 6 (1992): 416–440.

52. Okazawa-Rey, Robinson, and Ward, "Black Women and the Politics of Skin Color and Hair," p. 100.

53. M. Root, "Treating the Victimized Bulimic: The Functions of Binge-Purge Behavior," *Journal of Interpersonal Violence*, 4 (1989): 90–100.

54. L. Villarosa, "Dangerous Eating," *Essence* (January 1994): 19.

55. S. Bordo, *Unbearable Weight: Feminism, Western Culture and the Body* (Berkeley: University of California Press, 1993).

56. While it is important to recognize the ways in which the bodies and voices of women of different ethnic and class backgrounds are influenced by material forces in society, it is also necessary to challenge the extent to which such influence is totalizing, given preexisting dispositions (physical as well as cultural), situated knowledge, and fractured identities. See E. Martin, "Science and Women's Bodies: Forms of Anthropological Knowledge," in M. Jacobus, E. F. Keller, and S. Shuttleworth, eds., *Body/Politics* (New York: Routledge, 1990), pp. 69–82; D. Haraway, *Simians, Cyborgs and Women: The Reinvention of Nature* (New York: Routledge, 1991).

7. What We Can Do

1. H. Cordes, "Generation Wired: Caffeine Is the New Drug of Choice for Kids," *The Nation* (April 27 1998): 11.
2. Center for Science in the Public Interest, "Liquid Candy," *Nutrition Action Healthletter,* October 20, 1998.
3. Cordes, "Generation Wired."
4. Ibid. Not only are fast food chains located right in schools, but a reported corporate goal of one of the largest chains, McDonalds, was "to have no American more than 4 minutes away from one of their restaurants" (Ibid., p. 11). See also United States General Accounting Office: Report to Congressional Committees, "School Lunch Program: Role and Impacts of Private Food Service Companies," August 1996.
5. D. Stead, "Corporations, Classrooms, and Commercialism," *New York Times,* January 5, 1997. Corporate funding is also pervasive in after-school programs. The Boys and Girls Club of America, for example, accepted 60 million dollars from Coca Cola in return for making the company's products the only brands sold in more than two thousand clubs nationwide. See Center for Science in the Public Interest, "Liquid Candy."
6. R. P. Troiano, K. M. Flegal, R. Kuczmarkski, S. Campbell, and C. Johnson, "Overweight Prevalence and Trends for Children and Adolescents," *Archives of Pediatric and Adolescent Medicine,* 149 (1995): 1085–1091.
7. Ibid.
8. M. Root, "Treating the Victimized Bulimic: The Functions of Binge-Purge Behavior," *Journal of Interpersonal Violence,* 4 (1989): 90–100.
9. The opportunity to pilot an intervention for teen-aged girls based on what we had learned from the Teen Lifestyle Project was made possible by funding from Canyon Ranch, a health spa located in Tucson, Arizona. Over a nine-month period, our intervention was implemented with seventy girls at three field sites, allowing us to test the applicability and effectiveness of the project among girls of different ages and ethnic groups in both community and after-school settings. There were no control groups. The three sites were a community setting (a Boys and Girls Club), a largely African-American church-related after-school program, and a high school. The discussion in this chapter focuses largely on the high school setting. For a complete review of the three interventions see M. Nichter, S. Parker, N. Vuckovic, C. Sims, and N. Teufel, *The Final Re-*

port of the Looking Good, Feeling Good Health Promotion Project (unpublished report, University of Arizona, 1996).

10. Conducting the sessions outside of the classroom also gave us flexibility not possible during the school day. After-school and Saturday sessions allowed us to schedule longer time periods during which members of the group could explore personal topics in depth and interact in a variety of ways.
11. D. L. Franko and P. Orosan-Weine, "The Prevention of Eating Disorders: Empirical, Methodological and Conceptual Considerations," *Clinical Psychology: Science and Practice,* 5 (1998): 459–477.
12. S. Harter, "Self and Identity Development," in S. Feldman and G. Elliot, eds., *At the Threshold: The Developing Adolescent* (Cambridge, Mass.: Harvard University Press, 1990), pp. 352–388.
13. L. Steinberg with W. Steinberg, *Crossing Paths* (New York: Simon and Schuster, 1994).

Appendix A: Research Strategies

1. Mimi Nichter, "Body Image, Dieting, and Smoking: Parental Influences on Their Adolescent Daughters" (Ph.D. diss., 1995, Department of Family Studies and Human Development, University of Arizona).
2. This data-collection strategy was adapted from the methodology of the Continuing Survey of Food Intake of Individuals (CSFII-85 and CSFII-86).

Acknowledgments

T his book and the Teen Lifestyle Project upon which it is based have been very much a collaborative effort. Along the path of research and reflection, I have been fortunate to have many excellent guides and helpful colleagues.

Most important, I would like to acknowledge the girls who so willingly and honestly spoke about their lives, their bodies, and their families during the years of the study. The stories these girls told were the inspiration for this book. I would also like to acknowledge the girls who participated in our intervention project; they helped us understand how necessary it is to consider health and nutrition in relation to beauty and identity work.

Mark Nichter, one of the principal investigators of the project, contributed significantly to all aspects of the study. His careful readings of my evolving manuscript, his readiness to discuss newly emergent ideas at any time of day or night, and his thoughtful suggestions have been a constant source of insight and support. Cheryl Ritenbaugh, also a principal investigator on the study, taught me much about adolescent nutrition and enthusiastically guided me toward new directions of inquiry. Nancy Vuckovic was my co-researcher throughout the five-year project and the one-year intervention that followed. Her insights and continuous enthusiasm during our many discussions on topics ranging from "fat talk" to the "perfect girl" have contributed immensely to previous publications and to various chapters of this book. To Sheila Parker and Colette Sims, I owe immeasurable thanks for helping me understand the world of African-American girls.

I am extremely grateful for the excellent interviewing skills and careful transcription work of project team members, including Marybeth McPhee, Brooke Olsen, Elizabeth Cartwright, Dawn Curry, Dalia Rock, Suzanne Bieger, and Robin Lerner. Thanks also to Melissa Blackwell, Beebe Axelrod, and Lori Lerner for their painstaking work coordinating and entering the dietary data at various points in the study. Mikel Aickin did an admirable job of analyzing the complex dietary data, as did Gilbert Quintero, who processed much of the quantitative survey data.

I greatly appreciate the funding provided by the National Institute of Child Health and Human Development for the five-year longitudinal study and the one-year minority supplement, and by Mel Zuckerman of Canyon Ranch for support of our intervention work. Funding from the University of Arizona Provost's Author Support Fund helped with the final preparation of the manuscript.

Susan Silverberg Koerner, my dissertation advisor in the Department of Family Studies and Human Development, University of Arizona, was a careful and perceptive reader of the many drafts of my dissertation, which forms the basis for Chapters 4 and 5 of this book. The thoughtful insights she shared with me about the field of adolescence and the family are very much appreciated.

I am also grateful to many people who encouraged me through various stages of my writing. My friend and colleague Norma Gray read the book in pieces and finally in its entirety, and always had thoughtful and encouraging comments. Holly McCarter and Barrie Ross gave me helpful feedback on earlier drafts of the manuscript and were always willing to engage me in discussions about women and weight. My mother, Essy Beeber, my sister, Deborah Riverbend, and Bea Nichter and Melanie Wallendorf encouraged me to keep writing and settle for nothing less than my best work. Two excellent research assistants, Laura Tesler and Rhae Adams, helped in the prepa-

acknowledgments

ration of the final manuscript. I am also thankful for the comments and suggestions for revision from two anonymous peer reviewers on an earlier draft of the manuscript. At Harvard University Press, I deeply appreciate the support of my editor, Elizabeth Knoll, whose gentle prodding and thoughtful questioning helped move the book to completion. Christine Thorsteinsson's careful editing of the book is very much appreciated.

Finally, on a personal note, the men and boys in my life—Mark, Simeon, and Brandon—have each contributed in their own way to my writing. Mark has been present as a continual source of encouragement. My sons, Simeon and Brandon, patiently tolerated my long absences while I conducted research and wrote. Their presence grounded me and enabled me to see the world of teens more clearly. Watching them both as they enter and move through adolescence has added enormously to my experience as a parent and my personal understanding of what it means to be a teen today.

Index

Early versions of some chapters appeared elsewhere in a different form and are reworked here by permission: Chapter 2 as M. Nichter and N. Vuckovic, "Fat Talk: Body Image among Adolescent Girls," in N. Sault, ed., *Many Mirrors: Body Image and Social Relations* (New Brunswick, N.J.: Rutgers University Press, 1994); Chapter 3 as Mimi Nichter, C. Ritenbaugh, Mark Nichter, N. Vuckovic, and M. Aickin, "Dieting and Watching among Adolescent Females: Report of a Multimethod Study," in *Journal of Adolescent Health*, 17 (1995): 153–162, copyright 1995 by The Society for Adolescent Medicine; Chapter 6 as S. Parker, Mimi Nichter, Mark Nichter, N. Vuckovic, C. Sims, and C. Ritenbaugh, "Body Image and Weight Concerns among African American and White Adolescent Females: Differences That Make a Difference," *Human Organization*, 54:2 (1995): 103–114; and Chapter 7 as M. Nichter, N. Vuckovic, and S. Parker, "The Looking Good, Feeling Good Program: A Multi-Ethnic Intervention for Healthy Body Image, Nutrition and Physical Activity," in N. Piran, M. P. Levine, and C. Steiner-Adair, eds., *Preventing Eating Disorders: A Handbook of Interventions and Special Challenges* (Philadelphia: Brunner/Mazel, 1999).